Interviews are ubiquitous in modern society, and they play a crucial role in social scientific research. But, as Charles Briggs convincingly argues in this book, received interviewing techniques rest on fundamental misapprehensions about the nature both of the interview as a communicative event, and of the nature of the data that it produces. Furthermore, interviewers rarely examine the compatibility of interviews as a means of acquiring information with the ways in which their subjects typically convey information to one another. These oversights often blind interviewers to ensuing errors of interpretation, as well as to the limitations of the interview as a means of acquiring data.

To confront these problems, Professor Briggs presents an analysis of the "communicative blunders" that he himself committed in conducting research interviews among Spanish-speakers in northern New Mexico. By focusing on these errors and exploring how they may be avoided, he is able to propose new techniques for designing, implementing, and analyzing interview-based research. These rest on identifying the *subjects'* resources for conveying information, and the relative compatibility of the shared rules and understandings that underlie their strategies with those associated with interviews. Critical of existing paradigms of interviewing, which he sees as deriving from Western "folk" theories of reality and communication, Briggs shows that the development of more sophisticated interviewing methodologies requires further research into interviewing itself.

Briggs's conclusions provide a basis for the reexamination of current uses of interviews in a wide range of contexts – from social science research to job applications, welfare and health care delivery, criminal and legal investigations, journalism and broadcasting, and other areas of everyday life. His book will appeal to linguists, sociologists, anthropologists, historians, psychologists, as well as to other readers whose research or professional activities depend on the use of interviews.

Studies in the Social and
Cultural Foundations of Language No. 1

Learning how to ask:
A sociolinguistic appraisal of the role
of the interview in social science research

Studies in the Social and Cultural Foundations of Language

The aim of this series is to develop theoretical perspectives on the essential social and cultural character of language by methodological and empirical emphasis on the occurrence of language in its communicative and interactional settings, on the socioculturally grounded "meanings" and "functions" of linguistic forms, and on the social scientific study of language use across cultures. It will thus explicate the essentially ethnographic nature of linguistic data, whether spontaneously occurring or experimentally induced, whether normative or variational, whether synchronic or diachronic. Works appearing in the series will make substantive and theoretical contributions to the debate over the sociocultural–functional and structural–formal nature of language, and will represent the concerns of scholars in the sociology and anthropology of language, anthropological linguistics, sociolinguistics, and socioculturally informed psycholinguistics.

1. Charles L. Briggs: *Learning how to ask: a sociolinguistic appraisal of the role of the interview in social science research*
2. Tamar Katriel: *Talking straight:* Dugri *speech in Israeli Sabra culture**
3. Bambi B. Schieffelin and Elinor Ochs (eds.): *Language socialization across cultures**
4. Susan U. Philips, Susan Steele, and Christine Tanz (eds.): *Language, gender, and sex in comparative perspective**
5. Jeff Siegel: *Language contact in a plantation environment: a sociolinguistic history of Fiji**

*forthcoming

Learning how to ask

A sociolinguistic appraisal of the role of the interview in social science research

CHARLES L. BRIGGS
Department of Anthropology
Vassar College

CAMBRIDGE
UNIVERSITY PRESS

Published by the Press Syndicate of the University of Cambridge
The Pitt Building, Trumpington Street, Cambridge CB2 1RP
40 West 20th Street, New York, NY 10011-4211, USA
10 Stamford Road, Oakleigh, Melbourne 3166, Australia

First published 1986
Reprinted 1987, 1989, 1990, 1992, 1994

Printed in the United States of America

Library of Congress Cataloging-in-Publication is available

A catalogue record for this book is available from the British Library

ISBN 0-521-32225-1 hardback
ISBN 0-521-31113-6 paperback

The author gratefully acknowledges permission to reprint material from the following
sources:

Ivan Karp and Martha B. Kendall, "Reflexivity in Field Work," pp. 249-73 in
Explaining Social Behavior: Consciousness, Human Action, and Social Structure by P.
F. Secord (ed.), Copyright © 1982 by Sage Publications. Reprinted by permission of
Sage Publiations, Inc.

A Guide for Field Workers in Folklore by Kenneth S. Goldstein (copyright © 1964 by
Folklore Associates, Inc.; reprinted by permission of Gale Research Company),
Folklore, 1964.

For two viejitos de antes
Federico Córdova
Aurelio Trujillo
and for
Silvianita Trujillo de López
George López
Costancia Trujillo
Lina Ortiz de Córdova
expert pedagogues and patient friends

Contents

Foreword by Aaron V. Cicourel   *page* ix

Preface   xiii

1   Introduction   1

2   The setting: *Mexicano* society and Córdova, New Mexico   31

3   Interview techniques vis-à-vis native metacommunicative repertoires; or, on the analysis of communicative blunders   39

4   The acquisition of metacommunicative competence   61

5   Listen before you leap: toward methodological sophistication   93

6   Conclusion: theoretical quagmires and "purely methodological" issues   112

Notes   126

References   132

Index   149

Foreword

The most ubiquitous aspect of social science research is its reliance on talking to people about their experiences, attitudes, opinions, complaints, feelings and emotions, and beliefs. There is by now a huge literature on the problems of obtaining information from informants, respondents, and subjects. Why another book on interviewing? When I agreed to review this book for Cambridge University Press I posed hypothetical questions about the possible content of the manuscript and the types of issues it could raise. I did not know Charles Briggs at the time but was told he had been trained in anthropological linguistics and folklore. I was pleased to find that Briggs had used a sociolinguistic approach to interviewing and that he was preoccupied with a central issue of field research: the researcher's discovery of errors in her or his tape-recorded interviews. Although such errors are inevitable, they need to be pointed out to the reader at all times. I immediately agreed with several key points by Briggs: Interviewing errors are seldom reported, and the interview technique invariably imposes one set of communicative norms on the setting while researchers ignore the extent to which a speech community is organized along opposing lines.

Social scientists use interview techniques in field settings while ignoring the nature of communication in the different cultures in which they conduct these interviews. The same point can be made about those researchers who only conduct research in their own culture and ignore the wide range of communicative repertoires that exist. A key aspect of the book, therefore, is the author's insistence that we pay more attention to the communicative norms and speech forms used in a community.

Briggs examines the extent to which the metacommunication statements which report, describe, interpret, and evaluate communicative acts and processes which emerge during the interview tend to be ignored by the researcher. We don't know enough about the different kinds of practical native metacommunicative events that go unreported by researchers. Are coding procedures being employed that systematically eliminate these kinds of information? Does the researcher use such information without reporting it to the reader despite relying on such materials when interpreting data?

The existence of native metacommunicative repertoires goes to the heart of the validity of social science research. As Briggs notes, there is an incompatibility between standard interview techniques and native systems of communication. We need empirical research on the inter-view as a communicative event. How does this event contrast with other forms of communication in the community or region? How do we decide on the boundaries of a given speech community?

Briggs raises another important point: To what extent do the native's own discourse rules infiltrate the interview? Sociologists often assume that appropriate interviewers can be identified and trained to adjust to differences in repertoires, but we seldom find these issues examined conceptually and empirically. The social roles and goals of the re-searcher and respondent are also part of the communication problem and Briggs reviews these issues in his book.

A general issue that emerges from reading Briggs's research is the different ways a person can enter into a field situation and pursue certain research goals. When does a researcher feel that certain kinds of questions can be asked of informants? What sort of participation is necessary in order to begin asking questions? Social roles and goals and the way a social situation gets defined for participants are often emergent aspects of the interaction. What norms of interaction are observed that enable participants to assume that what is taking place is fairly standardized and well known? We need to distinguish between norms which seem to be fairly regularized across communicative events but where the norms can nevertheless vary according to the pragmatics of a specific context of interaction. I raise these questions and issues here to underscore the importance of Briggs's insistence on examining a society's categories of speech acts in social situations, and the related problem of avoiding the imposition of the researcher's conversational forms on the respondent's or informant's modes of responding.

Briggs's book forces the reader to recognize that non-native ethnog-raphers often enter a society lacking the background necessary to ob-tain or elicit information according to native communicative compe-tence. The researcher often pursues her or his own interests at the outset instead of trying to understand the native's communicative com-petence. The researcher can make things worse by seeking information on topics possessed by only a few members of the community. The ways in which topics are pursued can easily violate local norms of turn-taking and topicalization and the way natives order them. The researcher's interests can thus shift topics in a way that is disruptive to the informant, and such conditions may inhibit the informant from speaking about matters known to her or him in a language and style in which a topic is likely to appear in routine conversation. The use of interviews, therefore, should occur with an awareness of native meta-communicational skills or repertoires used in the community.

The problems carefully reported by Briggs emerged from research in a small community. His research is ethnographically informed at all times. The lessons we can learn from this research, however, apply with equal force to social scientists working in organizational or societal settings that are larger in scale. When research is conducted in communities or societies with which researchers consider themselves to be members then they are likely to ignore many of Briggs's important observations and suggestions. Briggs's detailed accounts of his field research problems and the specific issues he identifies can become the basis for a reexamination of current uses of interviews in communities and societies that are larger in scale. In particular, we can begin to reexamine the metacommunicative repertoires of interviews when people apply for jobs, higher education, welfare, health care delivery, criminal and legal investigation, and additional areas of everyday life. This research would enable scholars to observe and document the extent to which these exchanges reveal errors of interpretation or misunderstanding that may derive from socioeconomic and ethnic differences and communication problems inherent in all social interaction.

Aaron V. Cicourel

University of California, San Diego

Preface

This book has been a real challenge to write, and I hope it proves equally challenging to its readers. Nothing is harder than opening up questions that we already think are solved, finding crevasses and quicksand in what everyone sees as solid ground. Overcoming our reluctance to open Pandora's boxes is especially acute when it comes to "purely methodological" issues. Collecting data is viewed as an intrinsically sound, if not necessarily glamorous, pursuit. The realm of pure theory is exciting and important, even if empirically minded skeptics are likely to dismiss one's efforts as vapid. But methodology loses on both counts, being generally regarded as both mundane and unimportant.

These prejudices guided my initial work on the subject. More than a decade of fieldwork with *Mexicanos* in northern New Mexico had sensitized me to ways in which the interview, as a speech event, limits speakers' abilities to use expressions, such as proverbs, that are deeply rooted in a given interaction. This induced me to review field recordings of interviews in examining the nature of this mode of communication and the problems it presents. I was not surprised to find that my initial interviews (in 1972) had encountered numerous sociolinguistic obstacles (see Chapter 3). I subsequently adopted many features of the dialect, learned some basic social skills, became acquainted with the residents, and gained a sense of their background and present concerns. This enabled me to collect a fair amount of data on a broad array of topics, particularly concerning the local wood-carving industry, language use, and the oral history and folklore of the community as well as its ritual life. It thus came as a great shock to learn that many of the communicative difficulties I encountered initially continued to operate, if more subtly, in my most recent interviews.

This prompted me to perform a systematic sociolinguistic and conversational analysis–oriented investigation of my research methodology. I found that my *communicative blunders* were not a simple product of ineptness or personality but reflected a deep and pervasive pattern that was inherent in received interview techniques as used in a wide variety of disciplines. These blunders followed from the imposition of one set of communicative norms – those embedded in the interview situation – on a speech community that organized talk along opposing lines.

Comparing these results with my experience in quantitative research using questionnaires (Smith and Briggs 1972), conversations with other researchers, and the literature on interviewing convinced me that the difficulties I had faced in interviewing *Mexicanos* were symptomatic of obstacles to social-scientific and linguistic research in general. This realization motivated the two basic goals of this book. I consider it of vital importance to stimulate researchers to think seriously about these questions. This entails examination of the procedures they use in their own research, during planning, active research, and analysis phases. But looking deeply into these questions also opens up basic issues regarding our relationship to the subjects of our research. I thus hope to stimulate sociologists, anthropologists, linguists, sociolinguists, and other practitioners who conduct interviews or use interview data to ponder the theoretical roots of this methodological crisis. I do not believe that these problems are insurmountable; we now possess the conceptual tools to assess where interviews will succeed and where and how they will fail in a given research project. I accordingly propose a set of procedures for overcoming many of the problems that are inherent in received interview techniques.

Given the scope of the problem, I would be the last to claim that one short book can settle the turbulent waters. Providing a single "solution" would, in any case, circumvent the process I am trying to foster. My aim is rather to convince the reader that it is worth setting aside preconceptions regarding the triviality of "purely methodological" questions for a moment. It is important to invert the means–ends formula of research in broaching these issues, highlighting the research encounter itself. I am attempting not to take away the right to conduct interviews, only to help dispel the cloud that keeps us from seeing them clearly.

Michael Herzfeld invited me to contribute to a panel and book that proposed the application of a semiotic perspective to fieldwork. My response formed the basis of the argument developed in Chapter 3. The discussant, James Fernandez, provided both helpful criticism and generous encouragement. Dell Hymes commented on this article and invited me to draft a related paper for *Language in Society,* part of which is included in Chapter 4. The following persons read one or more of these papers and provided valuable suggestions: Thomas

Buckley, Paul Friedrich, Allan Hanson, Cornelia Kammerer, Robert McAulay, Lee Miringoff, and Marque Miringoff. Julián José Vigil submitted the texts and analyses to a meticulous reading. Beth Goldring and Barbara Fries offered excellent editorial critiques of the manuscript as a whole.

Three teachers at the University of Chicago – Marshall Sahlins, David Schneider, and Michael Silverstein – challenged me to give up some of my preconceptions and experiment with new perspectives on reality, each in his own way. Michael Silverstein's work has contributed greatly to the theoretical underpinnings of the book. Selected by the Press as a reader for the manuscript, Aaron Cicourel provided an unparalleled twenty-eight-page response. I take this opportunity to gratefully acknowledge his insights; the final version has profited enormously both from the individual criticisms and from his encouragement.

Three elderly couples in Córdova, New Mexico – Lina and Federico Córdova, Silvianita and George López, and Costancia and Aurelio Trujillo – were equally expert pedagogues. Their efforts to teach me how to learn, to overcome my need to define and control our educational encounters, provide the basic message of this work. I can only hope that my effort to translate it into a different type of speech event has not rendered their words incomprehensible.

Financial support for the various fieldwork periods was provided by the International Folk Art Foundation, the National Institute of Mental Health, the National Science Foundation, and the Research Committee of Vassar College. A research grant from the National Science Foundation provided funds for a return to the field in 1983 and for completing the analysis. An Andrew W. Mellon Faculty Fellowship in the Humanities in the Committee on Degrees in Folklore and Mythology at Harvard University has provided me with an ideal atmosphere for completing work on the manuscript. To all individuals and institutions who have helped me along the way, *¡mil gracias!* To Barbara Fries, Jessie Fries-Kraemer, and Feliciana Diodati-Briggs, who shared the journey, a fond salute.

1. Introduction

Interviewing has become a powerful force in modern society. Starting almost from birth, we are confronted by questions posed by educators, psychologists, pollsters, medical practitioners, and employers, and we listen to flamboyant interviewers on radio and television. Our skill at playing the role of interviewee influences our success in education and employment; our answers will help determine whether we receive such basic services as bank loans or disability pay. On a societal level, polling "pundits" are no longer employed exclusively by such specialized agencies as the National Opinion Research Center in Chicago or the Gallup Poll. Major corporations spend millions of dollars on market surveys that estimate customer wants and resources. Pollsters form integral members of major political campaigns, and their findings have a profound effect on the way candidates approach the voters. "Exit polls" now enable the media to advise West Coast residents as to how the East Coast has voted in national elections – even before the polls have closed.

Research in the social sciences is the great bastion of the interview. Estimates suggest that 90 percent of all social science investigations use interview data (cf. Brenner 1981b:115). Interviews are used in a wide variety of social contexts. A central component of the anthropological tool kit, interviews have produced a good bit of the information we possess about contemporary non-Western societies. Interviewing is, however, also a mainstay of research within modern industrial societies. We use interviews in exploring people's beliefs about the future (e.g., "Who do you think will win the election?") as well as their recollections of the past. The validity of a great deal of what we believe to be true about human beings and the way they relate to one another hinges on the viability of the interview as a methodological strategy.

Our faith in the interview is not entirely unexamined. An overwhelming mass of literature in psychology, sociology, anthropology, linguistics, political science, folklore, oral history, and other fields has

1

focused on interview techniques. Many of these works are of the "cook-book" type, providing recipes for better baking using interviews yet without seriously considering the nature of the interview or its inherent weaknesses. Others are devoted to analysis of the factors that "bias" interviews, skewing the results in a particular direction. The latter body of material has substantially increased the level of awareness with respect to the possibility that the interviewer's gender, race, political beliefs, linguistic characteristics, and the like may distort the results.

Given the ubiquity of interviews and the proliferation of works on the subject, I would hardly blame the reader for asking why we need one more book on interviewing. The reason is simple: We still know very little about the nature of the interview as a communicative event. Worse yet, because the interview is an accepted speech event in our own native speech communities, we take for granted that we know what it is and what it produces. One major problem is that the interview is most unusual, as communicative routines go. Accordingly, researchers base their interview strategies and the way they interpret the data on a number of false assumptions. This is, unfortunately, not a simple, naive mistake; I argue in later chapters that our methodological shortsightedness reflects our reluctance to face some thorny theoretical issues.

This mystification of the interview emerges primarily in three ways. First, interviews provide examples of *metacommunication,* statements that report, describe, interpret, and evaluate communicative acts and processes. All speech communities possess repertoires of metacommunicative events that they use in generating shared understandings with respect to themselves and their experiences. As I argue in Chapter 4, these native metacommunicative events are rich in the pragmatic features that root speech events in a particular social situation and imbue them with force and meaning. Unfortunately, researchers seldom gain competence (in Hymes's [1974a:92–97] sense of the term) in these repertoires, relying instead on the metacommunicative routine that figures so prominently in their own speech community – the interview. This practice deprives the researcher of an adequate sense as to how the information she or he obtains fits into broader patterns of thinking, feeling, and speaking.

An even more serious problem is inherent in the structure of the interview. By participating in an interview, both parties are implicitly agreeing to abide by certain communicative norms. The interview moves the roles that each normally occupies in life into the background and structures the encounter with respect to the roles of interviewer and interviewee. Attention is concentrated on the topics introduced by the researcher's questions. Preliminary "small talk" may highlight the participants' present states of mind and body ("How are you?") and their relationship ("It's good to see you. I appreciate your letting me interview you again"). But the initial question then shifts the focus away from the interaction to another time, place, or process ("Now tell me about . . .").

The problem here is that this movement away from the interview as a speech event mystifies researchers to such an extent that they generally retain this focus in the course of their analysis. What is said is seen as a reflection of what is "out there" rather than as an interpretation which is jointly produced by interviewer and respondent. Since the context-sensitive features of such discourse are more clearly tied to the context of the interview than to that of the situation it describes, the researcher is likely to misinterpret the meaning of the responses.

A third difficulty arises because suppression of the norms that guide other types of communicative events is not always complete. Some potential respondents are drawn from communities whose sociolinguistic norms stand in opposition to those embedded in the interview. This is likely to be the case in groups that do not feature the interview as an established speech-event type. Lacking experience in this means of relating, such individuals are less likely to be able and willing to adhere to its rules. The farther we move away from home, culturally and linguistically, the greater the problem. This hiatus between the communicative norms of interviewer and researcher can greatly hinder research, and the problems it engenders have sometimes abruptly terminated the investigation. If the fieldworker does not take this gap into account, he or she will fail to see how native communicative patterns have shaped responses; this will lead the researcher to misconstrue their meaning.

It has not been possible to limit the discussion to a critique of interview methods alone, however, because broaching these methodological issues raises much broader questions. Why are interviews ubiquitous in the human sciences? Why is the nature of the interview process so poorly understood, and why has it not been more adequately researched? Why are we so reluctant to modify our research methodology, particularly in the light of theoretical advances? The answer is easy: *Interview techniques smuggle outmoded preconceptions out of the realm of conscious theory and into that of methodology.* Both our unquestioned faith in the interview and our reluctance to adopt a more sophisticated means of analyzing its findings emerge from the fact that the interview encapsulates our own native theories of communication and of reality.

The refusal to rely more heavily on native metacommunicative repertoires as sources of information and our unquestioned belief that we have the right to impose interview techniques on our consultants have serious political implications. They indicate that social research is characterized by less sensitivity and willingness to expose oneself to other modes of learning than we may have imagined. By leaving the interview situation itself out of the analysis, we have cleverly circumvented the need to examine our own role in the research process. A clearer understanding of the interview will accordingly not only enhance its usefulness as a research tool but will greatly expand our consciousness of what studying our fellow humans is all about.

Lest the reader gain the wrong impression, let me make my position on the interview clear. *I am not trying to persuade researchers to abandon interviewing altogether.* In addition to being utterly unrealistic, such an attempt would undermine my project entirely. The presentation of a simple and unfeasible solution would ultimately lead most interviewers to lose interest in the task of critically examining the nature and limitations of interview techniques. The point is that the communicative underpinnings of the interview are tied to basic theoretical as well as methodological issues. My goal is to elucidate the nature of the interview as a communicative event and to contribute to our understanding of these basic methodological and theoretical problems.

I will approach this task in four primary ways. As I will argue in later chapters, one of the most important tasks confronting students of the interview is to examine transcripts of interviews in great detail. The point here is not simply to explain the problems that become explicit in the course of the interview. This is the orientation of many researchers who have focused on the problems of rapport-building and bias. My approach is rather to study transcripts (and tape recordings) as a whole in order to ascertain exactly what was said (the linguistic forms), what each question and reply meant to the interviewer and interviewee, and what the researcher can glean from these data. This technique reveals the points at which interviewer and interviewee have misunderstood each other and where one or both are likely to be misinterpreted by the researcher, even when such misunderstandings do not become explicit in the interview.

Unfortunately, it is difficult indeed to obtain verbatim transcripts of complete interviews in the published literature. I have accordingly concentrated my analysis on interviews I conducted over a thirteen-year period in a Spanish-speaking community in northern New Mexico. (A brief account of *Mexicano* society and the research site is provided in Chapter 2.) The reason for choosing these data is that I have tape recordings of interviews covering the span between my first few days in the community and my most recent research. The interviews are of a number of types, from the most nondirected and informal to quantitatively oriented formal interviews that utilized questionnaires. The research foci consisted of material culture (the production of carved images of Catholic saints), oral history, political economy, sociolinguistics, and folklore (oral literature). My ability to interpret the interview data is thus aided by systematic study of sociolinguistic patterns and social relations. I also conducted a social survey of a city of 14,000 inhabitants (Smith and Briggs 1972) and am currently studying job interviews between college seniors and prospective employers. Although these investigations have informed my understanding of interview techniques, they do not form primary sources of data.

The second basic thrust of my analysis is an exploration of the communicative roots of the interview. This approach emerges mainly from my training in sociolinguistics and discourse analysis. These fields utilize concepts derived from other types of linguistic analysis, anthropology, sociology, psychology, and literary criticism in studying the way language is used in a variety of settings. Discourse analysis has focused a great deal of attention on the heretofore neglected study of conversation. My purpose here is to see what types of linguistic and social norms are presupposed by the interview and to compare them with the norms characteristic of other types of speech events. This task should reveal the basic communicative features that are most likely to prove problematic in interviews.

The third dimension is the presentation of steps that might be taken to overcome the problems posed by these communicative obstacles. I argue that one of the most important facets of this process is the development of a heightened awareness of the theoretical problems that lie behind methodological naiveté. This discussion is taken up primarily in Chapter 6. A practical approach to this task is developed in Chapter 5. The basic steps in designing, conducting, and interpreting research using interviews are outlined to show how investigators can make the best possible use of interviews.

These suggestions are addressed to interviewing in the social sciences as a whole as well as in linguistics, folklore, and oral history. Most of the examples will be drawn from fieldwork conducted in another society. This reflects the fact that the data used in this study were collected in the course of a fieldwork project and that the bulk of my training was in anthropology and linguistics. The book is addressed, however, to all practitioners who use interview and/or survey data in their research. Some of my remarks are directed specifically at one type of interviewing or to the way in which interviews are used in a particular discipline. I have nevertheless tried to avoid spelling out the implications of each point for the different fields in order to avoid burying the argument in excessive complication and tedium. The reader will thus find it necessary to assess the bearing of my remarks on her or his own concerns.

The process of critically examining the nature and limitations of interview techniques involves another step as well. As I noted above, an impressive number of sources have examined the way interviews are (or should be) used in research. This literature has increased the sophistication with which interviewers deal with problems of sampling, bias, the wording of questions, and so forth. Unfortunately, very few writers have contributed significantly to our understanding of the nature of the interview as a communicative event and of the metacommunicative norms it presupposes. This oversight leaves us without a clear understanding of the problems that result from gaps between the metacommunicative norms of the interview and those connected with other types of speech events. The result is that most students of the interview seem unaware of many of the basic obstacles confronting this type of research. In other words, the literature on interviewing has also contributed to the *mystification* of the interview. Given the influence these sources exert on the way interviews are conducted, an examination of these works is a necessary starting point for any effort to rethink the interview.

Previous research on the interview

The task of summarizing the literature that deals with the methodology of the social sciences is daunting. My treatment of these sources is confronted by two constraints. On the one hand, I seek to point out problems that confront a wide range of different types of interviews. I must perforce deal with sources on interviewing that emerge from a number of disciplines. My goal in this book is, however, to analyze unexamined aspects of interviewing, not to produce a monographic summary of the literature. I will accordingly treat selected sources that deal with interviews as used by ethnographers, oral historians, folklorists, sociologists, and political scientists. The point in each section will be to grasp the basic problems that underlie the body of literature in question, not to adumbrate each relevant work.

A couple of definitions might help prevent interdisciplinary confusion. I will use the term "interview" to cover a wide range of research activities from the most "informal," "open-ended" interviews to the use of "formal" instruments in survey research. In order to be considered an interview according to my definition, the collection of data must occur in a face-to-face situation. The interaction must also occur in a research context and involve the posing of questions by the investigator. I thus exclude such events as telephone polling, the use of written questionnaires, and employment interviews. Although many points of my analysis apply to them as well, they also present special problems that I cannot elucidate in the course of this study. I will also use the term "fieldwork" in its anthropological sense to refer to research that involves intense interaction between a researcher and a given population over a substantial period of time. Fieldwork generally includes a number of different research modalities, including interviews of one or more types. My usage is thus to be distinguished from a common use of the term in sociology; here "fieldwork" often involves observation and other procedures *rather than* interviewing.

Anthropology

Classically, anthropologists have used a combination of observation and open-ended interviews in conducting fieldwork. Observing is not constituted in formal terms as it is, for instance, in the study of nonverbal communication. The classical paradigm is provided by Kluckhohn's article on "The Participant-Observation Technique in Small Communities" (1940). She urges fieldworkers to assume roles, such as housewife, teacher, and the like, that will afford extensive contact with members of the community in areas of interest to the research. In the eyes of Kluckhohn and of most anthropologists, participant-observation is not opposed to informal interviewing; the former rather provides opportunities for the latter.

Ethnographers generally rely on open-ended interviews rather than on surveys or questionnaires. Even those practitioners who urge fieldworkers to use surveys suggest that formal instruments should be introduced after basic cultural patterns have been established through observation and informal interviewing. Ethnographers use open-ended interviews in two basic ways. The basic thrust of the first type is captured by Powdermaker (1966:156–7):

I used no interviewing schedule, but I had well in mind the problems to be discussed, and the interviews tended to follow a general pattern. They were always by appointment and usually in the informant's home. The tone was that of a social visit. After an exchange of polite greetings, my hostess often made an admiring comment on my dress or suit. I might note a photograph on the mantel over the coal grate fireplace, and the informant would point with pride to the members of the family in it and this often led to talking about them. My questions were open-ended, and directed towards certain areas for both factual information and attitudes.

This account pertains to her work with blacks in Mississippi. Many ethnographers arrange interviews more informally, without appointments. Sessions are often conducted in the ethnographer's residence in order to isolate the interviewee and obtain privacy. The basic pattern of inaugurating and ending the session with "normal conversation," the absence of a formal instrument, and the direction of the discussion toward the research goals of the ethnographer is, however, quite common.

The second major type is "key-informant interviewing." In the course of conducting informal interviews with a number of members of the community, ethnographers generally form close working and often personal relationships with a few consultants. These individuals are then singled out for much more intensive interviews on a more frequent basis, and, as Edgerton and Langness (1974:33) note, "most anthropologists . . . come to rely upon certain persons for much of their detailed or specialized information." The possible dangers of too great a reliance on a few individuals, particularly with regard to sampling and observer effect, have often been described (cf. Young and Young 1961). Why, then, is key-informant interviewing used to a high degree?

The rationale emerges in a statement by Pelto and Pelto (1978:72) that "humans differ in their willingness as well as their capabilities for verbally expressing cultural information. Consequently, the anthropologist usually finds that only a small number of individuals in any community are good key informants." This motive is reiterated by such authors as Chagnon (1974:60), Edgerton and Langness (1974:33), and Kobben (1967:42). As I will argue in Chapters 4 and 6, this facet of ethnographic interviewing is quite revealing with respect to the communicative basis of ethnographic interviewing in general.

Finally, formal interviewing has been used to a limited extent in fieldwork. Obtaining a census of the population that contained basic demographic and economic information used to be de rigueur. This was generally accomplished in small communities by a door-to-door survey using an instrument with both open-ended and precoded questions. Taking a census seems to have lost its general appeal in recent years as ethnographers have become increasingly problem-oriented in focus. Nevertheless, anthropological fieldwork has come under attack from sociologists and quantitatively oriented anthropologists as being too reliant on "subjective" and nonquantitative observation and informal interviewing. As Pelto and Pelto (1973:267–70) report, many fieldworkers have accordingly turned to survey research as a means of providing more "controlled," "objective," and quantifiable data on their research foci. A number of sources have reported attempts to create a rapprochement between formal and informal techniques (see, for example, Bennett and Thaiss 1970; Brim and Spain 1974; Burawoy 1979; Cancian 1965; Denzin 1970; Freilich 1970; Mitchell 1965; Myers 1977; Speckman 1967).

The literature on ethnographic methodology. The literature on methodological aspects of fieldwork is substantial. One of the most common types of work in the area is the presentation of an anthropologist's experiences in one or more societies, drawing out his or her research design, methods of data collection, and mode of interpretive data. A few of the better-known examples of this type of study are Beattie (1965), Berreman (1962), Chagnon (1974), Freilich (1970), Georges and Jones (1980), Golde (1970), Henry and Saberwal (1969), Lawless, Sutlive, and Zamora (1983), Middletown (1970), Powdermaker (1966), Spindler (1970), and Wax (1971). A related body of literature describes the personal experiences of anthropologists in the field. Belmonte (1979), Dwyer (1982), and Rabinow (1977) provide leading examples of this type of discussion.

Several volumes feature articles that deal with specific aspects of fieldwork (see, for example, Jongmans and Gutkind 1967; Naroll and Cohen 1970). A large body of articles undertakes this task as well, much of which has been published in the "Field Methods and Techniques" section of the journal *Human Organization*. A number of manual-type publications have also been written, many with the beginning fieldworker in mind. (See, for examaple, Agar 1980a; Brim and Spain 1974; Edgerton and Langness 1974; Langness 1965; Langness and Frank 1981; Paul 1953; Pelto 1970; Pelto and Pelto 1973, 1978; Spradley 1979; Whyte 1984; Williams 1967). A number of works have appeared that treat fieldwork in historical perspective (cf. Firth 1957; Stocking 1968, 1974, 1983).

A critical assessment. This body of literature has produced insights that hold the potential for increasing the sophistication with which we view the fieldwork process. The work of Agar (1980a, 1980b; Agar and Hobbs 1982), for example, has helped us understand the way in which interview data reflect both the events described and the context of the interview itself. Berreman (1962) has increased our sophistication with respect to the complex ways in which both "natives" and ethnographers present themselves at different times to different people and regarding the effect of their shifts on data collection. Karp and

Kendall (1982) have questioned the misplaced analogies that have shaped our conception of the role of the fieldworker and the limitations of a positivistic conception of "social facts." Owusu (1978) questions the way in which fieldwork reifies basic Western cultural conceptions by "finding" theoretical constructs in the field.

Unfortunately, these pioneering efforts have not succeeded in turning the ethnographic enterprise onto itself in such a way that the nature of the interview and other research strategies would be revealed. Although a number of authors suggest that we must look at the interview itself as a cultural encounter (e.g., Agar 1980a:91–2, Conklin 1968, and Mintz 1979), no author has yet presented an in-depth statement of how this can be undertaken. Ethnographers accordingly fall back on their own native understanding of the interview. As I will try to show in later chapters, this view is based on a systematic distortion of the nature of the interview as a speech event. In the absence of an adequate grasp on the nature of the interview, the bulk of the literature thus gives the appearance of a host of reiterations of the status quo in terms of basic interviewing procedures and descriptions of how these have been applied in given fieldwork cases.

The lack of an adequate grasp of the interactional and communicative norms that underlie the interview is matched by a failure to grasp the importance of studying the correlative norms of the society in question. Ethnographers sometimes note that other groups have differing kinds of restrictions on who may ask what questions of whom in what circumstances. It has also been argued that questions may not mean the same thing to a member of another speech community, even if translated "accurately" (Edgerton and Langness 1974:44; Hollander 1967:12–13; Leach 1967; Paul 1953:447). These sorts of problems are cited as reasons for remaining critical of the potential of *formal* interviews as fieldwork tools.

The problem here is that rejection of surveys may serve as a cover for the failure to systematically explore the possibility that informal interviewing may suffer from the same sorts of problems. This can only be accomplished by a careful consideration of the compatibility of native communicative patterns and the norms presupposed by the interview and by a careful examination of interviews for hidden misunderstandings. Not only has this task not been accomplished, but the importance of undertaking it has been articulated only rarely. A great deal of attention has been devoted to the idea that "natives" frequently lie and/or give inconsistent answers. Such distortions do occur, but they are dwarfed in comparison with the effects of communicative disparities between ethnographers and their consultants.

Folkloristics

The field of folkloristics exhibits a nearly schizophrenic character with respect to methodology. On the one hand, generations of amateur and professional folklorists have compiled masses of oral material through the most naive means. Collectors have traveled to communities with folkloric traditions for very short intervals, frequently only days or weeks. Once there, collectors query passersby with respect to the identity of the person "who knows the most" ballads, tales, or what have you. When permission to tape-record or transcribe the material is given, the informant is asked to tell (or sing) all the items that he or she knows in the desired genre. The collector may take notes on the performer and the social setting. The result is the collection of a vast number of items in a relatively short period of time. Although this approach is by no means as prevalent now, it is still used by a substantial number of practitioners.

During the past two decades, a new generation of scholars in folklore and related disciplines has discredited this orientation. Many of these individuals have been influenced by linguistic training, thus developing greater interest in the formal properties of performances. Scholars such as Bauman (1975) and Hymes (1981) have shown that the "tell me all the X that you know" technique generally produces reports or summaries of the content of folkloric traditions rather than performances. In other words, the presentation of materials in such an artificial situation transforms the overall structure and the stylistic details of the traditions. Worse still is the collector's lack of awareness that such a transformation has occurred, thus distorting the process of interpretation.

The influence of the old methodology has been countered by a growing emphasis on fieldwork methodology. Graduate students in folklore frequently take classes in sociolinguistics and ethnography, and courses in folklore methodology are generally de rigueur. Goldstein's *A Guide for Field Workers in Folklore* (1964) has become the standard reference work. Here, Goldstein stresses the importance of *systematic* use of a variety of techniques as well as a heightened awareness of the need to take the collecting situation explicitly into account in analyzing the materials (see also Ives 1974; MacDonald 1972). Like ethnographers, folklorists rely mainly on observation and informal interviewing in collecting folkloric items and related materials.

A technique developed by Goldstein, the *induced natural context,* has also gained in popularity (1964:87–90). This involves an initial assessment of the situations in which a given genre is usually performed. An "accomplice" is then induced to invite other performers to a gathering; the real purpose of the meeting is not announced. The collector arrives "unexpectedly," thus theoretically minimizing the effects of his or her presence. Goldstein reports that this technique produces results closer to the "natural contexts" of folklore performance than to those explicitly structured by the fieldworker ("artificial contexts").

Two major methodological shortcomings remain. First, Goldstein and others have successfully identified some of the limitations on the usefulness of the interview for collectors. They also have a sense of the effects of the researcher's presence on the form and content of what is collected, whether in "natural" or "artificial" situations. Like ethnographers, however, folklorists have seldom gone beyond a commonsensical perspective on the interview. This leads them to misconstrue the nature of the interview as a speech event and thus the status of the data it yields. This prompts Goldstein (1964:104) to argue, for example, that the interview "supplies the collector with an insider's view of the individual, his culture, and his folklore" and of the way in which the informant conceptualizes and orders this knowledge (1964:109, 123). Discourse generated by interviews is structured, however, by the communicative norms of this type of speech event and by the role of the interviewer.

This lack of sophistication with respect to the nature of the interview and the role of the interviewer prevents folkloristic methodologists from providing their readers with clear guidelines for assessing the role of these factors in the generation and interpretation of interview data. This hiatus is all the more important because "Interviewing is the most common field method employed by folklore collectors" (Goldstein 1964:104).

A second major problem is tied to the concept of "context." Although the new generation of folklorists have laudably pointed to the importance of the social and linguistic setting in which materials are collected, this has not led to the development of a sophisticated view of the nature of contextual components. As Cook-Gumperz and Gumperz (1976) argue, the context of a speech event is not simply the sum total of elements present at the time it emerges. Contexts are not given, a priori, before the event begins. Contexts are interpretive frames that are *constructed* by the participants in the course of the discourse. The presentation of a checklist of elements in the social and physical setting that are seen as constituting "the context" is thus theoretically misdirected, as is the notion that "the collector has a clear duty to place the total situation of record as he observes it" (MacDonald 1972:410). Analysts would be better advised to look closely at the *form* of the performance in order to see how the participants are providing each other with signals as to the situational elements relevant to the meaning of what they are saying. The common practice of observing the "context" in "natural" performances and recording the texts in interviews thus creates a dangerous chasm between text and context (cf. Briggs 1985a).[1]

Oral history

In turning to oral historical interviewing, the same basic methodological schizophrenia is encountered. We find, on the one hand, a number of manuals that describe the way in which oral historians generally design and implement their interviews and interpret their findings. The authors generally include some tips as to how interviews are best undertaken. These pertain to techniques for establishing rapport, expressing interest in the interviewees' memories, avoiding "loaded" questions, and the like in addition to suggestions regarding tape-recording and transcribing interviews (cf. Baum 1971; Davis, Back, and MacLean 1977; Garner 1975; Hoopes 1979; Ives 1974; Moss 1974; Neuenschwander 1976; Shumway and Hartley 1973; Sitton, Mehaffy, and Davis 1983).

These discussions simply assume, however, that both the authors and their readers know what interviews are, how they work, and their compatibility with the process of articulating one's experiences. They similarly eschew any serious concern with the fact that the products of interviews are dialogic texts that are largely structured by the interviewer. Several authors have argued, for example, that oral historians must compensate for "biases" on the part of either interviewer or respondent that reduce the reliability and validity of interview data (cf. Cutler 1970; Hoffman 1974). As I argue in the section on sociology, conceptualizing the interview process in terms of the way specific "biases" can "distort" the data ultimately succeeds in further obscuring the real problem – the dialogic, contextualized nature of all discourse, including interviews.

A number of works that have appeared recently do take up some of these issues (see, for example, Allen and Montell 1981; Friedlander 1975; Joyner 1975, 1979; Thompson 1978). These writers help dispel the notion that oral historians collect, even in ideal terms, reflections of historical events. Thompson has articulated the point well. Speaking of social statistics, written documents, published sources, and oral history interviews, he notes: "They all represent . . . the *social perception* of facts; and are all in addition subject to social pressures from the context in which they are obtained. With these forms of evidence, what we receive is *social meaning*, and it is this which must be evaluated" (1978:96; emphasis in original). Joyner (1979:48) echoes Thompson's concern with context, arguing, "What is necessary is a full description of the context in which the testimony was taken." The point has similarly been made that interviews impose different kinds of constraints on speech than "ordinary" conversation does (Allen and Montell 1981:40–44). Some of these insights were anticipated by Vansina's (1965) study of the social relations that condition the transmission of historical tradition in Africa.

Such writers offer a new level of methodological sophistication to the discipline. Their efforts have not, however, succeeded in resolving two basic problems. First, the nature and significance of context in oral history interviews is not sufficiently appreciated. The task of examining the context is equated with a description of the physical and social setting of the interview. As Cook-Gumperz and Gumperz have argued, however, contexts are not simply extralinguistic givens that surround the spoken word. Context rather enters discourse as "perceptual cues which must be actively and continuously monitored in the course of the interaction" (1976:8). The point is thus to look into the verbal (and nonverbal) exchange itself for clues as to how the participants are drawing on their surroundings in interpreting each other's remarks.

Some of the most significant contextualization cues are so-called fillers and crutch words. Nearly all writers, however, urge researchers to delete these cues (cf. Davis et al. 1977:39–40; Thompson 1978:198). Ives (1974:49) and Thompson (1978:179) even suggest that the interviewer should avoid responding with "uh-huh" or "yes" for fear of cluttering the tape and transcript. In spite of recent efforts to call attention to the importance of context, the oral historians' own procedures are robbing their works of contextual information.

This problem reveals a deeper issue. The goal of oral history is to elicit information about past events. Researchers have noted the selectivity of memory. Yet a lack of awareness is apparent with respect to the fact that oral history interviews produce a *dialogue* between past and present. Interviewees interpret the meaning of both the past and the present, including the interview itself. Each query presents them with the task of searching through their memories to see which recollections bear on the question and then fitting this information into a form that will be seen as answering the question. Oral history interviews are thus related to the present as systematically as to the past. This is not to say that oral historians are entirely unaware of this process; great strides have been made in recent years toward becoming more sensitive to these issues. This growing awareness has, however, largely failed to stimulate researchers to thoroughly rethink the way they structure interviews and analyze interview data in light of the bifocal, synthetic nature of oral history.

Sociolinguistics

I am using the term "sociolinguistics" in a broad sense to refer to research on the ethnography of communication (Gumperz, Hymes), the quantitative study of linguistic variation (Labov, Sankoff), and the macrosociology of language (Fishman). The labels and boundaries associated with work in these areas are problematic because leading practitioners have all expressed some ambivalence regarding the term "sociolinguistics." Practitioners are concerned with the description and analysis of language use and the way it relates to cultural and social patterns. Quite different approaches to these problems are present in the field, and these discrepancies motivate contrastive views on methodological issues.

The field of sociolinguistics presents us with a paradox of a rather different sort when it comes to methodology than was the case with folklore or oral history. On the positive side, sociolinguists have provided us with systematic comparative data on language structure and use. Researchers have emphasized the diversity that is evident in forms, contexts, functions, and speech event types as well as in the way these phenomena are viewed in different communities. A crucial move for the development of sociolinguistics was Hymes's (1971a) emphasis on the study of sociolinguistic competence; this involved the expansion of Chomsky's (1965, 1968) stress on formal features and rules to include the communicative norms that underlie their use. Superficial attempts to correlate social–cultural and linguistic patterns are increasingly giving way to studies of the subtle ways in which alternations in linguistic features (from phonetic changes to changes from one language to another) are intimately related to shifts in interactional patterns. In spite of its theoretical difficulties, Austin's (1962) work on the performative force of language has stimulated much research on the dynamics of this process.

Another major effect of sociolinguistic research was to provide new sources of rapprochement between linguists and practitioners in such areas as education, social–cultural anthropology, folklore, sociology, and psychology. The point has been made by Cicourel (1964, 1974a, 1982b), Grimshaw (1969), Hymes (1969a, 1971b, 1972), Labov (1972a,

1972b), and others that the success of social-scientific research depends on awareness, generally implicit, of the ways in which the groups in question use language. Unless these sociolinguistic patterns move, at least in part, from the role of means to that of ends of research, the errors that are lodged in our own ethnocentric conceptions of linguistic processes may be built unknowingly into the results. Just as importantly, these practitioners have stressed the need to examine the results of educational, anthropological, folkloristic, sociological, and psychological research in developing a broader understanding of linguistic patterns. The present study is an attempt at deepening and systematizing both of these lines of attack.

Social-scientific research draws on a host of different types of communicative events. With its emphasis on speech acts and on the communicative norms that underlie them, sociolinguistics holds tremendous potential for revealing the nature of the social-scientific research enterprise. The beginnings of this process are apparent in the work of a number of leading researchers.[2] Hymes (1969a, 1971b) points out to political scientists and social anthropologists the fact that their methodologies rely fundamentally on linguistic processes; the devotion of greater attention to the communicative dimensions of data acquisition is thus requisite to methodological adequacy and a means of enhancing one's comprehension of the data. Grimshaw (1969) similarly encourages his readers to see "language as obstacle and as data in sociological research." Irvine (1978) argues that the elicitation of cross-cultural psychological data in artificial environments may lead to gross distortion. Gumperz (1972) notes that "the interview setting . . . is often formal and contrived and almost always quite different from the settings within which people usually interact." He thus urges sociolinguists to utilize a broader range of elicitation techniques. Labov (1966, 1972b, 1972c) proposes an expansion of the range of elicitation techniques that are included in the interview in order to collect a more diverse and controlled range of data.

This research offers important insight into research interviews. Its major limitations emerge from the interview's being generally treated in passing, not as a primary research focus. Albert's study of speech patterns of the Barundi provides a case in point. Her data were taken from "informants' verbalizations, spontaneous or by elicitation" and "the comparison of the interview protocols of a variety of informants" (1972:74–5). In her conclusions, Albert noted that "For Barundi (and possibly for a number of similar societies in Africa and the Mediterranean countries), rules of procedure for data gathering included: (1) avoiding direct questions, except in such matters as asking which road leads to Kitega or Nyabikere" (1972:98). Realization of the difficulties involved in obtaining information through direct questioning did not induce her, however, to question her own use of elicitation and interview protocols or to propose an alternative methodology for interviews. Indeed, she includes "systematic questioning" in her list of suggested methods for obtaining "a comprehensive view of speech behavior" (1972:104).

This case is not isolated – the insights that have emerged have failed to produce a systematic critique of sociolinguistic methodology. In fact, sociolinguists are relatively conservative, methodologically speaking. Practitioners rely primarily on familiar ethnographic and linguistic methods. Grimshaw (1974) has summarized the most common data-collection procedures under four headings: (1) the observation of "natural" speech in "natural" settings; (2) the observation of "natural" speech in contrived settings (i.e., experimental situations or those organized by the researcher); (3) the elicitation of speech through direct inquiries; and (4) the use of historical and/or literary materials.[3]

This is not to say that no methodological progress is apparent. Chomsky's reliance on the linguist's utterances and intuitions have been rejected in favor of data from native speakers. Tape- and video-recording has greatly increased the precision of data collection, and a great deal of attention has focused on the range of contexts in which recordings are made. The problem is rather that these methodological insights have not stimulated systematic sociolinguistic investigations of the speech events that researchers use in collecting their data. Proposals for methodological progress are still based to a high degree on preconceptions regarding the communicative underpinnings of observation[4] and interviewing; neither of these activities has formed the primary subject of in-depth sociolinguistic research. These insights have not even produced greater interest in methodological issues.[5]

An obvious and important exception is provided by Labov's work on speech variation in New York City (1966, 1972a, 1972b, 1972c). Labov has devoted considerable attention to methodological issues; this springs, at least in part, from his interest in combining elicitation techniques from linguistics, sociological survey methodology, and sociolinguistic concern with the contextual dimensions of speech. Labov's central methodological innovation consists of an attempt to increase the diversity of speech acts recorded in interview settings.

Interviews were structured in such a way as to produce five classes of data. "Casual speech . . . the every-day speech used in informal situations, where no attention is directed to language" (1966:100), emerged "spontaneously" before and after the interview and during interruptions, and during asides. Labov also obtained "casual speech" (Style A) by eliciting childhood rhymes and emotionally charged personal narratives. A second type (Style B) consists of "careful speech"; he argues that the formality of the interview setting induces the interviewee to focus greater attention on his or her own speech. Labov also increased the formality of the situation even more by asking interviewees to read short texts (Style C) and word lists (Style D). The interviews provided data on the socioeconomic characteristics and linguistic attitudes of each interviewee in addition to data for each of the contexts on five phonological variables (1966:137).

Labov's work is praiseworthy for the seriousness that is attached to methodological issues and for his attempt to base methodological innovations on the communicative norms of interviewees.[6] The value of his contribution is marred, however, by a number of crucial assumptions. Labov is centrally concerned with the way in which "the formal interview itself defines a speech context in which only one speaking style normally occurs, what we may call *careful speech*" (1966:91; emphasis in original). Several problems are apparent here. Interviews are quite complex and multifaceted speech events. Their communicative properties are highly reflective of the specific type of interview and of the relationship that is established between the involved parties. Discourse analysts and ethnomethodologists have similarly shown that what Labov terms "casual speech . . . the every-day speech used in informal situations, where no attention is directed to language," is much more formally and functionally complex and varied than Labov's definition would suggest.

Labov's reformulation thus ultimately relies on commonsensical assumptions regarding the nature of both interviews and "ordinary" discourse rather than on a systematic investigation of their communicative underpinnings. His distinction between "careful" and "casual speech" is similarly based on a naive concept of "formality"; as Irvine (1979) has argued, our judgments regarding the "formality" of a speech event reflect a broad range of frequently contradictory criteria. As Wolfson (1976) points out, Labov evinces little understanding of the way in which the unique features of interviewing shape the form and content of the sum total of utterances that constitute it, even in the course of "spontaneous," emotionally charged responses.

The commonsensical basis of Labov's view of interviewing is apparent in the way he uses the interview "to gather the information which is the ostensible subject of the questions being asked" (1966:137). As his focus shifts away from phonological variables, he is no longer concerned with the role of the context and style. In other words, he seems to think that the referential content of the responses can be interpreted without serious consideration of the role of the interviewer, the setting, and the formal features of the question. This appears all the more questionable because Labov places a great deal of importance on questions dealing with "subjective evaluation and linguistic attitudes" (1966:137). We are, however, not presented with any evidence that such data are less sensitive to contextual variation than phonological features: The stability of the referential content is simply assumed.

Sociology

Compiling a summary of the literature on methodology in sociology is a daunting task indeed. Sociologists as a whole take methodological issues seriously. Sociologists are often heard to criticize other social scientists as being insufficiently "rigorous." Classes in methodology are required in most sociology programs, even at the undergraduate level. The literature on methodology is enormous; a comprehensive survey would constitute a monograph in and of itself, and a long one at that. A substantial amount of research has focused on methodology, particularly on interviewing. Good critical studies of the interview have been emerging since the time of the classic study by Hyman et al. (1954), *Interviewing in Social Research.*

This should not be taken to mean, however, that the basic methodological issues that confront the discipline have been solved. Contradictions are certainly apparent here as well. The literature on methodology ranges between introductory manuals that codify received interviewing techniques and sophisticated critiques that point to basic underlying problems. Beyond the limitations of the literature on methodology itself lies the fact that many of its most significant findings have yet to be incorporated into interviewing practice.

Types of sociological research. Sociologists rely on a wide range of research activities. *Field research* or *participant observation* was utilized extensively in the pre–World War II period, particularly by members of the Chicago School of sociology; it played a central role in such classic sociological investigations as Lynd and Lynd's (1929) *Middletown,* the study by Warner and his associates of Yankee City (Warner and Lunt 1941), and Whyte's (1943) *Street Corner Society.* After a long lapse in interest, observation has gained prominence again in recent years (cf. Brogdan and Taylor 1975; Johnson 1975; Schatzman and Strauss 1973). As Riley and Nelson (1974:6) note, the term "observation" is used in sociological parlance to include a wide range of activities that revolve around "watching the behavior of the group, listening to its members, and noting its physical characteristics." The designation sometimes includes combinations of interviewing and observation, while it is also used to distinguish between research that includes interviewing and that which does not. Some sociologists have gone so far in attempting to circumvent the problems inherent in interviewing that they have developed techniques, termed "inobtrusive measures," in which the observer cannot be seen by the subjects (cf. Webb et al. 1966).

With respect to interviewing, sociologists make a basic distinction between *standardized* and *nonstandardized* interviews. The former type involves the use of a common set of questions with all respondents, whereas the latter does not. Standardized interviews are further categorized as *scheduled,* where both the wording and order in which the questions are asked is specified, or as *nonscheduled.*[7] In the latter case, the interviewer is free to present the questions in the way in which it seems most suitable for each interviewee. Data obtained through the use of scheduled interviews are thus much more amenable to statistical analysis than those from unscheduled or nonstandardized interviews. Scheduled interviews can be either of the *fixed-alternative* or *closed-ended* type, in which case the respondent chooses from a predetermined list of answers, or *open-ended,* where the range of possible answers is not specified. The actual list of questions that is used in an interview is generally termed a *schedule.* It thus contrasts with a *questionnaire,* a list of questions the subject reads and completes without the assistance of the researcher.[8]

Sources on methodology

Some basic categories of sources can be distinguished in the vast literature on interviewing. A number of manuals present introductions to interviewing and, in some cases, related research techniques. Some of the most widely used are those by Babbie (1973), Backstrom and Hursh (1963), Bailey (1978), Denzin (1970), Gorden (1975), Hoinville and Jowell (1978), Kahn and Cannell (1957), Kerlinger (1964), Richardson, Dohrenwend, and Klein (1965), and Simon (1969). A number of collections of essays on methodology have appeared (e.g., Riley 1963; Franklin and Osborne 1971).

Other works deal with particular types or aspects of interviews. Gorden (1969) suggests that these can be classified with respect to whether they focus on the type of respondent or the type of interviewer.[9] In the first case, we find works that concentrate on the aged (Kastenbaum and Sherwood 1967), parents (Langdon 1954), children (Rich 1968), elites (Dexter 1970), potential employees (Turner 1968), and other groups. Sources that treat particular types of interviewers often deal with the use of interviews in such professions as nursing (Bermosk and Mordan 1964), medicine (Froelich and Bishop 1969), psychiatry and counseling (Davis 1971; Erickson and Shultz 1982; Labov and Fanshel 1977; Sullivan 1954), journalism (Sherwood 1969), and social work (Fenlason et al. 1962; Garrett 1942).

With few exceptions, these works fail to provide a critical perspective on interviewing. Most authors simply assume that they and their readers already know what interviews are all about. These writers thus rely on their status and that of their audience as members of a society in which interviews are an established speech-event type. The presumption seems to be that native speaker status enables the authors to forgo the need to examine the nature of the interview as a communicative event. The underlying argument seems to be as follows: "We all know what interviews are and why they are important. We will thus simply assume this knowledge and go on to present techniques for improving the quality of interviews or to explicate the nature of specialized forms of the interview."

The "bias" theory

It is, of course, nearly de rigueur to include a consideration of interview problematics. This generally comes under the aegis of examining the way in which interviewer-induced *bias* can reduce the validity and reliability of the findings. The inclusion of such considerations certainly helps to alert readers to certain types of problems. Discussions of bias emerge, nevertheless, from a highly problematic theoretical premise. The claim is that the influence of one or more of a range of independent variables, such as the age, gender, race, political views, personality, or interactional style of the researcher and/or interviewee, can "bias" responses to questions. The assumption here is that if you could strip the interview situation of all of these factors, the "real" or "true" or "unbiased" response would emerge. This ideal response is sometimes referred to as the "individual true value," abbreviated as the ITV (cf. Brenner 1981b). The thrust of the argument is that the researcher should attempt to ensure, insofar as is possible, that none of these factors has any special effect on the data. In analyzing the responses, such distortions should be factored out.

Becoming sensitive to the role of such factors is certainly laudable. Two implications of this line of reasoning are less so. First, this approach leads most practitioners to believe that if no particular source of "bias" is present or if such overt "distortions" have been accounted for, the researcher can treat these data as if they were a direct reflection of the interviewee's thoughts. In other words, once the problem of "bias" has been treated in this way, one can forget that the statements were made in the course of a particular interview. This facilitates the comparison of data from different interviews, interviews with different persons, and data collected through "participant observation" and interviews.

A second implication involves the generally implicit assumptions that lie at the base of this picture of interviewing. The "bias" theory reflects Durkheim's (1938) notion that social facts exist independently of the observer and can be perceived from without. It is similarly based on individualistic and positivistic assumptions regarding, in Karp and Kendall's (1982:251) terms, the stability and observability of social facts. A response lies within the interviewee, and the problem simply consists of extracting it from her or him as directly as possible. The truth value of an informant statement is measured vis-à-vis its correspondence to the "real" object "out there," as somehow grasped "objectively," independently of the manner in which it is communicated to the researcher. Note the way in which such advice encapsulates our own folk epistemology, conceiving of "the truth" as being singular, unequivocal, and semantically transparent, once it has been identified. It goes without saying (or does it really?) that this reassuringly places the researcher in the position of final arbiter of what is "correct" and "objective." It also strongly biases the analyst in favor of responses that seem to bear a direct relationship to the "reality" in question. Statements whose meaning is clearly affected by the situation in which they are uttered are deemed less reliable.

One of the difficulties encountered by this approach is that an individual's knowledge and attitudes emerge from a complex web of relations with other human beings. Interviewees do not draw, even ideally, on a fixed idea or feeling in answering a question, but connect questions with some element or elements of a vast and dynamic range of responses. Because the interview is itself a social interaction, it provides another impetus for generating new reactions. Moreover, the response is often less a selection of one element of this complex whole than an index, in Peirce's (1932: 2.305) sense of the term, of the relation between conflicting or competing elements (Cicourel 1974c:20). The goal of getting the "individual true value" for each question thus greatly oversimplifies the nature of human consciousness. As Dean and Whyte (1958:38) have pointed out, the interviewer's task is thus not that of fishing for "the true attitude or sentiment," but one of interpreting the subtle and intricate intersection of factors that converge to form a particular interview. The social situation created by the interview does not simply constitute an obstacle to the respondent's articulation of his or her beliefs. Like speech events in general, it shapes the form and content of what is said.

This becomes apparent in, inter alia, the way in which responses comment metacommunicatively on the interview situation itself (see Chapters 3 and 5 of this volume).

This is not to say, however, that interviews are just like any other speech event. As Wolfson (1976) has argued, interviews constrain the presentation of many types of forms and of certain topics and alter the manner in which observed features are presented. One rule takes precedence over others – the need to adapt the form and content of the information in order to make it apparent that it provides an answer to the question. In interview-elicited narratives, for example, features such as the conversational historical present tense (e.g., "And so he says to the guy . . .") are absent (Wolfson 1976, 1979). Similarly, as Wolfson (1976:192) notes, "there is often elaboration and emphasis on the specific part of the story which answers the question that has been asked." The interview is thus probably the last place where one should forget that the statements were made in a particular context.

The emergence of a critical understanding of the interview

A number of sources have appeared that provide us with important insight into the limitations of the interview as a research method. Their contribution lies in two key areas.

Reliability and validity. First, these works have clarified the thorny issues that surround the important problems of reliability and validity. These two concepts are discussed in most works on methodology, because they provide the benchmarks by which data analysis and collection are measured. "Reliability" refers to the probability that the repetition of the same procedures, either by the same researcher or by another investigator, will produce the same results. "Validity" refers to the accuracy of a given technique, that is, the extent to which the results conform to the characteristics of the phenomena in question.

Hyman et al. (1954:20–1) pointed out that very few studies in the methodological literature were concerned with validity. Emphasis was rather placed on decreasing inter-interviewer variation, that is, in reducing the extent to which inter-interviewer differences affect the reliability of data. As Hyman et al. note, this presents a strong force for methodological conservatism. It also suggests that such efforts toward methodological reform may have no positive effect whatsoever on the degree to which procedures enhance our understanding of the questions they investigate.

The work of Hyman et al. and others has increased the degree to which questions of validity are taken seriously, although a bias toward studies of reliability is still apparent (Gorden 1969:6). The degree to which such work has affected interview practice is, however, far from clear. Cicourel provides us with insight into why this is the case. He argues that Hyman and his associates fell short of resolving the dilemma due to their failure to question the premise that underlies the reliability versus validity issue – the idea that procedures can be designed that will be both reliable *and* valid (Cicourel 1964:93).

Cicourel (1982a) raises the question of *ecological validity*. This concept pertains to the degree to which the circumstances created by the researcher's procedures match those of the everyday world of the subjects (cf. Neisser 1976). The problem is that competing demands are placed on the researcher. Standardization, a crucial device for promoting reliability, leads interviewers to attempt to present each question in exactly the same manner to each respondent. Bailey (1978:171) even suggests that "the interviewer's inflection and intonation should be the same for each respondent."

This raises two issues. First, true standardization would be achieved if the *meaning* of the question were the same for each respondent. This leads writers such as Gorden (1969:61) to suggest that differences in social backgrounds between respondents will force the interviewer to change the question wording in order to maintain the validity of quantitative measures. The problem runs deeper than this, however, because, as Cicourel (1974c:20) and Dexter (1970:144) note, interviewees respond not simply to the wording of the question but to the interview situation as a whole.

A second issue emerges from the fact that each interview is a unique social interaction that involves a negotiation of social roles and frames of reference between strangers. As Hyman et al. (1954:80–1) show, "bias" seldom appears as the interviewer's imposition of her or his own ideological slant on the respondent. "Bias," meaning inter-respondent and inter-interviewer differences in the presentation of questions and the perception of responses, *is rather an interactional resource* that is used in accomplishing the task at hand.

As this task becomes more onerous – for example, if the schedule is long and complex, questions are repeated, or the material is socially sensitive – it becomes more difficult to obtain answers. The negotiation process becomes more critical at this stage, and the interviewer must draw upon a wider range of conversational resources in narrowing the gap between the standardized questions and the background knowledge and communicative norms of the interviewee. Interestingly, writers are divided on the issue as to whether or not this is a good thing. (Compare, for example, Bailey 1978 with Gorden 1969.) Cicourel's point is that such divergences emerge from the fact that reliability and validity are incompatible goals.

The concept of context and the nature of interpretation. This realization has led to a deeper understanding of the role of the context in interviews. As noted earlier in this chapter, many writers conceive of "the context" as being the sum total of physical, social, and psychological stimuli that exist at the time of an interaction. This definition conveniently allows the analyst to decide what counts as "the context" on the basis of his or her own assessment of the situation. It also dichotomizes the analysis of "contextual variables" from that of the verbal components of the discourse. Given the fact that responses address the total situation, this dichotomization is methodologically problematic.

Brenner (1978, 1980, 1981a, 1981b), Cicourel (1974c, 1981, 1982a, 1982b, 1985), Dexter (1970), and Mehan (1979) have challenged this separation. They argue that the context is a phenomenological construct that is created jointly by the participants. Not only are contexts not simply situational givens, they are continually renegotiated in the course of the interaction. The words of the interviewer and interviewee do not simply occur within this frame; along with nonverbal components, they are the very stuff of which the context is constructed. Each utterance thus reflects this ongoing process, just as it contributes to it. As Cicourel (1974c:88) notes, "the actor's remarks in the interview, even when termed spontaneous, are often the product of a carefully monitored kind of presentation."

This immediately calls into question the naive concept of the interviewer as the medium through which the respondents' attitudes and beliefs are conveyed to the reader. The interviewer rather stands as a co-participant in the construction of a discourse. This view also challenges received procedures for the interpretation of interview data. Researchers generally draw on their a priori, commonsense understandings of the meaning of the questions; these are then used as frames for the interpretation of responses. If questions and responses rather constitute small-scale models of interviewer–interviewee interaction, this mode of analysis will radically distort their significance.

Unresolved issues

In a nutshell, then, the sociological literature on interviewing consists on the one hand of myriad studies that presuppose and accordingly reify the very nature of the phenomena in question. On the other hand, a limited number of studies have revealed some of the basic

problems that underlie interview techniques. This work has not succeeded, however, in producing a methodological reformulation that
would tell practitioners how they can best cope with these problems.

One of the most pressing needs in this regard is a more detailed
analysis of the ways in which these difficulties emerge in interview data
and a method for identifying them. Most professional interviewers will
not be satisfied by general statements regarding the problematic nature
of their enterprise. Methodological reform will also require the presentation of concrete ways in which these findings can translate into
procedure.

Another central goal is the development of a greater understanding
of the nature of the interview as a communicative event. As Wolfson
(1976) has argued, the interview is a unique speech event that is patterned by a complex array of communicative features, many of which
are not shared by "ordinary" conversation. The precise nature of the
norms that underlie interviewing are, however, still very poorly understood. As Grimshaw (1969) and Cicourel (1964, 1974c, 1982a, 1986)
have argued, interviewing must be seen as a research subject in its own
right and not simply as a useful tool.

Finally, Cicourel (1974c) cuts to the very heart of the matter when he
notes that the linguistic and sociolinguistic background of the interviewee may differ from that of the researcher. Given that the two
parties are generally separated by lines of class, ethnicity, and/or cultural background, this is more than a remote possibility. This problem-
atizes the notion that the questions and responses mean the same things
to interviewee and interviewer. Cicourel (1974c:19) rightly suggests that
the only solution to the dilemma is learning about the commonsense understandings and the sociolinguistic background of both parties.

What is needed is a means of exploring the nature of the communicative norms brought into play in the interview. A clearer grasp on the
norms that are presupposed by the interview vis-à-vis those characteristic of the respondents' speech communities is a prerequisite for progress in these areas. One major limitation of the studies mentioned in
the previous section is that they fail to draw on data on a wide variety
of speech events in characterizing the background knowledge the interviewee brings to the encounter. If interview data alone are used in this
capacity, the argument becomes circular.

The roots of methodological conservatism

The work of Brenner, Cicourel, Dexter, Grimshaw, Hyman, Mehan,
Wolfson, and others certainly provides a basis for revamping our approach to the subject. Why, then, have the past few decades produced

almost no changes in the way in which most practitioners use interviews in their research? Interview techniques not only continue to reign as the major tool in social research but are still used in a highly uncritical fashion. This lack of awareness of the issues raised by the use of interviews in social-scientific research in general has been noted by Dexter (1970:157):

Professional interviewers have for the most part assumed without analysis the nature of the process in which they are engaged. Until that process is itself viewed as problematic, something to be analyzed and explored, we will not be ready to determine what it records and measures, let alone how it can be used to draw valid inferences, etc.

The ensuing decade has witnessed few responses to Dexter's challenge.

Some of the major obstacles to progress along these lines can be linked to basic, recurrent crises in social-scientific and linguistic theory. An exploration of this complex web of theoretical and methodological issues must be based, however, on a fuller understanding of the status of the interview as a communicative event, and I will thus postpone it to the last chapter. One factor promoting stagnation, of course, is that most practitioners see no reason to question their own methodology, given the uncritical acceptance of the role of interviewing in research manuals, in social-scientific and linguistic writings, and in modern society as a whole.

Even if practitioners recognize the need for methodological change, however, accepted canons of interview technique render it nearly impossible for them to do so. The development of a more sensitive approach to the use of interviews is obstructed by a number of fundamental contradictions in the communicative norms that guide such encounters. These revolve around the way in which the communicative norms of the interview and those of the interviewees' speech communities place competing demands on the researcher.

As I argue in Chapters 3 and 4, the interview presupposes a set of role relations, rules for turn-taking, canons for introducing new topics and judging the relevance of statements, constraints on linguistic form, and so on. This effects a displacement of many of the norms that guide other speech events in the local community. Even in the most "unstructured," "open-ended" interviews, the interviewer has a great deal more control over the development of the discourse, and the respondent is primarily confined to answering the questions. Indeed, as many writers have argued, interviews are not *supposed* to be conversations.

The natives are not all willing, however, to permit this substitution of imported for indigenous modes of interaction. The greater the distance between the cultural and communicative norms of researcher and consultants, the more likely it becomes that this hiatus will generate interpersonal tension and misinterpretation in interviews. This commonly leads to difficulties in inducing the respondent to answer the question, producing seemingly irrelevant or incomplete replies or even silence. If the social roles and communicative patterns of the interview stand in opposition to basic moral values and/or patterns of interaction, it can bring the interviewing process to a halt. Interviewers attempt, either consciously or unconsciously, to avoid such friction by drawing on the everyday sociolinguistic norms of the respondents in creating a "friendly atmosphere." Such rapport-building speech events include introducing oneself, making "small talk" before and after the interview and perhaps between questions. It is often necessary to permit respondents to "wander off the point" and provide "irrelevant" information at times, that is, to permit a bit more egalitarian distribution of the control over the interaction.

The interviewer is thus subjected to conflicting pressures. She or he expects to be able to keep the interaction within the confines of the interview. The very success of that interview depends, however, on the researcher's capacity for allowing native communicative routines to work their way into the interview situation. This ambiguity also provides conflicting bases for evaluating interviews. Does the ability to maintain a focus on the research interests of the interviewer and his or her plan for the interaction constitute success? Or do the best interviews emerge from a more egalitarian cooperation in which both fieldworker and consultant contribute to the interview agenda and to the form of the discourse? The dilemma also raises the familiar issue of reliability versus validity. The interviewer's attempts to increase reliability by standardizing the presentation of the questions thwarts her or his ability to achieve ecological validity.

These contradictions emerge from the same underlying problem. Our refusal to examine critically the communicative norms of the interview in light of those implicit in the interviewees' metacommunicative repertoires has forced these two sets of sociolinguistic patterns into a relationship of unreconcilable opposition. Unfortunately, methodologists of the interview have failed to illuminate the nature of these contradictions, let alone attempt their resolution. This has clearly hampered their ability to assist researchers in escaping a sort of methodological "double bind" (cf. Bateson et al. 1956) inherent in the received research methodology.

Plan of the book

Dismal as this portrait of the state of interviewing in the social sciences and linguistics may seem, the situation is far from hopeless. This book

seeks to demonstrate that we already possess the tools to place methodology on a solid footing. The main thing that is needed is a new point
of departure. My contention is that investigating the metacommunicative repertoire of the group in question is the necessary starting point
for research. This thesis cannot be argued in vacuo, that is, without
grounding the argument in the analysis of the communicative patterns
observed in a given speech community. This work thus focuses on the
way in which a group of Spanish-speakers in the United States exchange messages about their own cultural and linguistic system. An
analysis of *Mexicano* metacommunication provides me with a basis for
arguing the incompatibility of standard interview techniques with the
native system and for demonstrating the richness of these metacommunicative routines themselves as a source of linguistic and anthropological data. Having placed the interview in its social and communicative
context, I am able to look more deeply into the theoretical and political underpinnings of the received methodology.

Chapter 2 sets the stage for this analysis by providing background on
Mexicano society. The work is predicated on the notion that linguistic
patterns cannot be understood independently of social and cultural
patterns and vice versa. Most particularly, comprehension of a number
of central *Mexicano* genres that are collectively termed 'the talk of the
elders of bygone days' is predicated on knowledge of the profound
socioeconomic transformation that overtook the *Mexicano* residents of
northern New Mexico around the turn of the century. Losing their
subsistence base forced *Mexicanos* into a much more intimate and
economically dependent relationship with 'the outside world' and par-
tially displaced timeworn patterns of social interaction.

Chapter 3 focuses directly on the interview. The analysis points to
the ways in which interviewers commonly pose questions in such a way
that interviewees cannot answer them. The focus is on the communicative components of the interview situation that can obstruct the process
of obtaining responses and interpreting their meaning. The data are
drawn from the communicative blunders I committed in research with
Mexicanos in northern New Mexico.

My goal, however, is not simply to identify and describe such problems. The development of greater methodological sophistication is also
contingent on examining their cultural and communicative roots. A
basic thesis of this work is that such illumination will only follow from
awareness of the native metacommunicative patterns in the interviewees' speech communities. Chapter 4 thus traces the way in which *Mexicanos* acquire metacommunicative competence. I argue that moving
through the various levels of skill involves a progression from observation to imitation to performance; the competence of individuals is

continually reassessed on the basis of their control over appropriate speech forms and the pragmatic force of their words. This analysis points to the potential of native metacommunicative routines as sources of socio-cultural and sociolinguistic data. A comparison between the norms presupposed by these events and those involved in interview-centered research is used in isolating the sociolinguistic bases of some of the most fundamental problems introduced by placing too much reliance on interview techniques.

In Chapter 5, I utilize the preceding analysis of what is likely to go wrong in interviews in developing a proposal for setting them straight. I argue that fieldwork should begin with an investigation of native communicative patterns, particularly those pertaining to metacommunicative routines. The focus then shifts to detailing the way these results can be used in shaping research design, in periodic evaluations of the effectiveness of the methodology, and in interpreting interview data.

Chapter 6 suggests that the problems inherent in interviews are of much more than "purely methodological" significance. I try to show that the popularity of interview techniques is based on the fact that they encapsulate our folk theories regarding the nature of social reality and of communicative processes. Interviewing has thus enabled us to retain some of the basic preconceptions that we have striven so hard to banish from the domain of explicit theory. Our inability to come to terms with methodological issues thus greatly hinders theoretical advancement, just as it points out that we have not been entirely successful in extirpating a number of rather disturbing political implications of the research process.

2. The setting: Mexicano society and Córdova, New Mexico

The data were collected in Córdova, a community of about 700 inhabitants in the mountains of northern New Mexico. The residents are *Mexicanos*, with the exception of one recent Mexican immigrant, two middle-aged Anglo-Americans who have married Córdovans, and occasionally a few transient Anglo-American youths. *Mexicanos* are descendants of primarily Spanish and Mexican citizens who settled in New Mexico and southern Colorado during the seventeenth, eighteenth, and nineteenth centuries. Their ancestry includes a significant Native American element, but the *Mexicanos* consider themselves to be culturally Hispanic.

Córdova lies in the extreme southeast corner of Rio Arriba County (see map, Figure 1). The foothills area that includes the community is bordered on the east by the Sangre de Cristo mountain range; Córdova lies at the base of the highest peak in this section of the range, the Truchas Peak, which stands at 13,102 feet of elevation. The foothills extend some fourteen road miles to the west, where they are severed by the area's major water course – the Rio Grande. Córdova is situated in a small enclosed canyon, the Quemado Valley. The valley, which runs roughly east and west, is 6,800 feet above sea level. The surrounding hillsides can boast only sparse range grasses, cacti, and small trees, primarily piñons and junipers. The scarcity of arable land and the harshness of the environment are compounded by the scant and variable rainfall – an average of ten to fifteen inches per year (Maker, Folks, Anderson, and Link 1973:6–7). Elevations above 8,000 feet are characterized by more precipitation, denser stands of range grasses, and tall conifers (yellow and ponderosa pines, spruce, Douglas fir, aspen, etc.).

Most of the Córdovans' houses are built on the hillside that extends from the north bank of the Rio Quemado to just below the mesa above. Residents note that the selection of this location was motivated by the requirements of their defensive posture vis-à-vis nomadic tribes and in order to reserve the valley land for agriculture. All of the

31

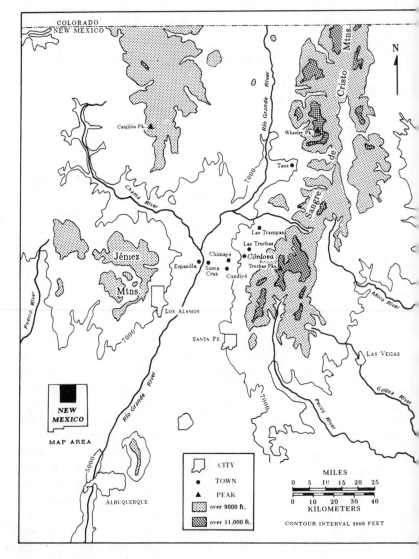

Figure 1. Northern New Mexico

houses were grouped around the community chapel in a roughly rectangular pattern until the twentieth century. The compactness, both physical and social, of the community and the appearance of the earthen homes and chapel are visible in turn-of-the-century photographs. The familiar Hispanic *plaza* or grid-pattern settlement (Simmons 1969; Stanislawski 1947) was complemented by the construction of *ranchos* 'isolated farm/ranches.' These have been built primarily on the south hillside, and the first such *ranchos* were founded in the initial decades of this century. The last three decades have witnessed the erection of numerous *ranchos* on the irrigated valley lands themselves.

These changes in settlement patterns are associated with fundamental changes in the mode of subsistence of the inhabitants. Córdova was founded between 1725 and 1743 (cf. Briggs 1986). The predominant mode of livelihood for almost two centuries was small-scale, subsistence-oriented agricultural and pastoral production. Modest harvests of corn, wheat, beans, legumes, and other crops were supplemented by meat, milk, and cheese from goats and, to a lesser extent, the meat of sheep and cattle. The construction of *ranchos* in the twentieth century, however, is associated with a growing displacement of the importance of agricultural and pastoral production in favor of first migratory and later daily wage labor. This movement from the central plaza to the isolated *ranchos* also reflects the growth of individualism in production and the social life of Córdovans in general.

Only a minute fraction of the residents' livelihood now comes from the land. Small herds of cattle are grazed during the summer on the surrounding uplands; most of this area is now part of the Carson and Santa Fe national forests. A few Córdovans raise alfalfa or hay for winter feed, and a number of residents keep small garden plots. The majority of the work force is now employed in the "Atomic City" of Los Alamos, New Mexico (see Figure 1). Although most work for the Zia Corporation (which provides janitorial and construction services), some are employed by the Los Alamos National Laboratory itself. Like the Lawrence Livermore Laboratory in California, Los Alamos is primarily devoted to designing and testing nuclear weapons and other projects under contract with the Department of Energy. Córdovans also work elsewhere in Los Alamos; the women are frequently employed as domestics in the scientists' homes. Additional jobs are found in Santa Fe and Española. Nearly all of the Córdovans who have jobs in these three cities commute daily to their work, and car pools are now common.

A few residents have secured jobs in and around Córdova. These include a postmaster and the owners of two small stores. Several Córdovans are employed by a Community Action Program–sponsored Head Start facility in Córdova and by the Mountain View Elementary School, which lies between Córdova and neighboring Truchas. Others perform unskilled and semiskilled labor in the homes of fellow Córdovans. Upward of thirty-five residents gain income through marketing their wood carvings to (primarily) Anglo-Americans, although such funds provide supplemental rather than primary employment for all

but a few (cf. Briggs 1980). Not all Córdovans have been accommo-
dated by these new sources of livelihood. Many are dependent on
Social Security, Aid to Families with Dependent Children, food
stamps, workmen's compensation, and other types of aid. Cutbacks in
such programs between 1980 and the present have created additional
hardship. Some have reacted to the scarcity of employment by working
outside the community part of the year or even by moving to cities in
New Mexico, Colorado, Nevada, and California.

What factors produced this situation of poverty for some and reliance on outside resources for all? The past hundred years have constituted a period of rapid change for Córdovans. Until the early part of
this century, the residents subsisted mainly on the produce of their
farm plots in the valley and dry farms in the uplands along with their
herds of goats, sheep, and cattle. This mode of livelihood entailed
access to irrigated land in the Quemado Valley and to the pastures,
fuel wood, timber, game, and other resources of the uplands. Documents dating as early as 1743[1] demonstrate that Córdovans possessed
rights to a grant of land that was bounded

on the east, by a small hill which is commonly called "Los Burros," on the
summit of the mountain, on the west Las Peñas Negras, commonly called
Centinela, on the north, the edge of the ridge (*riberas de la ceja*), on the
south, the Pajarito mountain, adjoining the grant of Cundiyó [Catron Papers,
case #212].

This tract corresponds to the area that the residents of Córdova and
surrounding villages had recognized as belonging to the community. It
measured roughly thirty miles east to west and fifteen miles north to
south (Catron Papers, #212). In a mountainous and semiarid environment, this quantity of land was vital to survival.

The Treaty of Guadalupe Hidalgo of 1848, which ceded the area to
the United States, formally guaranteed the property rights of Mexican
citizens. Unfortunately, the following century witnessed the expropriation of a great deal of the *Mexicano* land base, particularly community
common lands, by Anglo-American and *Mexicano* land speculators
and by the U.S. government (cf. Briggs and Van Ness 1986; Van Ness
1979; Westphall 1983). Córdova fared poorly in the land struggle. In
the absence of the original grant papers, the Court of Private Land
Claims rejected the residents' claim to the Pueblo de Quemado Grant
in 1898 (Court of Private Land Claims, case #212, SRCA). No attempts were made to deny rights to valley lands or home sites, and the
decision had little impact on Córdovans for two decades. The uplands
were included in the newly created Santa Fe National Forest in 1915,
however, and the implementation of various grazing regulations soon

deprived Córdovans of nearly all the subsistence that they had formerly gained from pastoralism. As the elders put it:

A: Everything has ended. Oh, there used to be lots of goats, sheep, and . . .
B: There used to be lots of everything.
A: The uplands used to be open, but that is no longer true. Now there is the fence and there is the government.

Since Córdovans had never been able to subsist entirely on garden produce, this undermining of their subsistence base forced them to depend on outside employment. This phenomenon was not wholly new; Córdovans had worked outside the community since the Spanish colonial era. After 1915, however, Córdovans had to sell their labor to an unprecedented degree and to work for employers of a different cultural background. This situation, along with the transition from a predominantly barter to a predominantly cash economy and the replacement of locally produced with mass-produced goods, created a growing need for cash income.

Córdovans resorted to a number of types of migratory wage labor in coping with this situation. Building railroads and working in mines and other nonagricultural enterprises in the area, harvesting sugar beets, onions, potatoes, and other crops in Colorado, and herding sheep in Colorado, Utah, Wyoming, Montana, and New Mexico all provided opportunities for outside work (Harper, Córdova, and Oberg 1943:77; Siegel 1959:38; Soil Conservation Service 1937:2). It has been estimated that before the Depression, 7,000 to 10,000 workers from the villages of the middle Rio Grande Valley, the land drained by the Rio Grande between Elephant Butte and the New Mexico–Colorado line, left each year to engage in these types of migratory labor (Harper et al. 1943:76–7). This pattern created a large dichotomy between the experience of those born around the turn of the century and that of previous generations.

Although Córdovans and other *Mexicanos* had become highly dependent on such employment, this source of income was sharply curtailed with the onset of the Great Depression. After the Depression gained momentum, earnings from outside work were reduced by as much as 80 percent (Harper et al. 1943:77). Widespread starvation was prevented by the implementation of many federal work and aid projects, but this was merely a stopgap solution.[2] The Depression proved to be a bitter cup to swallow for many rural *Mexicanos,* as this constriction of outside employment made the residents even more painfully aware of the expropriation of land resources.

A more permanent solution for this acute impoverishment followed the influx of population into New Mexico during and after World War II. Much of this growth was associated with the federal installations in Albuquerque and Los Alamos. The Los Alamos National Laboratory and the service industries that grew in its shadow provided opportunities for daily wage labor, a new source of cash income for residents of the area. The participation of Córdovans in the national economy was further enhanced by improved accessibility to the community. Before 1946, the road to Córdova was little more than a trail, and daily travel to Sante Fe or Los Alamos was impossible. In that year, however, the road that traverses the plain above Córdova was graded and maintained with gravel, and in 1953 it was paved.[3]

Depriving rural *Mexicanos* of their subsistence base placed them in a position of political–economic dependence on 'the outside world,' that is, modern industrial society. This in turn induced great changes in the way they related to each other. Corporatism, stressing the identity of individuals vis-à-vis their membership in the group, was a central feature of *Mexicano* society through the early twentieth century. This ethic was celebrated, as it were, in the importance of cooperative labor as well as in communitywide religious feast days and in dances. Corporatism similarly pervaded interpersonal relations; a person who refused to give or lend a possession to someone in need was sanctioned. But because the men were forced to spend months away from the community as migrant laborers or to leave each day for Los Alamos, they were no longer able to be on hand for community events. Working for wages in an Anglo-dominated world also fostered the adoption of individualist and materialist values. This has been reflected in recent decades in the construction of more "modern" homes on isolated valley or hillside plots away from the *plaza*. It thus became increasingly difficult to realize basic cultural values in production and social relations.

The residents of Córdova and similar communities were able, nevertheless, to preserve their ability to express their sense of themselves and their culture by retaining their language. All native Córdovans are fluent in Spanish, and Spanish is still the predominant language. Many residents over fifty know little or no English. The intimacy of the connection between language and *Mexicano* identity is enhanced by the distinctiveness of the dialect. The features of New Mexican Spanish were recognized through the pioneering work of Aurelio M. Espinosa, Sr. (1911, 1930) and Juan B. Rael (1937). New Mexican Spanish contrasts with the standard on primarily phonological, lexical, and suprasegmental grounds.[4]

Dialectal differences are closely related to social and cultural experience. Using Castilian or Standard Mexican Spanish in northern New Mexico immediately alerts native speakers of New Mexican Spanish that the person in question has emerged from a vastly different social, cultural, and educational background and, more than likely, a higher social class. A person learns New Mexican Spanish not in formal academic settings but by living with *Mexicanos*. A stranger who speaks New Mexican Spanish is thus assumed to have a substantial body of experience in common with those who share the dialect. In some cases, this process operates on an even more intimate level. Córdovans systematically substitute the *sh* sound [š] in words containing a *ch* /č/; the residents of surrounding villages can accordingly tell that a person is from Córdova simply by detecting this feature in her or his speech.

The connection between self-conception and communication exists not only in language structure but in language use. *Mexicano* culture has always been rich in spoken and musical folklore (see, for example, Campa 1946, 1979; Espinosa 1910–16, 1953; Rael 1951, [1957]; Robb 1980). Proverbs, folktales, scriptural allusions, ballads, hymns, and other forms are referred to collectively as *la plática de los viejitos de antes* 'the talk of the elders of bygone days'. This points to their status as central encapsulations of the approach to life that was embodied in former generations. The present elders view the transmission of this 'talk' as crucial to the survival of *Mexicano* culture and to the well-being of its members.

Although the elders do not reject all the accoutrements of modern society, they see its individualistic and materialistic mores as responsible for the growing erosion of *Mexicano* values and the unraveling of the community's social fabric. Teaching about the past and its values is the most important task awaiting an individual in his or her final years. Production and social relations may have lost their status as means of embodying the key values of working the land, treating fellow human beings with respect, and trusting in the will of God. Performances in these genres have, however, retained their potency as means of expressing one's beliefs and of conveying them to children and grandchildren.[5]

Such performances do not involve a simple repetition of timeworn oral texts. Individuals do gain respect for the ability to use a large range of examples and to perform in various genres. But community members place primary emphasis on using folkloric examples *para traer el sentido* 'in order to convey the sense, meaning, or significance' of a given situation. This involves utilizing a genre appropriate to the context at hand and then selecting just the right example to prove one's point. The proverb or what have you is then *embedded* in the conversation. This involves shaping the text to render it clear and comprehensible to interlocutors and complementing it with features (such as introductory and closing phrases, quotation-framing verbs, exegesis, etc.) that will point out its bearing on the issue in question. The best speakers thus draw on a body of texts that carries great moral force and on rhetorical devices for demonstrating the relevance of tradition to matters of immediate concern in speaking elegantly and persuasively. Rhetorical competence is highly valued, and an individual's verbal capacity is closely related to her or his reputation in the community.

Mexicanos thus place a great deal of emphasis on oral communication, and speech itself forms a frequent subject of discourse. A political meeting, for example, will form the subject of debate for days or weeks afterward. Discussion will center both on the force of each speaker's claims and on the élan with which the claims are presented.[6] *Mexicanos* are no less concerned with the substance of a person's remarks and the bearing of his or her words on future events than anyone else. But the way in which they learn how to use language renders them particularly sensitive to the stylistic cues, especially those alerting the hearer that a message carries important implicit meanings. *Mexicano* views of the communicative process thus heighten awareness of the political dimensions of speech, and the political-economic transformation of their society has underlined this politicization of language use. *Mexicanos* have a great deal to teach us about the beauty and complexity of oral communication. But alas for newcomers who lack sensitivity to the rhetorics and politics of language use; they are destined to learn these lessons the hard way.

3. Interview techniques vis-à-vis native metacommunicative repertoires; or, on the analysis of communicative blunders

As noted in Chapter 2, *Mexicanos* draw on a wide range of accepted speech forms, and they know intuitively which types of expressions are appropriate for which social contexts. Growing up in a given speech community presents the language learner with innumerable opportunities to discover the rules that relate form, context, and meaning. When a researcher leaves her or his own native speech community and establishes contact with another group of human beings, however, no such common body of experience is available to smooth the initial encounters. The same problem arises when investigators work with a different social class or ethnic group within their own society. In filling this gap, researchers commonly draw on the communicative device their speech community views as the best means of obtaining large bodies of information in the least amount of time – the interview. The implicit reasoning seems to be that interviews allow the researcher to assume control of the type and quantity of information being conveyed. This enables him or her to circumvent the usual constraints on the transmission of knowledge (e.g., kinship, age, degree of intimacy, gender, initiation, etc.)

I will argue that this process is really not quite as smooth and successful as we seem to imagine. Our ability to banish the native communicative norms that operate in other environments is far from complete, and the natives' own discourse rules have an odd way of infiltrating the interview. Unfortunately, researchers are seldom adequately aware of this process; most are hampered by their failure to learn how such features operate in the speech repertoire as a whole. This results in a communicative impasse – the researcher thinks she or he is engaged in an interview, whereas the "interviewees" believe themselves to be involved in a very different type of speech event. This hiatus greatly impedes the communicative process, disrupting interviews and rendering the analysis of the data a most precarious enterprise. Since the resultant errors are systematic rather than random, they are not "canceled out" through the standardization of questionnaires and the application of sampling techniques.

The data are drawn from interviews I conducted in Córdova. I am thus primarily concerned with informal, open-ended interviews, since most of my interviewing in northern New Mexico has been of this type. I will address the bearing of these findings on survey-based research that the investigator conducts in her or his own community in Chapters 5 and 6.

Speech events are multifaceted phenomena; interviews are certainly no exception. Given the complexity of the interview process, it is necessary to break down the task of examining the problems that can arise in interviews into conceptually manageable parts. A useful segmentation is provided by Jakobson's (1960) analysis of the components of the communicative event, which was subsequently expanded by Hymes (1964, 1972). I have couched the following analysis in its terms in order to pinpoint the sources of different types of communicative difficulties encountered in interviews. Because it is not tied to any specific language or speech event type, it can serve as a heuristic device for use by other fieldworkers in keeping in mind the sorts of factors that are crucial in planning, conducting, and analyzing interviews. This chapter draws on the model as a means of analyzing interview data; it can also serve as a means of obtaining information on native metacommunicative repertoires for use in devising a research plan (a subject discussed in Chapters 4 and 5).

A model for the analysis of interviews

A schematic representation of some of the principal components of the interview is given in Figure 2. The primary participants are termed the INTERVIEWER and the RESPONDENT(s). The MESSAGE FORM consists of the signals, both auditory and visual, that serve as sign vehicles in interviewer–respondent(s) communication. The REFERENT roughly corresponds to Peirce's (1932:2.230–1) "Object" and Saussure's (1959) *signifié,* the "something else" that is represented by the sign vehicle. Because the cognitive or referential function of transmitting information is dominant in interviewing, much of my analysis will be devoted to difficulties in establishing and maintaining reference. Communication also depends on opening one or more CHANNELS, physical (generally, visual and acoustic) and psychological circuits between participants. As in all forms of communication, a number of CODES, both linguistic and nonverbal (proxemic, gestural, etc.) must be shared by interviewer and respondents in order to permit the encoding and interpretation of messages.

Some components relate to two or more of the preceding factors.

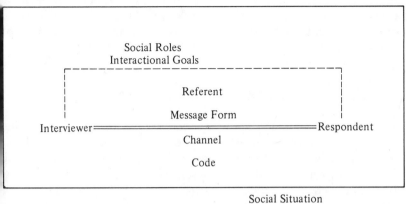

Figure 2. Components of the interview situation

The SOCIAL ROLES assumed by interviewer and respondent(s) prove to be of special importance to the success of the interview. INTERACTIONAL GOALS, the motivation of each of the participants for engaging in the interview, are frequently divergent in interviews. SOCIAL SITUATION refers to the context in which the interaction takes place, including the time (of the day, of the week, in terms of seasonal cycles, etc.) and location in which the interview transpires. These considerations may be crucial, because an interview will proceed differently if it is the central activity and other participants are excluded or if it takes place while planting, attending a ceremony, or the like.

Likewise, the interview itself will be placed within one or more of the society's categories of TYPES OF COMMUNICATIVE EVENTS, such as making a few bucks or imparting an esoteric tradition. The importance of the particular social roles, the overall social situation, and the type of communicative event that pertain to a given interview are revealed in their joint role in defining norms of interaction. Such norms determine who can participate, what sorts of information can be conveyed, how much can be said, what linguistic forms can be used, and so forth.

As Jakobson (1960:353) has noted, any of the basic components can play a dominant role in characterizing the verbal structure of a message and in defining the major communicative function of the event. Jakobson also argues that the subordinate factors still play vital roles in conveying the meaning of an utterance. It is especially important to keep some sort of inventory of such factors in mind in analyzing communicative problems, because such failures may result from the "malfunction" of any one of these components (or, of course, from some combination). This is not to say, however, that this model is exhaustive or that such representations are themselves exempt from the need for critical analysis.[1]

Key concepts defined

To avoid the emergence of any communicative obstacles to the reader's comprehension of what I am trying to get across, a few definitions are in order. One of the most basic distinctions I will be making (and one that lies behind the Jakobson–Hymes model) contrasts referential and indexical modes of signification.[2] As I noted above, the *referential* function of language lies in its ability to point to persons, objects, events, and processes. Reference rests ultimately on a perceived correspondence between the "content" of expressions and some state of affairs in "the real world." Contrastively, *indexical* meaning is dependent on some feature(s) of the context in which the expression is uttered. Some signs are intrinsically indexical, since their meaning cannot be discerned without interpreting their relationship to the situation. The meaning of the first person pronoun, for example, is contingent on the identity of the person who uses it.[3]

Indexical meanings can also be conveyed through the use of syntax, prosody, gesture, and the like. Take an utterance such as "John is a *very* intelligent fellow." How will the meaning of the statement be affected if the pitch of my voice rises and then falls in an exaggerated fashion on *"very,"* perhaps accompanied by an elongation of the initial vowel and a raising of the eyebrows? This combination of prosody and gesture will signal the hearer that the intended meaning is antithetical to that conveyed by referential content alone: John is really a dolt.

Failure to recognize the importance of this distinction lies at the heart of methodological dilemmas in interviewing. It is not simply the case that some signs are indexical or that indexical meanings are simply "added on" to referential ones. As Silverstein notes, "the sign modes of most of what goes on in the majority of speech events are not referential" (1976:15). Interview discourse is highly indexical, because the meaning of responses is contingent on the questions that precede them, previous question–answer pairs, the social situation, the relationship between the interviewer and interviewee, and a host of other factors. Researchers often operate, however, in keeping with an unstated and untested belief that the meaning of interview discourse can be interpreted exclusively or at least primarily on the basis of its referential content. As I argued in Chapter 1, the standardization of survey questions constitutes an attempt to reduce or eliminate the influence of the context of individual interviews as a determinant of the meaning – or at least to standardize indexical meanings.

The referential–indexical distinction is closely related to another key concept, that of *communicative competence*. Chomsky (1965) established the importance of the concept of linguistic competence, which he defined as the ability to produce an infinite number of grammatical sentences from a finite set of syntactic rules. Hymes (1971a, 1971b) redefined the term, noting that the ability to communicate entails more than a knowledge of syntax and semantics alone. Acquiring communicative competence involves knowing which expressions can be used under what circumstances to convey which meanings. In other words, mastery of the referential power of speech must be complemented by proficiency in use of its indexical properties if an individual is to gain communicative competence.

One of the major goals of this book is to show that the design, implementation, and analysis of interview-based research must emerge from awareness of the nature of the respondents' communicative competence. If the ability to communicate effectively in interviews and to interpret the data is identified with the ability to encode and decode referential meaning alone, inaccuracy, distortion, and misunderstanding are inevitable. This problem is particularly acute with respect to large-scale studies conducted in the researcher's own society. The point is that referential functions evince much less variation along the lines of class, ethnicity, geography, social situation, and the like than do indexical ones. Researchers who attempt to justify their failure to address these issues with reference to the fact that they speak the same language and live in the same society as their research subjects are thus playing a dangerous game of self-delusion.

Procedural problems in the interview

I will term the obstacles to the success of the interview "procedural problems." Churchill (1978:89) uses the expression in reference to 'the technical problems involved in delivering a request so that [speaker] and [hearer] both find clear meaning in the utterance." I will use the term, in a somewhat broader sense, to describe difficulties created by the researcher's questions that prevent the respondent(s) from answering. Although most procedural problems result from the inability of the interviewee to respond appropriately, I will also use the expression in reference to cases in which the respondent understands the researcher's question but either cannot or chooses not to respond.

Some procedural problems affect all conversational situations. In-adequate competence in the language is a code consideration that can limit the fieldworker's ability to collect data in all speech situations. Similarly, a lapse in the acoustical and/or psychological engagement of the interviewer and the respondent can disrupt the transmission of any message. But I am particularly interested in procedural problems that pose special difficulties for the interview.

Channel

The classical interview presupposes the suitability of explicit, referen-tially rich, verbal transmissions for learning about a given topic. Never-theless, communicative groups differ widely in the norms that pre-scribe which messages are to be transmitted through primarily verbal means and which are not. One is reminded of the importance of drum-signaling in certain parts of Africa (Herzog 1945), the curled-lip ges-ture among the Kuna of Panama (Sherzer 1973), and the use of hand gestures to convey aggressive, obscene expressions in our own society. Some messages can only be transmitted nonverbally, whereas others may combine a minimally essential nonverbal component with verbal elaboration. In either of these cases, repeated attempts to delve into these areas through speech alone will fail repeatedly.

This problem is illustrated by my initial difficulties in interviewing Silvianita and George López. The Lópezes were quite interested in my research project, and we had developed a strong friendship by the time I began the formal research. Nevertheless, my initial attempts to elicit exegesis on the local carvers and on the carving process were almost complete failures. The problem only resolved itself once I began carv-ing with the couple, thus receiving comments on my work and on the wood-carving art as a whole.

This example illustrates the problem of referential restrictions in general. The carvers were not simply examples of the "inarticulate artist" stereotype; given the proper circumstances, they were quite able to explicate their work. The problem is rather that such artistic metacommunication was encompassed by a more comprehensive semi-otic. Certain technical and stylistic features were elucidated primarily through visual signs – demonstration by the master on the student's carving. It was possible to obtain verbal exegesis in most cases. Decon-textualized questions were, however, quite ineffective in eliciting this material. The relevant metacommunicative information was provided in response either to purely visual signs (the appearance of a problem on the student's piece) or by verbal indexes of visual signs (e.g., 'How do you do this?'). In similar contexts, efforts to obtain explicit verbal exegesis on such topics will meet with failure or will fail to reveal the semiotic richness and complexity of how people actually deal with such situations.

Social situation

Some sense of when questions are appropriate is a common concern among fieldworkers, even if violations of such norms of comportment may be equally widespread. Interviewees are particularly sensitive to the social and political implications of providing the desired information, because the interview process brings the referential or cognitive function of language to the fore. The posing of questions is entirely interdicted in some settings (cf. Goody 1978:21), while others simply place restrictions on the range of lexical items that may be used or the topics that can appropriately be raised. The fieldworker may, for example, have to place herself or himself in special circumstances in order to be able to broach lewd or sensitive areas with impunity. Communication is likewise impeded in certain cases by the proximity of would-be eavesdroppers. Some fieldworkers circumvent this restriction by transporting their consultants to another location for interviews (see, for example, Cancian 1965:197–8).

Such observations are commonsensical. But three components of this problem may be less obvious. First, normative associations of social settings and appropriate modes of verbal interaction are culture specific, and they generally vary between social classes or subgroups as well (cf. Grimshaw 1969, 1969–70; Strauss and Schatzman 1955).[4] Sensitive and effective interviewing thus presupposes awareness of the society's categories of speech acts and social situations and the rules for relating them (cf. Frake 1972).

Second, this information is not only requisite to avoiding egregious faux pas. The context in which a question is posed often affects the respondent's interpretation of the query and the nature of his or her response. Resultant variations in the received data thus range from the interviewee's intentional omission or falsification of material to subtle differences in pragmatic or indexical meanings. These problems are particularly important in the case of research that deals specifically with pragmatic issues.

Third, even though the referential or cognitive function is generally dominant in interviews, this does not, as Jakobson (1960:353) has noted, mean that other communicative functions are of no importance. As Austin (1962) pointed out, language does not simply provide us with a vehicle for *describing* nonlinguistic events. Speech also possesses a *performative* capacity, meaning that words are also means of *creating or transforming* a given state of affairs. The performative force of an utterance may include a transformation of the relationship between interviewer and respondent(s) or between the respondent(s) and other persons who are present.

I found it nearly impossible, for instance, to collect data on forth-coming events that involved some of my closest friends in Córdova. I eventually learned that members of semicollective groups of cooperat-ing households never announce the imminence of such occasions to each other, let alone issue direct invitations. An explicit request for the pleasure of a person's company at a baptismal celebration or the butchering of a pig carries a covert message: Come, but as a stranger (cf. Briggs 1981:158–72). My consultants' desire to incorporate me into their group prevented them from responding directly to questions re-garding such events. This provides another example of the importance of attending to the strategic dimensions of communicative processes in this society. Indirection appears to be operative in an analogous semi-otic system – the regulation of participation in Warm Springs (Native American) ceremonials (Philips 1974).

Key and genre

As I noted, the use of interview techniques presupposes a model of social interaction. The interviewer specifies the issues to be covered, while the respondent supplies the information. The focus of the partici-pants is on conveying the needed information as efficiently, explicitly, completely, and accurately as possible. Of course, the consultants' speech repertoire may not include an analogous category, or the set-ting for such an event may not be at all the same. Even insofar as the respondent can be convinced to play this particular game, however, she or he is likely to break frame, to use Goffman's expression.

Two ways in which this frequently occurs are through changes of key and genre. The term "key" refers to "the tone, manner, or spirit in which an act is done" (Hymes 1972:62). The point is that the same words, possessing the same semantic content, may be spoken for an entirely different effect, such as humor, sarcasm, or equivocation. The fact that such an utterance is not to be taken at face value is often signaled extremely subtly, and exclusive use of nonverbal markers (changes of expression, posture, and/or distance between participants, etc.) is common (cf. Kendall 1981:246). Given cultural differences in the contextual parameters of such changes of key and in the nature of the signals, the fieldworker can easily record the face value of statements that were designed to be taken otherwise. This problem is compounded by his or her expectation that the interviewee will respond in a straightforward, "serious," discursive manner.

The latter bias similarly handicaps the interviewer's ability to discern changes of genres. My early field recordings reveal numerous proverbs, jokes, scriptural allusions, and so forth. Because the formal and contextual clues that permit the hearer to identify an utterance as a token of one of these genres are quite complex and subtle, I frequently failed to distinguish them from unmarked ("ordinary") speech.[5]

The fieldworker's failure to discern a shift in genre presents two important problems for the research. First, she or he is accordingly unaware that special norms apply to the interpretation of that utterance. A literal reading of the referential content of the words generally yields interpretive errors, as is the case with our own literary genres. Second, overemphasis on the explicit, discursive, unmarked speech fostered by the interview situation makes it much more difficult to see that an important native metacommunicative event has just taken place. As I argue in Chapter 4, *Mexicano* scriptural allusions, oral history, political rhetoric, repetition elicitation formulas, and other routines simultaneously invoke the force of traditional values and comment on features of the ongoing interaction. Such utterances link the normative and contingent, the general and the specific, thus providing valuable exegesis on both spheres. If fieldworkers are not sensitive to the signals that mark such performances, however, such insights will be lost.

Interactional goals

It is clear that the meanings of utterances emerge from their location within a particular context. This is especially true of responses – "second pair parts" whose relevance is conditioned by a preceding "first pair part" (in Sacks's 1967 terms). However, as Goffman (1981:40–8) has argued, responses may address all or part of the first pair part and/or some other element of the context. In the case of interviews, the respondent's orientation toward the interaction as a whole may inform his or her responses. This is only remarkable in that the interviewer and interviewee's motivations for participation in the interaction are likely to be dissimilar. If the fieldworker simply posits an identity between her or his goals in the interview – especially that of the transmission of information – and those of the respondent, he or she may fail to discern the central role of the latter's orientation in determining the meaning of the responses (cf. Herzfeld 1980).

An example of this sort of difficulty emerges from an interview with an elderly Córdovan couple, Aurelio and Costancia Trujillo, regarding the history of social inequality within the community. The Trujillos and I had established a quasi kin relationship soon after I entered Córdova; they addressed me as *hijo* 'son', and I generally used the terms *mamá* 'mother' and *papá* 'father' in addressing them. They accordingly took it upon themselves to teach me how to behave in accordance with *Mexicano* norms. Mr. Trujillo, who was highly religious, was especially interested in imparting to me the basic tenets of *Mexicano* "folk" Catholicism. He responded to what I deemed a particularly important question – 'Were there any *ricos* ['very wealthy individuals'] here in bygone days?' – by noting that 'No, they were all poor, but they helped one another, they performed acts of charity. Now there is no one who would help another. And, if they help you, they say, "pay me." Everything comes to an end, and it has all ended.' His response thus focused on the religiosity of prior generations and effects of this faith in promoting harmony within the community.

Nevertheless, statements that had previously been made by Mr. Trujillo and by other consultants asserted that Córdova had boasted *ricos* in the past. I was thus forced to deal with this apparent contradiction in my analysis of the interview. After numerous auditions of the tape, I was able to see that the couple's orientation to the interview contrasted sharply with my own. Whereas I sought to gain information on the theological basis of social inequality and on the rise of a particular *rico*, they were using the interview to try and convince me of the prevalence of religiously motivated cooperation in 'bygone days' and of the superiority of this *Weltanschauung* over secular individualism. Mr. Trujillo thus interpreted my 'Were there any *ricos* here in bygone days?' as pertaining to a basic contrast between the "impoverished but united past" versus the "wealthier but divided" present. His response appeared inconsistent only in the context of my goals for the interview (and thus my interpretation of the question).

Type of communicative event

The preceding example brings up a related problem. If the category of "interview" is not shared by the respondent or if the latter does not utilize this frame in defining such interactions, then he or she may apply norms of interaction and canons of interpretation that differ from those of the interviewer. In other words, the data obtained in interviews are affected by societal differences in the interactional goals of the participants. Even though fieldworkers may define the situation as a focus on the explicit transmission of data, respondents may see the process as entertainment, pedagogy, obtaining cash income, protecting her or his neighbors from outside scrutiny, and so forth.

The implications are threefold. First, the interviewee's categorization of the interaction will profoundly influence what subjects may be addressed, how much information can be given, how many personal or collective "secrets" to reveal, what speech forms may be used, and the like. As was the case with the interactional norms, the frame that the respondent provides for the event will significantly affect his or her interpretation of the questions and thus the nature of the responses. If the type of speech event invoked by the interviewee does not emphasize the referential function, this will affect the reliability of the referential content of the responses as an index of their meaning. Therefore, a minimally adequate analysis of interview data entails awareness on the part of the fieldworker of (1) the society's (or subgroup's) categories of communicative events and (2) the signals that enable participants to discern the category (or categories) being applied to any given situation by those involved in the exchange.

Second, research on conversation has shown that interlocutors must process more than just the semantic content of discourse in order to grasp its meaning. Grice (1975) advances the notion of *conversational implicature.* He argues that utterances are shaped by the need to reflect "maxims of conversation" that constrain speakers to render their contributions relevant, factually grounded, perspicuous, and the like. Addressees draw on these maxims in trying to discern the manner in which the words they hear make sense in terms of the ongoing interaction. Cicourel (1974a, 1974c, 1982a) and Garfinkel (1967) emphasize the "common sense knowledge of social structures," the participants' background knowledge that guides their interpretation of the discourse. Cicourel in particular stresses the ethnographic or organizational information regarding persons, institutions, events, processes, and the like that become relevant in the course of an interaction.

The point is that different sorts of both conversational implicature and commonsense knowledge become relevant in contrastive communicative settings. A shift from one type of speech event to another thus prompts participants to draw on a new set of assumptions. This is illustrated by Cicourel's recent work on medical discourse (1982; personal communication, 1985). As the same case is represented in an interview with the patient, in the initial write-up, in informal consultation between physicians, and in the final report, the nature of the assumptions that inform interpretation of what are ostensibly the same facts changes radically.

Let us return to the problem of contrastive classifications of interview discourse. If participants do not share a common frame for the interaction, their interpretations of the meaning of what is said will be based on divergent sets of assumptions. Since these processes are largely tacit, the failure to recognize this divergence in classification will produce differences in interpretation that are similarly likely to go undetected. This issue is hardly of relevance to open-ended interviews conducted in another society alone. Few practitioners who conduct surveys concern themselves with the nature of the unstated assumptions that shape the respondents' interpretation of questions and the way they respond. The researchers' assumption seems to be either that acceptable questions are semantically transparent or that the respondents' assumptions will match those of the practitioner. Cicourel (1974c), in one of the few investigations of the problem, shows that such beliefs are mistaken. (See also Cicourel 1986.)

Third, conversational maxims are context sensitive. Insensitivity to the respondent's definition of the situation may accordingly lead the researcher to violate the speech norms evoked by the respondent's categorization. Such norms will, of course, restrict the range of interactional strategies that can be utilized in obtaining data as well as the variety of topics that can be addressed. Nevertheless, disregarding these "inconveniences" is quite detrimental to establishing rapport; a number of cases have even been reported in which such faux pas have brought research projects to a premature termination.

Reference

The procedural problems I have examined thus far relate primarily to the indexical or context-sensitive functions of speech. Both interviewer and respondent may share a common interpretation of the referential meaning of what is said and yet may differ widely on their interpretations of indexical meanings. This can create severe problems for researchers who have mastered the semantics and syntax of another language without gaining sufficient competence in subtle indexical functions. The consequences can be just as great, however, for researchers working in their own society who mistake a common syntax and lexicon for shared communicative competence.

I now wish to show, however, that reference is really not quite as simple and transparent as this discussion may have suggested. Even if the interviewee can identify the semantic content of the words contained in a given question, he or she may be unable to discern its referent(s). Similarly, the fact that a given reply follows a particular question does not necessarily mean that it constitutes an answer to that

question. The interviewee may have misunderstood the referent provided by the question or may be purposely shifting the frame of reference. In either case, the danger is that the researcher will overlook this
referential hiatus and thus misinterpret the response. The business of
establishing and maintaining reference in interviews is accordingly no
less in need of critical analysis.

Procedural problems of this type are sometimes corrected through
the operation of such devices as "side sequences" (cf. Jefferson 1972):

Int.:   What was your grandfather's name?
Resp.:   Which one?
Int.:   Your mother's father.
Resp.:   His name was José Rafael Aragón.

The interviewer and/or respondent are not always aware, however,
that the latter has failed to identify the referent. Such a response will
prove misleading if it is interpreted as a reply to the question. If the
researcher is repeatedly unable to establish a frame of reference that is
intelligible to respondents, this may seriously undermine the interviewing process itself. Given the importance of the referential function to
the interview, it is worthwhile to examine the business of establishing
and maintaining reference in some detail.

Establishing a referential frame. Reference is both a creative and
a powerful act, since it provides an intersubjective link between
speaker and hearer. One or more entities, processes, imaginative constructions, and so on are selected by the speaker from an infinitude of
referential possibilities and are re-created in the mind of the hearer.
As Garfinkel (1967) has noted, vagueness is never entirely absent from
an utterance, and this re-creation is always more or less approximate.
Nevertheless, a useful answer is obtained only through the presentation of a question (of whatever form) that possesses sufficient specificity to permit the potential respondent to discern what the speaker is
asking.

Identification of the proper referent is, however, only the first step.
If I was asked, "Tell me about your mother," I would find it quite
difficult to respond. Answering a question presupposes awareness not
only of the referent but of the type and quantity of information about
the referent that is being requested. This is particularly crucial in the
interview setting, where a broad range of types of information and
degrees of detail may be sought. An appropriate response to the preceding question might thus be "What do you mean? Who is she, what
does she do for a living, how did we relate when I was a child, or what
sort of person is she?" In other words, the question must not only

provide a referent but situate that referent within its larger conversational context – if procedural problems are to be avoided.

It is obviously impossible to reduce the complexity of the processes that underlie successful acts of reference to a single rule. Nevertheless, the countless examples of both referentially adequate and inadequate questions that appear in the tape recordings of my Córdovan interviews do reveal one critical feature. Each object, place, person, event, and so forth that figures in Córdovans' referential universe can be designated with a variety of lexemes and/or larger units. One of these expressions is, however, nearly always used in shifting the topic of discourse from a previous referent to the desired one, especially in the case of phenomena that pertain to the community's past. In other words, any one of these referentially equivalent lexemes or constructions can be utilized in posing a question about some aspect of the *current* topic. If the presentation of a question is to function simultaneously as a signal for a topic change, however, the conversationally marked designation must be included in the form of the question.

An example is provided by my research on Pedro Córdova, an extremely wealthy and influential Córdovan (the pun is illustrative of his position) of the nineteenth century. In initially broaching the subject with me, my consultants used such expressions as 'the great-grandfather of' X, *él que hizo la campana ahi en la capilla* 'the one who made the bell there in the chapel', or even 'there used to be a very, very wealthy man here; he was like a king. He was very rich; his name was Pedro Córdova'. The use of these forms in this context was motivated by the elders' belief that I had not heard of Pedro Córdova; some background information was thus deemed necessary. Subsequent attempts on my part to accomplish a change of topic to traditions regarding Pedro Córdova through the use of these expressions was ineffective. Such questions simply induced reruns, calls for reiteration of the question – *¿quién?* 'who?' By reiterating some of the material on the man that I had collected in previous interviews, I was eventually able to clarify my referent. But this did not provide a clear referential *frame* for the question, and my consultants were still confused as to what sort of information about Pedro Córdova was being solicited.

Perplexed, I listened to the manner in which my consultants brought up the subject. I found that they generally introduced the topic in conversations with persons who already knew the legends by beginning their utterances with *el difunto Pedro* . . . 'the late Pedro' . . . This phrase not only specified the referent but signaled that a discussion of the man, the extent of his opulence, the fate of his treasure, and even that period of Córdovan history as a whole was imminent. I was thus able to elicit a great deal of exegesis in succeeding interviews by asking questions such as *¿Tenía mucho tesoro el difunto Pedro?* 'Did the late Pedro have a lot of treasure?'

In other cases, however, the referential frame for a topical shift is provided not by the referring expression itself but by an adjacent lexeme or phrase. Locative and temporal expressions are common. For example, one of my consultants noted that *antes había muchos animales pa' 'cá* 'in bygone days there used to be lots of livestock here'. He announced his intention to open a discussion of Córdova's economy during the late nineteenth century by using the term *antes. Antes* is used in its unmarked or general sense to refer to any event that took place before the time of the utterance. In oral historical discussions, however, it is used to indicate that a given referent is associated with *lo de antes* 'things of bygone days', the era that ended in the first decades of this century. It is also used in a more highly marked sense to place the referent within the latest of three periods of the community's history, the epoch that extended from the time in which the present elders' grandparents were children until the time of the latters' death. It contrasts with *mucho más antes,* the first era of the community's history, and *más antes,* the intermediate period. The syntactic juxtaposition of a locative and a referring expression with *antes, más antes,* or *mucho más antes* thus signals the speaker's shift to a discussion of this general feature of existence (e.g., pastoralism and, more generally, a thriving subsistence economy) in the general area (here Córdova and environs) during that entire period.

Such designations possess a threefold role in discourse, and I will accordingly refer to them, extending a concept of Jakobson's (1957), as *triplex signs.* An initial function of such expressions is simply to index a given referent. They are equivalent at this level to other designations for the same entity. They contrast with referentially equivalent signs, however, with respect to a second function, that of indexing the entire referential frame in which they are included.[6] *El difunto Pedro* thus indexes the entire set of oral traditions that deal with the man, his legacy, and that period of Córdova's history.

Finally, such signs also constitute, in Jakobson's (1957:131) terms, messages that refer to the code. The code in this case is conversational structure, the demarcation of turns, topics, openings, closings, and so on and their combination in higher-level units. Triplex signs are conversational metasigns, indexing the status of the referent as the predominant topic of discourse at that point. Triplex signs are thus essential, powerful, and creative tools for structuring conversations in general and interviews in particular.

The role of triplex signs in providing a referential frame for discourse provides another clue in deciphering the factors that underlie the difficul-

ties encountered in interviewing. Fieldworkers generally gain initial insights into a given society's referential universe by observing its members.
Nevertheless, researchers are only able to initiate discussions of specific
referents once they have learned the relevant designations and can identify the terms that function as conversational metasigns. The status of
these signs as topical indexes is cryptotypic in Whorf's (1956:69–70)
terms – there is generally no overt formal marker of their metacommunicative function. This can be learned only through analysis (conscious or
unconscious) of the way that the various referring expressions operate in
the speech of one's consultants. Because the effectiveness of interview
questions is contingent on inclusion of conversational metasigns,[7] interviews will necessarily flounder until fieldworkers have become competent in this respect.

Specifying the scope of the response. Responses can address a
given subject from many different points of view and provide more or
less detail. The provision of a referential frame by the question (or in
the preceding discourse) assists the respondent in assessing the quantity and the type of information being sought. For example, *¿Antes
había muchos animales pa' 'cá?* 'Was there much livestock here *antes?*'
would, if addressed by a younger person to an elder, constitute a
request for a lengthy description of the pastoral economy of late nine-
teenth- and early twentieth-century Córdova. This question is referentially equivalent to *¿Tenía muchos animales la gente de aquí antes de la
primera guerra mundial?* 'Did the people here have much livestock
before World War I?' The latter question would not, nevertheless,
signal the respondent that the researcher was looking for a substantial
description of the economy of Córdova at this time. The interviewee
would have to call for a rerun, clarifying the status of the question as a
request for a general oral historical account, the names of the principal
sheep owners, the approximate percentages of goats, sheep, and cattle,
or something else again.

The establishment of a referential frame also constrains the type and
quantity of information that can be elicited by further questions on the
topic. Detailed descriptions and chronological assessments constitute
central features of accounts of recent events – for example, 'In what
year did you dig your well?' or 'What towns did you used to pass
through on your way to the mine?' Events that are preserved in the
community's oral traditions are reckoned, however, in terms of *antes,
más antes,* and *mucho más antes* periods and, within each, with respect
to culturally significant events (e.g., 'around the time of the big flood'
or 'soon after they cast the bell' [for the local chapel]). Dates are thus
irrelevant in determining temporal relationships between events which

transpired in 'bygone days,' and such questions as 'In what year did X take place' will elicit a *¿quién sabe?*

The basis for judging a 'good' answer (in my consultants' terms) similarly varies in accordance with the referential frame. It is the sheer quantity of detail as well as the accuracy of the description that is sought in characterizations of contemporary affairs. Wealth of detail is also valued in descriptions of persons, places, and events that relate to the 'outside' – the world beyond Córdova and surrounding communities. In statements about the past, however, it is one's ability to capture the *meaning* of events – by placing them within the broad scheme of *Mexicano* moral values and by contrasting them with the present – that is respected.

Evidence of invalid presuppositions. An otherwise well-formed question may present substantial procedural problems if it is based, in the eyes of the respondent, on one or more false premises. The classic example of such queries is "When did you stop beating your wife?" Such invalid presuppositions may appear on a variety of levels. Some cases, such as the following, involve a semantic error:

CB: What jobs did your father have? He was a *carpintero* ['carpenter']. . . .
SL: Oh, he made some window frames, door frames. (Looks at GL.) Right?
GL: That's right, he wasn't really a *carpintero*. No, he just made. . . . He used to make window frames and door frames, and then he would put in the window.

I had not realized at this point that *carpintero* possessed a more restricted semantic range in New Mexican Spanish than in English or Standard Spanish. José Dolores López, George López's father, made window and door frames, railings, and a wide range of furniture (Briggs 1980:31). To be designated a *carpintero* at the time, however, a person had to be skilled in installing pitched galvanized-steel roofs (with wooden frames) on top of the usual beam, stick, and mud roofs.

Invalid presuppositions can reflect simple factual errors. If the question presupposes an ontological assumption that contrasts sharply with native cultural premises, the situation will be rather more complex. I once asked Mr. López, for instance:

CB: How did [the wealthiest local family] make its money?
GL: There have always been wealthy persons all over.
CB: But how did the X's get so rich when everyone else was poor?
GL: ¿Quién sabe? ['Who knows?']

My question presupposed the common Anglo-American premise that a person becomes wealthy through a combination of will, hard work, and fortuitous circumstances. The query thus confused my consultants, because they believe that God bestows material blessings on persons who supplement very hard work with a spirit of cooperation and generosity and who act in accordance with His will rather than their own desires. Evidence of such grossly invalid presuppositions generally induced my consultants to (1) provide a response that seemed unrelated to the question, (2) request a rerun, or (3) signal the unsuitability of the question by responding with *¿quién sabe?* 'who knows'. The emergence of invalid presuppositions thus precludes the generation of an adequate referential frame by the question and often elicits a comment on the researcher's presuppositions rather than a response to the question (cf. Hobbs and Robinson 1979).

Social roles

As noted above, the structure of interviews generally dictates a number of components of the relationship between the participants. The typical interview situation grants the interviewer principal rights to topical selection by virtue of her or his provision of the questions. He or she further determines whether a response counts as an answer by choosing whether or not to reiterate the question during his or her next turn. The utterance of a new question releases the interviewee from the task of answering the previous one; the interviewer thus signals the respondent as to the adequacy of the "answer" by presenting or withholding a new question (among other means). It is similarly the researcher who creates the successive textual representations of the fruits of the interview. In sum, the interviewer maintains a great deal of control over the interaction; the respondent's principal means of subverting this power lies in breaking the frame of the interview.

Playing by the rules prompts the subordination of other components of the interaction to the mutual goal of the conscious transmission of interesting, accurate, and abundant information. When the system is working properly, the participants accept the roles assigned to them by the structure of the interview. Interviewers provide clear and interesting questions that enable respondents to exhibit their knowledge. These roles preempt the criteria that normally define these individuals' roles in society (age, gender, occupation, etc.). The latter factors come to the fore in interviews only when one or more of the participants fail to conform to the requirements of the interview situation.

A number of researchers have commented on the inclusion of the interview in the repertoire of speech events of middle-class speakers of American English (Grimshaw 1969, 1969–70; Strauss and Schatzman

1955; Wolfson 1976). When consultants are not accustomed to playing this particular game, however, they are unlikely to accept this suppression of normal social criteria. An understanding of the participants' social personas and the norms that inform interactions between such persons thus becomes crucial. Likewise, I have noted in preceding paragraphs that the respondent may frame the "interview" as another type of communicative event. This possibility must be considered, because other categories of events have their own structures of social roles. This new set of roles may in turn invoke distinct interactional norms and canons for the generation and interpretation of signs. Differences between the interviewer and the interviewees' perceptions of the roles they are assuming in the encounter will thus profoundly affect the sort of text that is produced and how it is to be read.

An example should bring out the importance of these considerations and illustrate the intimacy of the connection between social roles and types of communicative events. Having entered Córdova unmarried and only nineteen years of age, I was not seen as being fully adult. I was similarly ignorant of *Mexicano* culture and of local norms of comportment. Although I spoke Spanish, I was only beginning to learn the local dialect, and I had little grasp of New Mexican Spanish discourse structure. Quite properly (and most fortunately), the Lópezes and other Córdovans took it upon themselves to teach me to behave in accordance with basic *Mexicano* values. Given the community's distrust of Anglo-Americans, these individuals took this goal quite seriously. Conversational etiquette is obviously a central feature of proper comportment, especially in a society that places great emphasis on rhetorical ability.

In view of the fact that I had not yet reached even the status of *muchacho* (literally 'boy', meaning 'young man'), the culturally appropriate response to the situation would have been to spend a great deal of time around the elders, pay close attention to everything that was said, and to speak, by and large, only when a response was elicited from me. As I acquired more competence both socially and linguistically, it became appropriate as well to ask questions that related directly to statements that one of these individuals made in the course of his or her pedagogy. The generation of questions that did not directly spring from my seniors' discourse counted, however, as original utterances. The right to produce original questions or statements had to be earned, in this speech community, by demonstrating rhetorical competence. Although I achieved this level in time, this did not happen until I had aged a few years, spent a certain amount of time in the community, and acquired most of the features of the dialect.

Therefore, most of the utterances that were addressed to me, especially by the elders, were pedagogical in nature. The Lópezes regarded our conversations about Córdova and its carvers as expectable and necessary pedagogical sessions. They deemed it appropriate to convey the subjects of their own choosing through a combination of their own metacommunicative routines – primarily nonverbal lessons in wood carving and highly articulate performances of personal narratives, oral traditions, scriptural allusions, proverbs, jokes, and so forth.

I classified the communicative events as falling under the aegis of "interview," however, not as pedagogy. I accordingly made repeated attempts to convey to my consultants the nature of my involvement in the community as anthropological research. Conforming to my own definition of the situation, I posed basic questions about the carved images of the saints, the carving process, the earliest carvers in the community, and so on. The couple's responses consisted largely of *Ooo, pos, ¡quién sabe!* 'Oh, well, who knows!' and of one-sentence "answers" followed by 'that's it' or 'now you've got your story'. I eventually realized that the Lópezes were implicitly telling me that they could not accept my attempted reversal of the appropriate social roles. If the elders had allowed me to lure them into traditional interviews, they would have accepted a subordinate role in a conversation with a rhetorical incompetent.

Given the society's emphasis on maintaining patterns of respect for one's elders and of demonstrating rhetorical competence, the carvers had to preserve their control over topical selection and interactional strategy. Toleration of a reversal of social roles would have similarly undermined their position as my primary pedagogues in the community, in addition to being highly self-effacing. The political implications of allowing a younger person who was much less versed in the community's history and traditions to dominate the conversation were hardly lost on the Lópezes and their contemporaries.

The effects of my attempts to impose my own metacommunicative strategies on my consultants also made it quite difficult for me to see that they were presenting me with extremely valuable material. The nature of their resistance to my research strategy not only revealed a great deal of information about themselves and their art, but it articulated the location of this enterprise within a broader semiotic framework. Their pedagogy embodied the complex interpenetration of visual and verbal modes of constructing and transmitting artistic messages. The derivation of their pedagogical tools from their own metacommunicative strategies provides a striking illustration of the process of acquiring competence in this semiotic system. My epistemological preconceptions suggested to me, however, that exegesis was properly obtained by asking questions and obtaining explicit answers.

Fortunately my interest in gaining sociolinguistic competence facilitated my acquisition of conversational norms. I was thus learning other metacommunicative strategies, even though I still attempted to elicit exegesis through interviews. This permitted me to utilize a broader range of metacommunicative devices in my research (see Chapter 4) once I finally accepted the limitations on the usefulness of interviewing in this speech community.

From hindsight to foresight

This chapter has surveyed a number of different types of communicative problems that threaten the success of interviews and the interpretation of interview data. As an initial means of addressing this complex nexus of methodological issues, I focused on a number of basic components of the communicative event. I attempted to demonstrate how a lack of agreement between interviewer and respondent on the nature and role of any one of these components can jeopardize the interviewing process. This chapter did not, nevertheless, address two of the most basic questions.

First, my analysis was primarily directed at the problems that can be identified in a given corpus of interviews. Researchers should find it useful as a retrospective tool, for example, in sharpening their analysis of interview data. A thorough proposal for methodological advancement must also provide a means of *foreseeing* where interview techniques will conflict with native metacommunicative repertoires. This will assist fieldworkers in avoiding communicative blunders in the first place.

Second, the preceding discussion has focused on a description and analysis of common types of interviewing problems. I would like to suggest, however, that significant methodological headway can only emerge once a clear understanding of the roots of methodological problems has been gained. Given the close interrelation of methodological and theoretical issues, part of the task is to ferret out the problematic theoretical assumptions that have become embedded in methodological principles. I will devote myself to this problem in Chapter 6.

With respect to research in a particular society, discovery of the provenance of interviewing problems can only proceed from awareness of the norms that shape the way people talk about communication. My communicative blunders did not simply result from a lack of agreement between myself and my consultants with respect to individual speech-event components. *Mexicanos,* like the members of any speech community, have a repertoire of native metacommunicative routines that are used in teaching members how to describe, evaluate, and interpret communicative events. An adequate understanding of the source of interviewing problems must emerge from a comparison of interviews and native metacommunicative routines as wholes and of their role in the acquisition of social–cultural and linguistic competence. I accordingly move to an analysis of *Mexicano* metacommunication in Chapter 4.

4. The acquisition of metacommunicative competence

Chapter 3 took a corpus of interview data and attempted to isolate the sources of a broad range of procedural problems. The analysis may have provided some retrospective clarification regarding specific obstacles to the success of interviews and their interpretation. As I argued in Chapter 1, however, it is impossible to judge the effects of using interview techniques in a given speech community without learning something about the way language is used in other contexts. This limitation is imposed by the inverted logic that poses the interview as a starting point and then proceeds to the discovery of basic communicative norms as they impinge on the interview. This process will only result in an ad hoc, piecemeal picture of local speech patterns. A far better procedure is to concentrate initially on discerning the norms that govern speech in the local community and then to compare these with the patterns that underlie the interview. This chapter applies the latter approach to the *Mexicano* data.

The need to order the methodological process in this way is heightened by our using the interview for more than just obtaining assorted bits of information, particularly when we conduct research in another society or with members of another social class or ethnic population. The interview, along with observation, is generally the primary means of gaining the knowledge and skills required to develop a minimal competence in the native language and culture. We ask our consultants to be our teachers, to show us what it means to think, feel, act, and speak like a native, and we ask them to use the interview as their main tool for doing so. They evaluate and respond to both our request for instruction and our implicit specification of the way we wish to learn. As my initial experience with the Lópezes shows, native reactions to the two parts of the request may be quite different. Learning how the natives conceive of the educational process and what pedagogical techniques are appropriate will enable us to avoid such situations.

Since interviews are metacommunicative, I am especially interested in the natives' resources for describing, evaluating, and interpreting

61

the nature of communicative events. My analysis of such events will focus on what they tell us about the norms underlying the acquisition process and the points of compatibility and incompatibility of interview techniques. I will also outline the way in which native metacommunicative routines provide important sources of data on the questions of social-scientific and linguistic interest that are generally broached in interviews.

Analysis of native metacommunicative routines, such as the one presented in this chapter, provide the cornerstone for methodological sophistication in interview-based research. Unless we grasp the norms that underlie the way in which respondents convey information in other contexts, we will have no way of knowing how standard interview techniques are destined to conflict with these norms.

This is not to say that every research project must begin with a full-scale sociolinguistic investigation of the speech community in question. This would be impractical for anthropologists and folklorists who have a given amount of time to collect cultural or folkloric data in a given society. It would be equally unrealistic to suggest that large-scale survey researchers must fully investigate all of the speech communities to which their respondents belong. This does not mean that the need to investigate native metacommunicative repertoires is a goal that is realistic only for detailed sociolinguistic research. I rather wish to demonstrate the existence of relatively simple techniques for discovering the ways in which speakers articulate information about their own communicative systems to each other. I will outline some practical means by which this type of investigation can be incorporated into different types of interview- and survey-based research in Chapter 5.

Native models of socialization

I have argued that natives make judgments as to the appropriateness of interviews vis-à-vis other types of speech events as means of acquiring social–cultural and sociolinguistic competence. One of the major determinants of the course of such evaluations is the way people conceive of the learning process. As Ochs (1982) has argued, language acquisition, language teaching, and the evaluation of communicative competence are closely related to the views that the members of a society hold of the learning process. These considerations are important in the case of fieldworkers as well, because these are the models against which the researcher's efforts to learn about social–cultural and linguistic patterns will be judged. Ignorance of native theories of the acquisition process thus deprives the fieldworker of the resources needed to foresee how her or his attempts to gain competence will fare in the eyes of the natives. In the *Mexicano* case, the use of interviews for this purpose runs directly counter to the natives' sense of the proper mode of instruction.

My consultants frequently used an agricultural metaphor in explicating the manner in which a person acquires a skill or body of knowledge. You must have seeds in order to plant. These are equivalent in pedagogical terms to *talento* 'talent'. *Talento* refers to a God-given aptitude for learning a given thing. No one possesses *talento* in all areas, and individuals differ greatly in the number of spheres in which they are given *talento*. All persons, except the severely mentally retarded, have the *talento* for learning language; nevertheless, some have a 'quick talent' (*un talento liviano*) and will increase their verbal ability rapidly, whereas others are 'slow' (*despacio*). Only some speakers have the *talento*, however, for mastering such specialized speech forms as proverbs, jokes, and scriptural allusions or for leading hymns and prayers.

Talento will not develop, however, in isolation – it must be *desparramado* 'spread out' or 'scattered'. This refers to the need to observe those who have expertise in the endeavor. *Interés* and *concentración* are also required; a person must want to learn and be able to concentrate.

The next stage involves watering and weeding the growing plants. The allusion here is to taking the knowledge that has been gained through observation and intensifying and extending it through imitation. In the case of the acquisition of communicative competence, this refers to reiterating the words of one's seniors. A person who lacks *paciencia* 'patience', who wants to absorb a topic immediately and believes he or she can be an expert shortly thereafter, will not gain competence. Such attempted precociousness would also demonstrate a lack of *respeto* 'respect'. *Respeto,* a central cultural value, prescribes deferring to one's seniors' greater command of the pertinent skills.

If properly cultivated, the plants will grow to maturity and can be harvested. Another means of scattering your 'talent' gains importance at this point. A particular musician may be able to play well. If the person does not get out of the house and play for a wide range of audiences, however, she or he will not become a competent performer and will not gain a reputation as a great musician. This corresponds to the point at which individuals are expected to exhibit their rhetorical virtuosity. Once a speaker has mastered all the requisite skills, she or he must practice discussing community affairs, performing proverbs, singing hymns, or the like in public.

In short, the beginning of the acquisition process lies in observation. Frequent exposure to the behavior of one's seniors leads to the internalization of a sense of the pattern underlying what has been seen and heard. This permits the "student" to begin imitating the words and actions of others. Evaluating the success of such attempts is no less important for initial imitations than for other areas of rhetorical competence. Once an individual can adequately reproduce the forms provided by his or her seniors (see the next section), the time has come to make one's own judgments as to which utterances are appropriate in which environments. Such attempts to produce original utterances are met with evaluations with respect to his or her success both in providing the proper linguistic form and in interpreting the messages provided by others. Interestingly, the sequence posited by this native theory of learning – from comprehension to imitation to production – coincides with a leading theory of linguistic ontogeny (cf. Menyuk 1977:68–9).

This material provides insight into some of the communicative blunders I committed in research with *Mexicanos*. Let us contrast, for example, two strategies for inaugurating the wood-carving industry-research – theirs versus mine. I simply assumed that a knowledge of Standard Spanish, a research project that proved acceptable to the couple and their community, and the development of a friendship would enable me to begin interviewing. I similarly believed that interviews would provide the best means of gaining social–cultural and sociolinguistic competence and of gathering data on the industry.

As I argued in the previous chapter, however, providing the referential frame for a conversation about the past presupposes a great deal of knowledge about both this era and the folkloric expressions used in conveying it. Providing the frame also accords one a great deal of interactional power. Given *Mexicanos'* concern with the political dimensions of communication and with the evaluation of rhetorical competence, a serious issue was whether or not to allow me to assume such authority by according myself the right to pose the questions. Because I was ignorant of the community's oral traditions and lacked command of any of the requisite pragmatic skills, the elders had no choice but to regain control of the interaction by breaking the interview frame.

Recall, on the other hand, the Lópezes' preferred mode of instruction – handing me a piece of wood and a penknife and helping me learn how to carve. Because verbal directions were kept to a minimum, especially at first, this forced me to draw on what I had gained from watching them. My initial efforts consisted of attempts to imitate their actions. When I failed, they pointed out the source of my error either verbally or by taking my carving in hand and showing me how the step is performed, that is, providing me with a model for direct imitation. Once I had learned the basic techniques, they encouraged me to carve a more complex figure of my own choosing, such as a religious image.

Note that the course of our verbal interaction roughly followed this sequence. They initially expected me to pay attention to what was said and done without interjecting an excess of queries or comments. Once they saw that I was getting the point (in terms of both carving technique and interactional norms), they began to provide more detailed information on the carvings and their social–cultural and artistic background. I then found myself in the position of being able to gain additional information by repeating one of their statements, followed by a tag question: 'So your father used to be a great joker, did he?' Thus, once I had grasped the appropriate means of learning and had gained a minimal level of competence, the Lópezes were quite willing to provide me with information on the carving art. Fortunately, the couple allowed me to turn on my tape recorder at such times. This not only provided a wealth of background noise for my initial recordings, but it provided me with data on the way the Lópezes were teaching me to learn.

Analyzing metacommunicative routines: three examples

I would hardly want to suggest, however, that assessing the potential compatibility of interview techniques can be accomplished with reference to native models of the acquisition process alone. Such native models do not stand in a one-to-one relationship with the acquisition process itself. Some elements are beyond the conscious knowledge of native speakers, and native theories, like their academic counterparts, are interpretive rather than directly reflective of behavior. Specifically, the most pragmatically sensitive forms lie beyond the limits of awareness for native speakers (see Chapter 6 and Silverstein 1979, 1981b). This means that natives will encounter difficulty in describing the role of a number of sociolinguistic skills that are crucial to their own assessments of rhetorical competence.

Asking the natives about the learning process provides a good initial direction for studying the relationship between interview techniques and native communicative patterns. If used as an exclusive basis for such evaluations, however, it simply reinvokes the tautological process of asking people questions in order to assess the relationship between interview techniques and broader social–cultural and linguistic norms. I will accordingly analyze three *Mexicano* metacommunicative routines – the elicitation of repetitions from young children, the oration of adults in political disputes, and the use of scriptural allusions in the pedagogical discourse of elders – in drawing out the norms that impinge on the use of interview techniques in this society.

Observation and elicited repetition in early childhood

As Ochs (1982), Snow (1977:37), and others have noted, societies vary greatly in what is believed about and expected from children. In *Mexicano* society, caregivers are quite voluble with infants. This does not, however, reflect the assumption that infants are trying, if imperfectly, to communicate with them (as has been asserted of Anglo-Americans [cf. Bates et al. 1979; Shotter 1979; Trevarthen 1979]). Rather, it is believed that children must be able to observe a great deal of speech if they are to be expected to 'pick up' the language. Such verbal interaction also enhances the child's *interés* and *concentración,* ensuring that observation will promote learning. Several familiar features of "motherese" or "baby talk" registers, especially decreased rate of speech and increases in pitch range, are seen as facilitating the process of getting and keeping the baby's attention.

Questioning infants. During the first year of a child's life, the topics used most frequently by caregivers involve the child and her or his surroundings. The form most commonly used in these utterances is the interrogative, a strategy for drawing the young child into conversation in numerous societies. Caregiver discourse often consists of asking a series of questions over and over, varying pitch and word stress:

1. Father to six-month-old daughter[1]

Mi HIjita, mi HIjita (pronounced [mi:ta])	My DAUghter (diminutive), my DAUghter
¿Qué te PAsa?	What's going ON?
¿Qué te PAsa?	What's going ON?
¿Que pasó con la (child's name)?	What's going on with (child's name)?
¿Qué QUIEres, mi hijita?	What do you WANT, my daughter?
¿Quieres LEche?	Do you want some MILK?
¿Quieres PApas?	Do you want some FOOD? (literally, 'potatoes')
¿Qué QUIEres, mi hijita?	What do you WANT, my daughter?

The father was hardly asking informational questions; the point was simply to engage the child in mutually enjoyable verbal play.

Eliciting repetitions from young children. Once children reach the holophrastic or one-word-sentence stage, caregiver emphasis shifts from encouraging observation to eliciting responses from the child.

The point, however, is not to induce the child to come up with novel utterances. Caregivers assume that comprehension precedes production; the absence of an intelligible response thus is not necessarily interpreted as reflecting a complete lack of understanding. Observation alone, however, is not a sufficient developmental basis for gaining the ability to generate the proper forms in the appropriate social settings. "Imitation" is seen as a requisite intermediate stage between comprehension without production and the acquisition of true command over linguistic forms.

As children approach two years of age, one means of eliciting responses assumes a central role in caregiver–child interactions. Children are seldom alone with a single caregiver; other siblings, grandparents, aunts, uncles, cousins, other relatives, and neighbors are frequently about the household, which may be multifamily in any case. Any person who is about six years of age or older is likely to amuse herself or himself by directing the baby to 'say "X" to so-and-so.' The following tape recording was made while Linda (one year, nine months of age) was being held by her grandmother, Lupe. Linda's mother, father, grandfather, and her uncle Ben (Lupe's oldest son) were standing near a large woodpile. I was standing between the two groups, with my tape recorder pointed in the direction of Linda, María (Lupe's youngest child), and Lupe. María approached Linda frequently and gave a gentle yank on one of her legs, to the amusement of all.

2. Linda (age 1.9) with grandmother, uncle, and aunt

Lupe: ¡NO, María!	NO, María!
(María and Linda laugh for 6 seconds)	
Linda: María.	María.
(María and Linda laugh, followed by Lupe; total of 12 seconds)	
Lupe: DEjala, María.	Leave her aLONE, María.
(9 seconds of laughter by María and Linda)	
Lupe: ¡NO!	NO!
(Lupe begins laughing before finishing utterance; is joined by María and Linda)	
María: ¿A cuál? ¿Este?	Which one? This one? (Meaning 'which foot should I pull?')
(María and Linda laugh for 7 seconds)	
Lupe: "¡No!" dile.	Tell her, "No!"
María: ¿Este?	This one?
Lupe: ¡NO!	NO!
(but Lupe laughs with María and Linda)	

María: Siéntense y mírense.　Sit down and watch.
(Lupe laughs for 2 seconds, then
joins the adults' conversation; María
and Linda continue to laugh for 14
additional seconds)

The game continues intermittently for eight minutes; Lupe attends alternately to the adults' conversation and to María's and Linda's play. Ben pretends to charge Linda. She squeals with delight at first, but then cries. Lupe tells him to desist, using a serious tone of voice, and he does. María begins anew to pull Linda's feet, and Lupe then tries to end the game.

Lupe: ¡DEjala!　Leave her alONE!
(Linda starts to cry)

Lupe: ¡No! De todos rumbos la　No! They pull at her from all sides!
jalan!
(everyone laughs, including Linda)

Lupe: Como se ríe. Pobrecita.　How she laughs. Poor thing.
(all laugh)

Lupe: NO, María, LEAVE HER ALONE.　NO, María, LEAVE HER ALONE.
María: *Okay*.　Okay.

Lupe: No la jales.　Don't pull on her.
(said in singsong; María and Linda
laugh loudly)

Lupe: ¿Quieres que yo te jale los　Do you want me to pull on your
SHONGOS[2] de indio?　Indian BRAIDS?
María: No.　No.
(everyone laughs for 10 seconds)

Ben: Dile, "shongos de perro."　Tell her, "dog's braids."
Linda: [anos]　[anos]
Ben: Yah, "María, shongos de　Yah, "María, dog's braids."
perro."

Lupe: NO, MARIA, NO LA JALES!　NO, MARIA, DON'T PULL ON HER!
(previous utterance stated in stern,
serious tone)

Ben: "Shongos de perro," dile.　"Dog's braids," tell her.
Linda: [biyga]　[biyga]
Ben: No, dile "shongos de perro."　No, tell her "dog's braids."
Linda: [sagmiy, samiy]　[sagmiy, samiy]
Lupe: LEAVE HER ALONE, te digo.　LEAVE HER ALONE, I'm telling you.
Ben: "Shongos de perro," dile.　"Dog's braids," tell her.
Linda: ¿[miya]?　[miya]?
Ben: "Shongos de perro." That's　"Dog's braids." That's good!
good!
(Linda begins crying, and Lupe
puts her down on the ground and
begins looking for her doll)

Lupe: ¡NO! MARIA, ¿QUE ESTAS　NO! MARIA, WHAT ARE YOU DOING?
HACIENDO?
Trae el mono.　Bring the doll.
Dile que te dé el mono, mi hijita.　Tell her to bring you the doll, my
　little one (literally 'daughter').
¿WHACH YOU DO WITH IT, MARIA?　WHACH YOU DO WITH IT, MARIA?
María: ¡NADA!　NOTHING!

The game then ended; Linda was put down on the ground, and Lupe focused on conversing with the other adults.

At first glance, this text seems to offer little insight into the norms that underlie communicative competence in *Mexicano* society, particularly as they impinge on the process of fieldwork. Indeed, it is just a simple game that involves a young child and her older relatives. It is hardly rare; such play takes place with great frequency, and this episode is far from unusual. Nevertheless, a close analysis of the form and content of this interaction can provide us with a great deal of information regarding the role of basic cultural premises, social roles, and metacommunicative signals in speech.

Cultural premises. The interpretation of this conversation presupposes important cultural assumptions. One underlies the grandmother's ambivalence. She is obviously enjoying the game, but her admonitions to María and Ben are not entirely playful. Infants and young children are *inocentes* 'innocent ones'. They cannot be blamed for their own actions, because they are too young to know the difference between right and wrong. But they are also highly susceptible to supernatural harm, which can manifest itself as a potentially fatal physical illness, such as *mal de ojo* 'evil eye' or *susto* 'fright' (cf. Trotter and Chavira 1981:90–2). Playing with babies is enjoyable, but it is also potentially dangerous. If an infant or young child laughs loudly for an extended period of time, he or she becomes a potential target for supernatural illness. (Anglo-Americans are notoriously indiscreet in this regard. Because my daughter spent the first year and a half of her life in the field, I was continually being lectured on the inadvisability of eliciting too much laughter.) Lupe was becoming more and more concerned about this possibility throughout the interaction. This element seems simply to add to the tension, hence the humor, in the course of the game. Lupe's fear is beginning to outweigh her enjoyment during the second part of the text, and she brings the game to a halt shortly thereafter.

It should be noted that Ben's feigned attacks on Linda elicit quite different reactions from Lupe. Ben is immediately admonished *No me gusta que la agarres, Ben* 'I don't like your grabbing her, Ben'. The children's reactions are similarly contrastive – Ben ceases this form of play at once. He then picks up on Lupe's semantic lead by pointing out María's long and beautiful braids, thus becoming a second ally for Linda. This contrast in the children's behavior cannot simply be attributed to age or gender (María was six and Ben was fourteen). Two boys span this age gap in the family, and they persist longer in the face of such admonitions than María. It is, rather, necessary to understand the special role that accrues to the eldest male child, who is often referred to as the *papacito* 'little father' in *Mexicano* families. Because he is accorded a quasi-parental status, his responsibilities are much greater, the range of acceptable behavior is much narrower, and his rights are correspondingly greater than those of his siblings.

A third cultural premise involves the importance of fighting one's own battles and defending one's dignity. From the time that they are ambulatory, children are not picked up when they injure themselves slightly or are roughed up by other children. (Anglo-Americans are considered horrendously indulgent in this resepct; I was constantly being told that I was spoiling my daughter.) Constant interventions are said to prevent children from learning how to stand up for their own rights and to resist assaults on their person or reputation. Maintaining one's *dignidad de la persona* 'personal dignity' is the key to preserving self-respect as well as a good reputation in the community, and actions construed as attacking an individual's *dignidad de la persona* are treated with the utmost seriousness. Linda is still too young to fight her own battles. But Lupe is encouraging her to defend herself (rather than to rely solely on caregivers' efforts) by framing some of her admonitions as Linda's own words through the use of the *dile* formula.

These data strongly support Ochs's contention that the manner in which individuals gain communicative competence reflects and is based on "a particular set of cultural values and beliefs" (1982:88). Elucidating the meaning of this short conversation provides the analyst with a good point of departure for investigating *Mexicano* conceptions of the person and the importance of this cultural construct for social interaction. This is, of course, hardly surprising. As Cook-Gumperz and Gumperz (1976) and Ochs (1979, 1982) have argued, caregivers' speech often focuses on basic cultural knowledge as well as features of the communicative situation itself that are often assumed in adult–adult discourse.

Alternation of social roles. Interpreting this interaction also presupposes the ability to discern the manner in which the participants are moving between a number of different social roles. Lupe's participation, for example, is structured by her movements between two different role sets. On the one hand, she alternates between a mother role, playing with and supervising the children, and interacting with the other adults. Interestingly, she is the only participant who exhibits this flexibility. The other adults observe the children's play at various points and the children listen to the adults' conversation as well, but the members of these groups do not enter into the interaction of the other. Lupe plays two roles within the children's game, alternately "playing along" with and enjoying the game and trying to extricate Linda from a potentially dangerous situation. María similarly plays the part of the mischievous child, pretending to attack her niece, as well as that of the obedient daughter, responding seriously to her mother's admonitions ("okay"). She also distances herself from the child's role entirely at one point in the interaction by assuming the role of a dictatorial teacher (*siéntense y mírense* 'sit down and watch'). Note that this places both Linda and Lupe in the role of naughty students; Lupe apparently appreciates the humor of this sudden reversal, because she laughs heartily.

Ben enters the interaction, having just finished carrying a truckload of firewood to the woodpile, by displacing María in the role of mischievous attacker. After being scolded by his mother, he assumes the role of an older sibling who is admonishing his junior, María. He does not, however, discard his playful maliciousness entirely, but simply converts it into a means of playfully sanctioning the misbehaver. His allusion to 'dog's braids' is derogatory; it may be slightly off-color as well, equating María's braids with a dog's tail and thus its posterior, but I did not pursue this possibility with my consultants. Ben also distances himself from the child's role, assisting his mother in admonishing María. This movement is completed within the game when he switches into English and changes voice to play the role of parent with 'that's good!' Finally, both Lupe and Ben alternate between playing themselves and assuming Linda's part. The latter is accomplished by their creating lines for Linda and then reciting them themselves.

Within this short dialogue, Linda has been exposed to a broad range of familial roles. Each is similarly presented vis-à-vis complementary roles, providing insights into the norms for interaction between elder and junior siblings, parents and children, teachers and students, and so on. Exchanges between persons playing these roles also provide Linda with insights into the rights and obligations that accrue to individuals who stand in these relationships. Lupe's frequent reversion to a serious, parental position enables her to provide a running metacommunicative commentary on the appropriateness of these roles. Obviously, close observation and analysis of such interactions can provide fieldworkers with insights into areas of central socio-cultural and sociolinguistic importance.

The role of metacommunication. The preceding material raises the question of how both Linda and the fieldworker can perceive such alternations in the discourse. The answer to this question lies in the *contextualization,* in Cook-Gumperz and Gumperz's terms, of discourse. These authors argue that linguistic contexts are not, as many researchers seem to believe, simply inherent in the social situation and transparent to all present, including the analyst. It is rather the case that "context is communicated as a part of the total message" (1976:4). Communication is punctuated with "contextualization cues" that mark relevant features of the social and linguistic setting, thus providing interpretive frameworks for deciphering the meaning of other participants' signals and for shaping one's own contributions. As Cook-Gumperz and Gumperz (1976:8) note, speakers and hearers are constantly monitoring each other's behavior for verbal and non-verbal clues as to their interlocutor's meaning. In other words, contrary to the prevailing (mis)use of the term, contexts are (1) culture-specific sociolinguistic constructs and (2) are changing from moment to moment in the course of interactions

The central contextualization clues in the preceding text are changes in prosodic features and the elicitation of repetitions from Linda. Lupe, Ben, and María alter the pitch, quantity, rhythm and stress patterns, and the speed of utterance of their speech. In some cases, these are used in marking an utterance as motherese or baby talk. But they are also used by Lupe in framing the relative ludic versus admonitory character of her statements.

The best example of such variations is provided by the three ways that Lupe articulates *no*. *No*'s that are framed as feigned prohibitions feature a slight increase in pitch and quantity over that of the adjacent lexemes, with a slight prolongation of the vowel. Lupe marks another admonition (*no la jales*) as facetious through the use of a "singsong" intonation with exaggerated contrasts in pitch. Lupe also uses *no* in an elicitation device earlier in the game. Here the *no* in "*no," dile* ' "no," tell her' is distinguished by a greater rise in pitch on the word itself; the utterance as a whole is marked by a diminution in the quantity and by laryngeal constriction–the illusion of a "small" voice. All of Lupe's NO's following her initial "LEAVE HER ALONE" conformed to a third pattern. Here stridency was complemented by greatly increased pitch and quantity, creating a sharp, stern tone. The *no*'s followed by a laugh are perhaps the most interesting. They not only constitute a striking contextual clue to Lupe's simultaneous enjoyment in and fear of this situation but also suggest that she is at times playing this tension for dramatic effect.

María's first utterance on the transcript (*¿A cuál? ¿Este?*) is marked by laryngeal constriction, higher than normal pitch and volume, and an unusually slow rate of utterance, that is, baby talk. When she is playing the role of teacher, the pitch is lower than normal, the speech is relatively slow, and each word is enunciated with great care. Her conciliatory responses ("okay" and *no*) were not marked by alterations of pitch, speed, or volume, although the last syllable of "okay" featured falling pitch. Her final ¡NADA! indicated surprise (real or feigned), as if to say, "Who, me?"

Ben enters the scene as a wild animal, saying "rah rah" to Linda while raising and reaching out his "claws." Later, *shongos de perro* is uttered much more slowly, with careful enunciation, and at a higher pitch than the quotation-framing verb, as was the case with Lupe's repetition elicitations. This alternation complements syntactic and lexical markers in setting apart the embedded utterance as a quotation. 'That's good!' is marked by an increase in quantity and a decrease in pitch and speed of utterance, creating a "parental" tone of voice.

A second type of contextualization cue is provided by the repetition elicitation formulas. These are of two types. In the first, the speaker provides the hearer with a direct quotation of the utterance that the latter is to repeat. These are marked by the insertion of an inflection of *decir* 'to say' or 'to tell' in either pre- or post-position. When used with children, they are also marked, as I have noted above, by the prosodic features of baby talk. A rapid change in prosody thus occurs when the speaker moves from the verb-plus-pronoun frame (*dile*) to the embedded utterance (or vice versa). The second type of formula provides a report of the embedded utterance (i.e., indirectly quoted speech). Baby talk is not present, and there is no prosodic shift at the juncture between the frame and the utterance.

These formulas provide the child with a host of pragmatic information on the speaker's perception of the ongoing social situation. They are often used to draw the child into the interaction and to keep her or his attention. They provide a clear index of the caregiver's desires, telling the language learner whom to address and what to say. The formula specifies the types of assistance the baby can reasonably expect to obtain from the third party, thus illuminating the norms that govern such relationships. The utterance also informs the child as to which speech acts are appropriate for obtaining the desired effect. Lupe and Ben are using these formulas to teach Linda to tease, scold, and defend herself verbally in this case. Such formulas are also used in teaching children how to shame, insult, console, plead, demand, and the like. Repetition elicitation formulas provide a link between a particular conversational setting and the relevant social and sociolinguistic norms.

The question remains, however, as to the nature of Linda's involvement in the interaction. In this text, it is apparent that Linda has acquired the ability to identify the first part of adjacency pairs and to provide second parts, a skill that commonly emerges at about this age (Ervin-Tripp 1979:412). She repeats segments of the embedded utterances; her success in this pursuit at one year, nine months of age varies between being accurate if partial (María) and unrecognizable (*biyga,* etc.). Note that Ben evaluates her approximations and provides feedback.

Because I left the field soon after this episode, my next observations were taken when Linda was two years, three months old. At that time she had mastered this interactional pattern, providing accurate repetitions of forms – when she wanted to do so. An even clearer sign of the progress that had been made in this regard was apparent. Linda spends as much time at her grandparents' house as she does at her parents'. Family members thus often comment on the degree to which Linda is attached to Lupe. When asked, in English, "How much do you love your grandma?" she apparently once told Lupe "I love you eight-nine-ten." Everyone was so amused by this utterance that they rehearsed her by asking her to "tell your grandma 'I love you eight-nine-ten.' " Now, when other relatives or neighbors come to visit, a performance is elicited with 'Tell (X) how much you love your grandma'. In short, within six months Linda had not only mastered the art of responding to repetition elicitation formulas but was also able to negotiate a routine used in eliciting a quotation in English.

Interestingly, the distribution of this strategy for the acquisition of sociolinguistic competence appears to be quite widespread. Eisenberg presents an extensive description of the use of *dile* among recent Mexican immigrants in northern California. The similarity of the two sets of data is striking: "The children were told what to say to initiate interaction, to get their own way, to tease and joke, to greet, to apologize, etc. Rather than intercede for the young child in an interaction, the adult speakers pushed them to interact on their own" (1982:90). Ochs (1982) has reported quite similar data from her research on caregiver–child speech in Western Samoa.

Schieffelin provides a detailed analysis of the use of ɛlɛma 'say like this/that' among the Kaluli of Papua New Guinea. ɛlɛma and *dile* are remarkably similar, in terms both of their communicative functions and of their role in the acquisition process:

> The effect of the triadic interactions with ɛlɛma is that the young child is pushed into interactions with others by the mother who supplies him with the correct lines to say, before he can spontaneously and appropriately produce them himself. For example, the caregiver may use ɛlɛma to assist the child in requesting objects, information, or actions that the caregiver deems appropriate to the child in the situation. (1979:90)

How do we account for these striking similarities? I have tried to show that caregivers' speech contains contextualization cues that foreground a wide range of aspects of the present interaction. Children thus "read" these subtle cues, along with the wider context, in discerning their elders' perceptions of what is happening at that instant. These cues simultaneously point out the conventionalized expectations for these types of settings (cf. Cook-Gumperz and Corsaro 1976). Having both of these sorts of considerations in mind does not, however, constitute communicative competence. As Cicourel (1974b) points out, the real hard nut is figuring out "how children acquire (the interpretive) ability to articulate an experienced social setting with his or her understanding and memory of abstract rules or norms."

The solution to this puzzle lies in the *form* of the verbal and nonverbal messages. Caregivers construct their utterances in such a way that the formal features simultaneously index what they take to be the crucial dimensions of the present interaction and its socio-cultural background (cf. Cicourel 1970, 1974b; Corsaro 1979; Ochs 1979). Repetition elicitation formulas are particularly useful in this regard, because they convert conventionalized expectations into one of the parameters of the context – the child's speech. They constitute the clearest (although intentionally *not* the most direct) means of telling the child "this is how the normative background intersects with this particular interaction at this particular moment *for you*."

Bearing messages in later childhood. Repetition elicitation formulas continue to be of significance as the child grows older. These routines do not lose their importance, but their role changes. Beyond playing a part in the language acquisition process, they accord the child a meaningful position in the verbal economy of the community. Beginning at about six years of age, the *dile* formula is used in asking a child to relay a short message to a member of a nearby household. A child will be told, for example, *Dile al Santiago que me preste una pala* 'Tell Santiago to loan me a shovel'. The child will then go immediately to Santiago's house and tell Santiago (or, in his absence, another member of the household) in a very high-pitched and excited voice, *Dijo mi daddy si tienes una pala pa' prestarle* 'My daddy asked if you have a shovel to loan him'.

Note that the request itself foregrounds the nature of the utterance (as reported or indirect speech), the identity of the sender, the purpose of the visit, and the mode of transaction (a loan). Children of this age are thus expected to be able to interpret and generate a number of speech-act types. Because the child provides a report of the senior's speech (rather than a direct quotation), he or she must modify pronouns, verbal inflection, and syntactic form as well as transform one type of directive (an explicit request to convey information) into another (an implicit request by a third party for a material item).

What sort of communicative competence, then, do six- through ten-year-olds possess and how are these skills regarded by the community? As Goffman (1959:95–6) notes, children possess incomplete social selves. They can enter other households more freely than adults, and their visits do not require the residents to shift from intimate and mundane to formal and ceremonial presentations. As Hotchkiss (1967) suggests, this renders them perfect messengers for errands that would cause adults to lose face (e.g., requesting a petty loan) or would be nearly impossible (e.g., finding out what your neighbors are up to). Córdovan children are thus sometimes told by adults or older siblings to observe what is said and done at a neighboring household or in the street and to report back to their seniors.

This advantageous position is not, however, without its price tag. Children are not yet considered full-fledged actors on the household or community stage, and they accordingly are given few lines in the substantive dialogues. The youths' strictly linguistic competence is not at issue here. They have already mastered a broad range of speech acts and, as demonstrated by the verbal games they enjoy with peers, they can be quite subtle and imaginative in their use of language.[3] They are, however, expected to exhibit *respeto* for their seniors at all times, that is, to honor the latter's considerably greater access to the center stage of interaction. In short, they are expected to have mastered a set of complex metacommunicative skills relating to the transference/transformation of speech in a manner that will be deemed appropriate in a broad range of social settings. I noted above that repetition elicitation formulas provide younger children with crucial information regarding their rights vis-à-vis other children and adults. Carrying messages provides older children with models regarding adult privileges and responsibilities vis-à-vis other adults.

Repetition elicitation devices and interview techniques. Even if it is admitted that such simple formulas involve such complex skills, it is only fair to ask what bearing this has on the task that confronts the interviewer. I contend that these results are most telling in this regard. They point to the fact that observation and imitation are critical components not just of the native model of learning but of the routines used in the course of the acquisition process. They also show that observation and imitation demand a great deal more from the language learner than simply learning to mimic series of sounds. Participation in these imitative exercises exposes the initiate to the way underlying cultural premises, social roles, and interpretive frames enter into social interaction. Once the child has mastered the skills of observation and mitation, these are used in drawing her or him into a significant role in the communicative patterns of the community.

Interestingly, it is precisely the stages of observation and imitation that are avoided by relying on interviews early in fieldwork. Researchers who have just entered another society try to jump from a lack of social–cultural and sociolinguistic competence to the generation of original utterances – questions. Unfortunately, their inattentiveness to the preceding phases of language learning deprive them of a great deal of practice in interpreting and using context-sensitive expressions and of learning when and where they are appropriate. Given the importance of earning the right to produce original utterances of a given type by demonstrating one's ability to repeat and interpret them, it comes as little wonder that native speakers will resist this attempted circumvention of what they see as the proper means of gaining competence.

Political oratory and the rhetorical competence of adults

Once individuals have begun earning a living, married, started raising a family, and established a household, they are presented with opportunities to make their voices heard, so to speak, in interactions with members of their and their spouse's extended families. As they progress from age thirty to sixty, many assume roles of importance in religious voluntary associations, irrigation-ditch associations, parish affairs, domestic water and land-grant associations, and other intracommunity groups. If they prove themselves to be thoughtful and persuasive speakers, their statements regarding community affairs can come to be taken quite seriously by persons of all ages. These are the years in which men and women who possess *talento* for public speaking are expected to develop and exhibit their rhetorical facility. A great deal of prestige accrues to the community member who can sway an audience in the course of a meeting or other public gathering.

In studying the verbal skills that form the focus of the acquisition process during early and middle adulthood, I will draw on the procedure that I adopted in studying children's speech. This consists of tape-recording a fair amount of discourse in as wide a variety of situations as possible. This corpus can then be examined to see what metacommunicative routines are evident. A few of these can be selected for more intensive analysis. Having chosen an uneventful, everyday interaction in the analysis of the early years of language acquisition, I will deal here with a speech event that formed a focus of attention within the community, both during the time of its occurrence and for days thereafter. The analytic method will, however, be identical – a close examination of the tape and transcript to see why this particular set of expressions was used and how these lexical, syntactic, prosodic, and other features provide clues to the meaning of what was said.

The following transcript is taken from a tape recording of a meeting of the board of directors and the membership of an association of the users of the local water system. As is the case in any small community, an issue occasionally arises that creates a persistent dispute. Problems with the community water system had resulted in frequent shortages over a period of years. This serious and at least temporarily irreconcilable situation had produced a number of lasting rifts that surfaced during the meeting. One schism developed between two geographic parts of the community, while the other divided the association's board and its membership.

Both sets of issues emerged in this meeting. The president of the board used his opening remarks in directing the discussion toward the technical and legal dimensions of the situation. Everyone knew, however, that the members' feeling that the board itself was behind much of the difficulty was the true, if hidden, agenda of the meeting, and a room in the local school was accordingly packed. One member, whom I refer to as the "Disputant" in the following transcript, had been particularly vocal in denouncing the actions of the board in discussions with fellow members. He and other members had utilized a rarely invoked clause in the association's bylaws in forcing the board to call a special meeting. The Disputant interrupted the president's remarks with a series of questions. Other persons, including an equally vocal board member, entered the debate, but none had been able to induce the board members to address the central issue.

3. Dispute at board meeting[4]
Disputant:

1.	Lo que se NECESITA . . .	What is NEEDED . . .
2.	Yo soy de eso opinión.	I am of this opinion.
3.	A mí no me importa	It doesn't matter to me
4.	quien es usted,	who you are,
5.	de comisión o como	a board member or whatever
6.	quiera que SEA.	you want it TO BE.
7.	Para mí, todos son	For ME, all are GOOD.
8.	BUENOS.	(meaning 'I am impartial')
9.	Pero sí, digo una COSA.	But I WILL say one THING.
10.	Lo que se necesita	What is needed
11.	en este negocio	in this business
12.	[es que] se arregle	[is that] it work itself out
13.	y camine TODO	and that EVERYTHING proceeds
14.	como SOPONE caminar.	the way it is SUPPOSED to proceed.
15.	Y no que . . .	And not that . . .
16.	Y no camine bajo de,	And that it doesn't proceed under,

17. bajo de POLÍTICA	under [the influence of] POLITICS
18. o bajo de ENVÍDIA	or under [the influence of] ENVY
19. o bajo de esto y el OTRO.	or under this and THAT.
20. Es hacer . . .	It is to do . . .
21. Yo estoy alcanzando a conocer	I am coming to see
22. que aquí hay mucha ENVÍDIA,	that here there is a lot of ENVY,
23. tanto por un RUMBO	as much from one DIRECTION
24. como por el OTRO,	as from the OTHER,
25. ya estamos todos MAL.	so we are all WRONG.
26. A mí me gusta hacer CLARO	I like to make [myself] CLEAR
27. y me gusta decir	and I like to say
28. lo que voy a decir	what I am going to say
29. a un PÚBLICO.	in PUBLIC.
30. Yo no . . .	I don't . . .
31. Yo no le rodeo a NADIE.	I don't walk around ANYBODY.
32. Se necesita que TODOS nos	What is needed is for ALL of
33. trabajemos como HOMBRES	us to work like MEN
34. y que TODOS digamos la VERDAD	and for ALL of us to tell the TRUTH
35. y no la MENTIRA.	And not LIES.

Board president:

36. Y la verdad es/	And the truth is/

Disputant:

37. /Porque yo sé CIERTAMENTE	/Because I know with CERTITUDE
38. que hay muchas cosas	that there are many things
39. escondidas en esa LINEA.	hidden in that LINE.

Other board member:

40. ¿Sabe usted que lo que estoy	Do you know what it is that I
41. diciendo yo, [Disputant's name]?	am saying, [Disputant's name]?

Disputant:

42. Um hum.	Um hum.

Other board member:

43. Nosotros no tenemos NADA	We don't have ANYTHING
44. escondido aquí.	hidden here.
45. Yo sé que ustedes creen que . . .	I know that you believe that . . .

(recounts charge leveled by members against board)

The other board member then argued that the water shortage had been as hard on her household as on those of the general membership in attempting to refute the latter's charge that the board had been getting more than its fair share of water.

The Disputant's (hereafter D) words constituted a focal event in the meeting, and they were highly effective in bringing out the topic he wished to discuss. Wherein lies their efficacy? The *form* of the discourse is crucial. In comparison with the preceding statements, D's words were marked from the start by an increase in volume and a decrease in the speed of utterance. The pitch, loudness, and stress

evince a much greater range of variation than the surrounding discourse. The individual utterances are separated into clear tone groups
that come close to being poetic lines. The nucleus rests in the final
word in all utterances save 16, 20, and 30, which are false starts, and in
the last line (38–39). Each is followed by a longer than normal pause.
The speech is also segmented prosodically into quasi stanza-like units
(1–8, 9–19, 20–25, 26–31, 32–39). The end of each "stanza" is
marked by a sharp drop in pitch and an even longer pause.

D's words were preceded by a period of short turns with frequent
interruptions. Once D secured the floor in 1, all side conversations
ceased, and all eyes turned to him. Even when the board president
tried to prevent D from coming to the point in 36, D was able to retain
the floor. His slow, clear, measured, rhythmic, forceful speech marked
his statement as climactic. This formal elaboration highlighted his abilities as rhetorician, thus increasing the stakes, so to speak, of the success or failure of his efforts. When D shifted register, he signaled the
audience that the meaning of what he was about to say must be sought
less in its overt referential meaning than in the way in which the poetic
form provided clues to underlying, implicit meanings.

This strategy was crucial. D and his fellows had prompted the board
to call the special meeting in order to bring their charges against the
latter out into the open. This had not taken place thus far, and the
discussion of technical problems was becoming so tedious that many of
the participants were losing interest and beginning side conversations.
D had to bring the key issues to the fore soon if the momentum
produced by the special circumstances of the meeting was to be preserved. Nevertheless, to accuse the board directly of taking more than
their share of the scarce water and of covering up their actions would
have constituted a real affront. Such public accusations would contro-
vert the accused's *dignidad de la persona* 'personal dignity', and would
be likely to spark a real confrontation and engender lasting enmity. D
thus sought to force the issue without directly referring to it himself.

D accomplished this feat by juxtaposing allusions to three fundamental *Mexicano* values with implicit allusions to the basic conflicts that
underlay the meeting. Lines 3–8 express a basic ideal of interpersonal
relations – *tratarle igual a todos* 'to treat everyone equally'. One of the
highest compliments that can be paid a person is that he or she 'treats
everyone well' (*buenos*) or 'the same' (*iguales*). This value is seen as
following from Christ's love for all humans. Christian values dictate
the avoidance of pettiness, spitefulness, and conceit. D thus implicitly
contrasts his compliance with these norms with the members' assertion
that some board members feel that their position entitles them to a
greater share of the water. In other words, D is saying to the presi-

dent, "You may think that you, as a board member, are better than I am, but I treat everyone equally."

Lines 10–25 juxtapose a second value, corporatism, with another dimension of the conflict, that between the two sections of the community. *La gente* 'the people' should ideally be united, sharing labor and resources in times of need. This, too, has a biblical precedent; it is often said that 'we are all brothers and sisters, because we are all children of God.' This is the way that community affairs 'are supposed to go'. *Envidia* 'envy' and *política* 'politics' are major obstacles to realizing corporatism. D goes on in lines 21–25 to suggest that all parties have given way to *envidia*. The use of *rumbo* in this context is a double entrendre. *Todos rumbos* is the common expression for 'all over'. But the other side of the community is generally referred to locally as *el otro rumbo* 'the other side'. D's allusion to the internecine conflict thus similarly combines a veiled but clear reference to a basic aspect of the dispute with a value-laden exhortation.

A final juxtaposition of value and conflict involves D more directly. Before the meeting, D had personally queried most of the members with respect to their feelings about the board's actions. Because he had not yet spoken directly to anyone on the board, some of the commissioners accused him in private of being afraid to confront them directly. This constituted a serious charge. The inability to face one's opponent in person would constitute a loss of face and a diminution in one's sense of personal dignity. D asserts, on the contrary, that he likes to speak not only clearly but publicly, and that he doesn't 'walk around [i.e., isn't afraid of] anybody.'

Now that he has adumbrated both the conflicts and the perceived strength of his own position, D goes on to state his charge publicly – if still implicitly. Having declared himself to be forthright and truthful, he exhorts all participants to behave similarly and to tell the truth. The board president correctly perceives that D is just about to drive the last nail into the board's would-be coffin, so to speak, and tries to interrupt him in line 36. Not lacking in rhetorical strength at the moment, however, D concludes with 'because I know with certitude that there are many things hidden in that line.' This may seem cryptic at first glance. However, several of the key issues in the dispute revolved around a water line that passed next to the houses of several of the board members, and this line had been discussed at length in the preceding dialogue. *Linea* also denotes a line of reasoning, and the ambiguity is very much a part of D's strategy. In essence, D is telling the board directly that "we all know that your statements about the real cause of the water shortage are lies, and it is time to tell the truth."

D's plan worked. Without making any direct accusations, he managed to bring the charges out into the open. His allusions were so clear that it was necessary for the board members to refer to them directly in responding to D. The board member proceeded to summarize the people's feelings with respect to the board's actions and then to give a detailed justification of her own position. My analysis suggests that D's success rested both on his use of sub-rosa argumentation and on his juxtaposition of commonly accepted, traditional values with specific issues. These values provide an indisputable source of legitimacy for his points. They also enable him to interpret the events in line with his perspective on the situation.

D's use of a formal, quasi-poetic style highlighted the importance of his statement as well as his own rhetorical skills. By relating these current, specific issues to basic values, he enhanced their consequence. Gaining recognition for one's verbal abilities is an important part of the process of moving through the status of *muchacho* (literally 'boy', meaning 'young man') and into full-fledged adult status. Speaking out on the affairs of the community is the most important means of establishing one's reputation at this point in life.

Adults between the ages of about thirty and sixty have thus earned the right to produce original utterances, even on important public occasions. The focus is on developing the ability to draw out the moral values that are seen as embodying the way of life in the days of *los viejitos de antes* 'the elders of bygone days' and to show their bearing on a particular, ongoing interaction. Esteem is accorded to individuals who can relate the two so effectively that their position on the situation at hand is compelling. The rhetorical rights of persons between these ages is, however, still limited. Although they can use the values that emanate from 'bygone days' in legitimating their stance, they cannot do so explicitly, by framing their words as 'the *talk* of the elders of bygone days' itself. They similarly enjoy only restricted access to the folkloric forms, such as proverbs, oral historical vignettes, and scriptural allusions. Although persons under the age of sixty may *refer* to such forms, they are not generally accorded the right to *perform* them, particularly in front of their elders.

Such individuals can legitimately provide the communicative frame for conversations and other interactions, thus assuming a powerful role in their denouement. They have earned this privilege by demonstrating a high degree of rhetorical competence. (This does not mean, however, that everyone achieves as high a degree of verbal virtuosity as the Disputant.) They are still cognizant that the full range of referential frames is not open to them. Specifically, entrance to the crucial realm of the *viejitos de antes* is still gained primarily by the present elders.

Adults continue to draw their parents and other elders into 'talking about the past.'

What exactly is involved in producing and in interpreting political oratory? The Disputant's words are most revealing with respect to *Mexicano* norms of conversational implicature. It is clear that it is not always appropriate to adhere to such conversational maxims as the Gricean (1975) principles of "relevance" and "perspicuity." It is, rather, necessary at times to bury one's meaning in metaphorical allusions or in seemingly simple, transparent statements that carry "hidden" levels of meaning. Political rhetoric can similarly reveal a great deal about the use of commonsense knowledge as an important conversational resource. Only by making explicit the connection between the structure of the oratory and such knowledge can participants or analysts grasp the meaning of what is said. Deciphering such speech events can thus sensitize researchers to the norms that govern when information must be conveyed implicitly and how subtle indexical forms are used in doing so. Such analysis prepares the investigator to recognize the signals embedded in interview discourse that point to the fact that the speaker is "burying" his or her meaning.

Scriptural allusions and 'the talk of the elders of bygone days'

Los ancianos or *los viejitos* 'the old folks', females and males of about seventy years of age and older, are the legitimate bearers of traditional knowledge in *Mexicano* society. The central principle of *respeto* 'respect' constrains both what individuals can say and when they can speak. The oldest members of the community are obligated to preserve and transmit 'the talk of the elders of bygone days'; they are the only speakers who are accorded the right to use performances in specialized genres in doing so. Just as the more esteemed speech types and the knowledge they presuppose belong to the elders, theirs is the floor as well. A 'respectful' younger speaker will always yield the floor to an older person, will not contradict her or his senior, and will not grow angry if contradicted by a *viejito*. The elders thus do much of the talking, especially when two or more of them are present.

'The talk of the elders of bygone days' emerges in three main types of social situations. First, elders who are highly versed in these traditions enter into exchanges of oral historical vignettes, proverbs, and the like. These are true virtuoso performances. The participants are experts in presenting these speech forms; the young and inexperienced may watch, but they keep their distance. The texts are presented in an abbreviatory fashion, and they are not explicated.

Another context consists of discussions of the past by persons of roughly thirty to sixty years of age. These take place in informal situations, such as conversations between good friends and trips to the mountains. The material is generally drawn from the more recent past, and it is presented as the personal recollection of the speaker (e.g., *yo no tenía más que como diez años cuando . . .* 'I was only about ten years old when . . .'). Such exchanges of stories are seen as recreational, rather than competitive or pedagogical.

The third and most common arena for presentation of this 'talk' is pedagogical discourse. Here an elder or elders engage one or more younger persons in a dialogue about the past. The explicit object is to inculcate the basic moral values that exemplify the actions of 'the elders of bygone days' to succeeding generations to such a degree that they come to be reflected in the thought and action of the latter group.

Common settings for pedagogical discussions are informal gatherings in living rooms or kitchens; elders also frequently launch into pedagogical discourse on passing a local landmark on a walk or a trip into town. These conversations are generally initiated by the elder, although younger persons' questions regarding some facet of the past can serve as an entrée into a lengthy exposition. Elders have much more control over what will be discussed and how the conversation will proceed; nevertheless, pedagogical discourse is *dialogic* in nature. The elders often query their junior(s) as to whether she or he is comprehending what has been said by ending a statement with such questions as *¿ves?* 'you see?' *¿sabes cómo te digo?* 'do you know what I'm telling you?' or *¿verdad?* 'right?' Similarly, the "student" is free to ask for reiterations or further elaborations. Younger persons use questions (e.g., *¿verdad?* or *¿sí?* 'really?') or such exclamations as *sí* 'yes,' *um hum,* and the like in signaling the elder that they are comprehending the "lesson."

Having presented analyses of other genres elsewhere (Briggs 1985a, 1985b), I will draw on performances of scriptural allusions in illustrating 'the talk of the elders of bygone days.' Scriptural allusions are a fairly flexible genre, so to speak, since they can be used in a variety of situations and can incorporate texts of various degrees of length and complexity. They consist of the insertion of a text bearing on moral principles that is identified as scriptural into ongoing discourse. The following scriptural allusion was provided by Mr. Trujillo. He performed it in 1972, during our first extended conversation, six years before the exchange analyzed in Chapter 3. Mr. Trujillo was commenting on the growing reluctance of people to maintain their devotional practices.

4. Scriptural allusion

1. AT:	Pero al cabo que Dios	But in the end God
2.	los sabe premiar	knows how to reward them
3.	lo mismo que premia al	just as He rewards a
4.	((pecador)),	((sinner)),
5.	porque dice	because He says
6.	"perdonar al inocente,"	"pardon the innocent,"
7.	dice,	He says,
8.	"porque no sabe lo que	"because he knows not what he
9.	hace."	does."
10.	Y todos semos [sic] HIJOS,	And we are all CHILDREN,
11.	todos semos BROTHERS,	we are all BROTHERS,
12.	todos semos hermanos.	we are all brothers and sisters.
13. CB:	Sí.	Yes.
14. AT:	Y muchos no,	But not for many,
15.	porque tiene un nickel	because she or he has a nickel
16.	more que el otro;	more than the other;
17.	es ORGULLO.	it's PRIDE.
18.	Mire,	Look,
19.	la VANIDAD	VANITY
20.	se acaba,	comes to an end,
21.	no tiene fin.	it is pointless.
22.	EL DINERO se acaba,	MONEY comes to an end
23.	no tiene fin.	it is pointless.
24.	De modo que hay tres cosas	And so there are three things
25.	que no tienen fin.	that are pointless.
26.	Y la AMISTAD REINA EN LA VIDA.	And FRIENDSHIP REIGNS IN LIFE.

This scriptural allusion is metacommunicative in two major respects. The allusion is to Christ's invocation on behalf of his crucifiers (Luke 23:34). The term *inocente* refers to those who lack the knowledge of good and evil, and it is generally applied to young children and to imbeciles. The term is extended to all humans in the text, however, because we lack divine omniscience and our actions are fallible. God will accordingly forgive those who forget Him just as He forgives sinners. Mr. Trujillo extends this logic in this allusion and in two subsequent allusions to suggest that humans must love their fellow *inocentes,* regardless of what wrongs they may commit against them. Mr. Trujillo also lists what he sees as the three greatest obstacles to the expression of such brotherly–sisterly affection – pride, vanity, and avariciousness.

The second major thrust of this allusion – its bearing on the situation at hand – is especially clear. I had inaugurated my fieldwork in the community three weeks previously, and I met Mr. and Mrs. Trujillo four days before the present meeting. During this initial session, my position was quite ambiguous. I was a stranger, an Anglo-American, who came with a tape recorder and wished to conduct research. As a representative of the superordinate society who wished to write about the community, I possessed a high degree of status. I was, however, also a nineteen-year-old who obviously sought the Trujillos' friendship and wanted to learn from them. Mr. Trujillo's speech reflected this ambiguity. He used formal–deferential, *usted* forms while occupying the preeminent position in an asymmetric mode of interaction – pedagogical discourse.

Mr. Trujillo had an obvious interest, however, in playing down the deference-to-hearer and emphasizing the solidarity-with-hearer dimension (cf. Silverstein 1981a:5). His speech was accordingly pronouncedly performative in that he sought to create a close friendship and to be accorded the deference that he, being fifty years my senior, deserved. Like Mr. Trujillo's utterances in this conversation as a whole, a number of features of the scriptural allusion were carefully suited to this goal. His condemnation of pride, vanity, and avarice is not simply reflective of basic values – Anglo-Americans are commonly stereotyped as proud, vain, and avaricious. Moreover, these characteristics are believed to engender in Anglo-Americans a sense of superiority to *Mexicanos* and a reluctance to develop close friendships with them. Mr. Trujillo goes on to argue that friendship (*amistad*) conquers these obstacles. Mr. Trujillo indexes the fact that his remarks are directly applicable to Anglo-Americans (present company included) by inserting three English lexical items into the discourse.

Thirty-five seconds after this segment, Mr. Trujillo argues that the obligation to extend fraternal–sororal love to everyone admits no racial distinctions: *No importa quien sea, no importa que sea negro o que sea lo que fuere o austriago o lo que fuere* 'it doesn't matter who it is, it doesn't matter if she or he's black or she or he's whatever it may be or a foreigner or whatever it may be'.

Friendship did come to reign in the situation. The Trujillos became two of my best friends, central consultants, and major sponsors within the community. Mr. Trujillo shifted to *tú* forms before long, and we adopted kin terms for use in address a year later (I addressed them as *papá* 'father' and *mamá* 'mother', and they addressed me as *hijo* 'son').

Scriptural allusions thus provide metacommunicative commentary on the ongoing conversation in two primary ways. First, scriptural allusions draw upon a textual tradition shared by the speaker, his or her interlocutor(s), and their audience. Such phrases as *Dios dice* 'God says' or *dice mi Señor Jesucristo en sus evangelios* 'my Lord Jesus Christ says in His Scriptures' tell the hearer "these are not my words, these are the words of Jesus Christ." Use of a scriptural allusion thus places the highest source of legitimacy in the society behind the

peaker's words. Because the scriptural text is irrefutable, the legitimacy of the speaker's point of view can be disputed only by challeng-
ng the bearing of the text on the issue at hand.

The rhetorical force of scriptural allusions cannot be attributed en-
irely, however, to the connection of the discourse to this shared tex-
ual background. The effective use of a scriptural allusion uses this
source of legitimacy in advancing the speaker's view of an issue of
present concern. Text 4 adumbrates the values that Mr. Trujillo deems
central. It also affords us insight into his perception of *Mexicano–
Anglo-American* relations, our friendship, and of what was taking
place on an interactional level that afternoon. The scriptural allusion
thus functions as a blueprint or, in Peircean terms, a diagrammatic
icon of the speaker's view of a particular situation. This diagrammatic
function is two-sided, so to speak, because it also includes an iconic
condensation of one aspect of 'the talk of the elders of bygone days.'

In anthropological terms, scriptural allusions connect an ideal model
with a real, temporally bounded event, specifying how the former
applies to the latter. Such speech events thus show great promise for
ethnographers. Some fieldworkers collect extensive data on structural
principles or decontextualized ideals. Others are less concerned with
norms and meanings than with the details of "objectively" observable
behavior. The ideal and the real are, however, never equivalent, and
ethnographers encounter difficulties in relating the two. The study of
these sorts of speech events thus provides the ethnographer with a
large set of examples of how the people themselves envision the relationship between cultural norms and concrete situations.

Summary: the evaluation of metacommunicative competence

Taken as a whole, these materials point to the centrality of three types
of tasks to the developmental process. Lacking basic linguistic competence or command of a given type of speech event, individuals are
expected to learn initially through *observation*. Once the learner has
gained some grasp of the requisite skills, this mechanism is complemented by a second acquisition device – *repetition* of the words of one's
seniors. Once this reiterative capacity has been acquired, the focus
turns to practicing the *production* of original utterances in dialogue.

These skills roughly correlate with basic stages of the acquisition
process, with children observing and reiterating the words of their
seniors, adolescents producing original utterances in interactions with
peers, and adults creating increasingly sophisticated speech acts in public. Nevertheless, all three devices are utilized at each stage as well,

albeit in different social contexts. Young children, for example, are not encouraged to offer original contributions to adults' conversations. But they possess competence in and a right to perform verbal games that are hardly shared by adults. Similarly, although most adults of thirty to sixty years of age can speak freely on issues pertaining to wage-labor employment and community affairs, they are still restricted primarily to observation and repetition of the elders' presentations of 'the talk of the elders of bygone days.'

This progression continues through the life span, and a person normally reaches her or his point of maximum competence in these areas just before joining 'the elders of bygone days,' barring senility. Rhetorical facility and the right to perform the most esteemed genres are not, however, simply guaranteed by growing older. The degree of rhetorical competence requisite to discussing such "advanced" topics as oral traditions, ethnotheology, and moral values is thus gained in the course of a gradual and lengthy process of mastering social and linguistic skills. The combined effects of *talento, interés, concentración,* and *paciencia* render it possible for some persons to gain rhetorical competence earlier than others.

Two factors play a major role in assessing rhetorical ability. First, ceteris paribus, the greater the number of folkloric genres in which a person can perform, the greater his or her status as a rhetorician. The second factor entails the development of a heightened pragmatic sense. The best speakers select an utterance type, such as a joke, a story, or 'just words,' that best fits the social context of the conversation and the predominate topic. Likewise, the utterance does not falter (through slurring of words, a lapse in memory, etc.) and is accompanied with appropriate gesticulation, body movement, facial expressions, and prosodic features. A good speaker will maintain the cohesion of the discourse, making her or his hearer(s) aware, whether explicitly or implicitly, of the relevance of the utterance to the present situation. Such individuals thus subtly manipulate both linguistic forms and aspects of the social situation to lend compelling force to their utterances.

Rhetorical competence and interview techniques

Question–answer sequences play several distinct and quite important parts in the acquisition process. Young children repeat adults' questions to other adults and then convey the latter's answers to the former. Children are also accorded the right to pose permission requests to the appropriate adults, as in our society (e.g., "Mama, may I go to the store with Mary?"). This act presupposes a knowledge of appropriate age and gender roles and of authority relations, because unreasonable requests or queries directed to the wrong person would be ineffectual or even criticized.

At a much higher level in the rhetorical hierarchy, individuals are permitted to query their seniors with regard to "traditional" *Mexicano* knowledge – ethnotheology, oral historical traditions, spoken and musical genres, and so on. Posing questions in this way does not, however, resemble an interview. Persons who wish to acquire such knowledge frame a repetition of part of the elder's preceding utterance with an interrogative marker. Common questions thus assume the form of *¿Qué no dijo usted que . . . ?* 'Didn't you say that . . . ?' or *¿Qué quiere decir X?* 'What does X mean?' It is important to note (1) that the referential frame for such questions is provided by the elder's speech, (2) that the latter's pedagogical discourse provides the dominant conversational structure for the interaction, and (3) that the utterance of such a question presupposes both basic knowledge of this type of information (gained through observation) and the manner in which it is disseminated.

Standard interview techniques invert these conversational norms in three ways. First, fieldworkers enter the society lacking acquaintance with norms for comportment and speech. Instead of acquiring communicative competence by ascending through the established succession of developmental tasks, however, interviewers skip the stages of observation and repetition of their seniors' words to move immediately to the generation of original utterances – questions that emerge from their own interests. Furthermore, such questions frequently pertain to the most esoteric topics – those in which only the most advanced speakers are competent.

Second, control over the interaction lies in the hands of the interviewer. It is he or she who exerts the most control over the process of turn-taking, it is he or she who introduces topics, by and large, and it is he or she who decides when to move onto the next topic. This constitutes an inversion of the normative structure for the conveyance of information on such topics between a senior and a junior.

Finally, the interviewer's initial lack of familiarity with the relevant referential frames and accepted means of conveying information frequently renders her or his questions disruptive to the cohesion of the discourse and/or inappropriate for the social situation. These problems are compounded when the interviewer attempts to shift the discourse to a subject of greater relevance to his or her research interests or moves from topic to topic. Problems emanating from insufficient competence in the language or dialect or in basic cultural premises also undermine the effectiveness of the interviewer's speech. As I argue in the preceding sections, questions that contain such stumbling blocks are difficult to answer. The repeated emergence of procedural prob lems prompts the consultant to reassess the former's ability to engage effectively in this level of discourse.

The pragmatic effectiveness of a person's speech – providing the proper referential frame, avoiding significant formal or semantic flaws making one's remarks appropriate to the social situation, and main taining the cohesion of the discourse – is one of the two primary means of judging rhetorical competence. The emergence of such procedural problems thus suggests to the hearers that their interlocutor lacks suffi cient competence to enable the latter to generate original utterances. One's consultants are accordingly not obligated to repair the procedu ral problem, answer the question, and give the turn back to the ques tioner, as is prescribed by Anglo-American middle-class speech norms (Churchill 1978:89). It is indeed far more appropriate in the case of the fieldworker to signal her or him of the failure of her or his efforts to assume a sophisticated communicative role.

Attempts to circumvent the acquisition process

Nevertheless, inverting norms for the acquisition of metacommunicative competence is par for the course. Although some fieldworkers, such as Geertz (1972), provide notable exceptions, most ethnographers seek to impose their own metacommunicative norms on their consultants.‍ Rather than adopting native metacommunicative norms, consultants are taught a subset of the fieldworker's own metacommunicative devices – those pertaining to interview technique. This is the practice that I have termed "communicative hegemony." This refers to researchers' efforts to impose their own communicative strategies on their subjects or con sultants regardless of the possibility that these techniques may be incom patible with those persons' own communicative repertoire.

The legitimacy of this approach is enhanced by its enshrinement in manuals on ethnographic fieldwork. One of the most widely used dis cussions of anthropological fieldwork, Pelto and Pelto's *Anthropologi cal Research: The Structure of Inquiry,* suggests that "humans differ in their willingness as well as their capabilities for verbally expressing cultural information. Consequently, the anthropologist usually finds that only a small number of individuals in any community are good key informants" (1978:72). Note, of course, that the basis of the selection is the communicative norms of the fieldworker, not those of the na tives. Then, having selected the "right" person(s), "some of the cap abilities of key informants are systematically developed by the fieldworkers, as they train the informants to conceptualize cultural data in he frame of reference employed by the anthropologists" (1978:72).[6]

We are thus left with two fundamental and, it seems, commonly accepted assumptions regarding the epistemology of fieldwork. First, obtaining large quantities of ethnographic data entails (or is at least aided by) the training of one or several natives in the metacommunicative norms presupposed by the interview. Second, this process is facilitated by the selection of "key informants" from among the ranks of those who appear to have the greatest facility for operating within this mode of discourse.

I found the second premise to be quite accurate in my own fieldwork. My initial experience in interviewing Silvianita and George López in connection with my research on the Córdovan wood-carving art provides a case in point. In spite of our friendship and their commitment to the project, Mrs. López responded to nearly all of my questions with *Ooo, pos, ¡quién sabe!* 'Oh, well, who knows!' Mr. López alternated between this response and the provision of highly abbreviated replies.

On the other hand, I proposed a set of interviews to Federico Córdova, another community elder. He agreed both to the interviews and to their tape-recording. When I returned from my car, Mr. Córdova asked me 'Now, what is it that you wanted to know?' I provided him with one of the questions that had fared so poorly with the Lópezes. He then proceeded to produce a long, flowing narrative history of the local carving industry.

How are we to account for such differences? Some researchers might have worked almost entirely with the more "cooperative" of the three. But the ability and desire to communicate were not the problems here. After George and Silvianita López restructured our interactions by inducing me to carve wood with them, our collaboration became quite fruitful. The conversations that were structured by the couple turned out to be extremely fertile sources of data, since the form of the discourse provided crucial information on how the carvers perceived the history of the industry and their own participation in it.

I rather think that an awareness of the vastly different educational and linguistic experience between the three will bring us closer to understanding this situation. Mr. Córdova was fluent in English, and he was literate in both languages. Mrs. López, on the other hand, is virtually monolingual, while Mr. López possesses only rudimentary competence in English. Mr. Córdova gained his first extensive contact with English-speakers in World War I, and he mastered the language while attending teacher-training courses at the regional normal school. He then taught for many years in the local school. He later worked for the U.S. Forest Service, a job that involved extensive interaction with English speakers. Mr. Córdova often reads English-language newspapers. Interestingly, Lina Ortiz de Córdova, Federico Córdova's wife, who is monolingual, responded to my questions in the same fashion as the Lópezes.

Mr. Córdova had not only acquired the phonological, syntactic, and semantic systems of American English, but he had mastered its conversational structure as well. He had such a sophisticated idea of the interviewing process that he even thought to make sure that the tape recorder had been turned on before beginning his account. (The one stipulation he imposed in helping me was that I was to give him a copy of the final publication.) Why, then, was the latter interview so painless and so "successful"? Even though Mr. Córdova and I spoke in Spanish, the interview was bilingual, since the frame of reference and the conversational structure we used did not emerge from conversational patterns that related Córdovan youths and elders. Fortunately, this is not true of the sections of the interactions in which Mr. Córdova "wandered off the point," i.e., gained control of topical selection. Here the tape recordings reveal the same richness of metacommunicative routines and rhetorical structure that characterize the pedagogical dialogues with the Lópezes.

My research methods thus dictated the imposition of my own conversational norms on my consultants. The gap between American English discourse structure (especially interview techniques) and patterns that are characteristic of speakers of New Mexican Spanish is sufficiently wide that my initial position of communicative hegemony was successful only with a bilingual consultant. Fortunately, the Lópezes and other elders were so consistent in their refusal to allow me to structure our pedagogical interactions in keeping with my own "instincts" that I was forced to develop an alternative methodology. In Chapter 5, I systematize this process and attempt to show how it can be applied to interviewing in general.

5. Listen before you leap: toward methodological sophistication

I must admit to having painted a critical picture of the state of interviewing in the social sciences and linguistics. I initiated the discussion by pointing to a number of serious flaws in the literature on interviewing and by relating the persistence of crucial theoretical problems to a lack of methodological sophistication. Chapter 3 pointed to some of the procedural problems that can impede interviewing and can create serious problems in analyzing the data. I argued in Chapter 4 that native metacommunicative routines can inform the use of interview techniques in a given culture as well as provide precisely the types of data that are crucial for many problems in social scientific research.

It would thus be far from surprising if the reader were to have gained the impression that I am attempting to convince researchers to stop interviewing altogether. Indeed I am not. Interviews are highly useful tools for exploring a host of problems. As noted in Chapter 1, the theoretical and methodological insights that have emerged from such fields as the ethnography of communication, conversational analysis, language acquisition research, and other fields have provided us with the skills necessary for conducting and analyzing interviews in a more appropriate fashion.

Similarly, I am not arguing that greater methodological sophistication can only be gained through becoming a sociolinguist or at least developing more interest in the communicative dimensions of the interview than in the problems under study. This is hardly an all-or-nothing affair. It would be unrealistic to expect survey researchers who work with large populations to fully investigate the communicative norms of all potential respondents. Such a proposal would be seriously counterproductive, because it would lead most practitioners to dismiss these criticisms on the grounds that they could never satisfy them. It would also serve to widen the gap between researchers who lack interest in the ethnographic and linguistic communicative knowledge that underlies their data-collection techniques and practitioners who study communicative processes but lack interest in broader social issues.

This chapter is designed to forestall this conclusion by presenting some practical proposals for incorporating the study of native meta communicative routines into interview-based research. I will propose a four-phase approach to conducting interviews and interpreting the re sults. My thesis is that any type of interviewing will be plagued by serious procedural problems if it is not based on sensitivity to the relationship between the communicative norms that are presupposed by the interview and those that are more broadly characteristic of the population under study. This need cannot be addressed in the same fashion, however, by the fieldworker who works by herself or himsel in a small community as the research team studying a large and diverse sample. I will accordingly provide some sense as to how my sugges tions can be taken up in large-scale survey research.

Phase 1: learning how to ask

Adequate applications of interviewing techniques presuppose a basic understanding of the communicative norms of the society in question Obtaining this awareness should accordingly constitute the first item on researchers' agenda. In the case of fieldwork, the first weeks or months of a researcher's field stay are generally devoted to gaining an initial acquaintance with the native community and, in some cases, to learning the language. This is an ideal time in which to observe such simple facts as who talks to whom, who listens to whom, when people talk and when they remain silent, what entities are referred to directly and which are referred to indirectly or signaled nonverbally, and the like. An essential question is: What are the different ways in which people communicate? Hymes (1972) and others have outlined the pos- sible types of variation, and a number of descriptions of local verba repertoires are available (e.g., Abrahams 1983; Albert 1972; Gosser 1974; Sherzer 1983). Sherzer and Darnell's (1972) "Outline Guide for the Ethnographic Study of Speech Use" sketches the issues that might be raised. This is not to say that one must be a sociolinguist to conduct interview-based research. As I argued in Chapter 1, sociolinguistics itself is hardly free from methodological naiveté. The point is rather that overcoming procedural problems is predicated on developing a broader understanding of communicative processes.

The goal at this stage is to gain a sense of the range of social situa- tions in relation to the types of speech events that can take place in each. Learning the rules that relate the two is crucial. One way to facilitate this undertaking is to conduct an intensive analysis of selected

peech events, as was illustrated in Chapter 4. For each major segment
f the life cycle, select a frequently observed speech event. It is useful
ɔ take some events that are of special importance to native speakers
nd others that are unremarkable. It may also be necessary to take
ender, social class or caste, and other factors into account in choosing
xamples for intensive analysis. Each event type should be observed a
umber of times; I strongly recommend the tape-recording of at least
ne instance.

These examples should be analyzed with two objects in mind. First,
he fieldworker should ascertain the meaning of the event for the
articipants. Particularly if one's linguistic competence is still incom-
lete, help can be sought in transcribing, translating, and interpreting
he episode. Such exegesis should hardly be confined to obtaining
teral, referential meanings. The point is to discover the linguistic and
ocial–cultural knowledge that underlies the ability to participate in
nd interpret such events. Second, once an array of such events has
een analyzed, the data can be compared, attempting to discern the
asic norms that underlie specific communicative patterns.

Several issues merit special attention. Metacommunicative features
rovide particularly important clues for the fieldworker. As I argued in
Chapter 4, certain linguistic forms point to the speaker's view of basic
ocial–cultural processes and of the ongoing speech event. As Silver-
tein (1985) has argued for quotation-framing devices, metacommuni-
ative features often index the interpretation that the speaker ascribes
o the utterance. Developing an ability to read such metamessages
rovides the analyst with the ability to base his or her interpretation on
he participants' ongoing process of sorting out the meaning of what
hey are saying and hearing.

It is also important to learn how speakers frame queries. What are
he proper linguistic forms for different types of questions? How do
oninterrogative forms serve as questions in some contexts? Who can
sk questions of whom? Obviously, it is terribly important for the
ieldworker to discover the negative cases – what types of questions are
nappropriate in what circumstances? It is also crucial to study the
cquisition process, for example, the appropriate means of learning
hese rules. In order to become a good interviewer, the researcher will
ave to develop some degree of *competence* in these sociolinguistic
atterns.

Applying this component of the methodology to large-scale survey
esearch presents a real challenge. It would be difficult to document
he sociolinguistic repertoire of potential respondents in a large sample
hat is stratified along the lines of class and ethnicity and that covers a

substantial geographic area. It would be hard in any case to convinc
most funding agencies that a large amount of money should be allc
cated for research that is preliminary to an exploration of the ostensiv
goals of the study.

There are a number of ways in which researchers can, however, gai
greater awareness of communicative patterns in the population i
question within the temporal and monetary constraints faced by mos
survey projects. First, sociolinguists have now conducted studies i
urban environments; these range from microanalyses of small group
or specific situations to macro studies of the relationship between lir
guistic and social–cultural features of large populations. Labov, fo
example, has explored speech patterns in New York City from th
level of narrative construction by members of specific youth gangs t
broad correlations of phonological and syntactic features with suc
variables as class, ethnicity, education, and so on (1966, 1972a, 1972b)
Fishman (1964, 1966; Fishman, Ferguson, and Das Gupta 1968) ha
analyzed sociolinguistic patterns on an even larger scale. Some dimen
sions of communication in modern society, particularly in educationε
settings, have formed the subject of fairly extensive ethnographies c
communication. Obviously, not every problem and community hav
been studied, but the literature can be most useful in giving re
searchers a sense of the range of sociolinguistic variation they ar
likely to encounter once the interviewing has begun.

Researchers are also well advised to conduct a limited amount c
sociolinguistic fieldwork on the native metacommunicative routine
that relate to the focus of the survey. The idea here is to interact wit
members of the population in a variety of situations, particularly thos
in which the relevant matters are likely to be broached. It might b
possible, for example, to tape-record a public meeting where pertinen
issues are raised. A careful analysis of the transcript will reveal som
of the ways in which such topics are appropriately introduced in formε
settings.

An example of how a modicum of research on metacommunicativ
routines can improve interview techniques is provided by research
conducted with Sherolyn Smith in Gallup, New Mexico (Smith an
Briggs 1972). Our task was to provide the City of Gallup with data tha
would enable planners to gauge how a neighborhood facility cente
then under construction could best meet the needs of area residents. ₤
survey instrument was administered to a 10 percent random sample

The instrument had been pretested and revised. No effort was made
however, to conduct preliminary research on the ways in which resi
dents would discuss such topics in other contexts. The situation wa
complicated by the fact that the population of Gallup is ethnically quit

omplex, consisting primarily of Zuni and Navajo (Native American), Mexican-American, Black, and Anglo-American residents.

One question was designed to elicit information on the range of ervices in the facilities center that the respondent and her or his amily would use, if available. In conducting the interviews, I noted nat the numbers were much lower for Navajo respondents than for nembers of the other groups. These data seemed to lend themselves to ne interpretation that Navajo residents were less interested in using ne services than were the other residents.

Fortunately, I began conducting informal ethnographic research with Navajo and Mexican-American residents. After spending a minimal amount of time with Navajo families, I learned it was deemed highly nappropriate to speculate on the behavior or beliefs of others. The anger here is that such talk might be seen as a usurpation of the ndividual's own decision-making power, which would be construed as n attack on the person's integrity (cf. Kluckhohn and Leighton 1946: 02, 309–10). Speculating on the preferences of one's spouse and chil-ren would accordingly be deemed extremely rude. Rather than do so, Navajo respondents would estimate which services they themselves vere likely to use. The use of a probe to obtain data on other family nembers generally yielded statements such as "No, I don't think so." The data thus reflected a gap between the presuppositions of the ques-ions and the conversational maxims of native speakers of Navajo ather than a lack of interest in these services.

Simply using the question in a pretest did not expose the problem, ›ecause the pretest did not provide information on Navajo metacom-nunicative norms. The lack of such insight introduced a clear source of ›ias into the data, and it placed Navajo respondents in an uncomfort-ble position. The point is that the investment of a minimal amount of ime in discovering these communicative patterns *before* designing the nstrument would have circumvented the problem.

Phase 2: designing an appropriate methodology

Most practitioners have at least some idea as to the problem they plan to nvestigate and the research methods and methodology they will use ›efore inaugurating their research. It is nearly always necessary to mod-fy both to some degree in the course of the research. Freilich (1970) ecommends to anthropologists that the "active" phase of research, that vhich is focused on the fieldworker's own interests, be preceded by a ›eriod of passive research. The passive phase serves as a guide for eformulating plans for the active. Such changes are, however, generally undertaken on an ad hoc basis. The difficulty here seems to be that modifications of research methods have heretofore been seen as re sponses to specific obstacles. As Freilich (1970:25) puts it:

For example, a strict sampling may not be possible if local customs prohibit [the anthropologist] from interviewing particular people or groups; if the subject matter central to the project's goals is too sensitive to be researched due to the internal problems of the system being studied; or if important informants do not cooperate with the researcher because of his nationality, race, sex, or religious affiliation.

Such specific circumstances do need to be borne in mind. But this stopgap approach falls far short of an adequate adaptation to local social–cultural and communicative norms.

I suggest that systematic data collection should be guided by systematic examination of the best methods for conducting research on the chosen problem in the society in question. I see two considerations as being particularly important here.

First, the results of Phase 1 should inform an in-depth investigation of the points of compatibility and incompatibility between interview techniques and the local metacommunicative repertoire. This will suggest which topics can be explored in the course of interviews and which social situations are appropriate for interviewing. Again, the negative results are equally important – what issues will have to be explored by other means. This examination will also assist the re searcher in selecting the most suitable interview techniques and in modifying them in order to increase their compatibility with local communicative practices. As was suggested in Chapter 3, such an exercise will help the researcher avoid the procedural problems that threaten rapport, disrupt interviews, and greatly confound the analy sis of interview data.

Second, as I argue in Chapter 6, interview techniques rely primarily on the referential or descriptive function of language and on knowl edge that lies within, in Silverstein's (1981a) terms, the limits of aware ness of speakers. This means that interviews will be totally ineffectual in dealing with some topics, and they certainly will exclude important facets of those subjects that can be treated in interviews. It is thus crucial to design a methodological plan in such a way that interview data are systematically supplemented with other types of information whenever possible.

I pointed out in Chapter 4 that a close analysis of native metacom municative routines can provide rich data on problems of interest to social scientists. These routines, rooted in the society's communicative patterns and closely tied to the social context of the interaction, are less likely to be idealized or decontextualized than are responses to

nterview questions. Accordingly, they are less subject to the imposi-
ion of the researcher's own categories and presuppositions on the
lata. This recommendation is hardly unprecedented, because writers
vho focus on methodology often note that interviews should be sup-
olemented by observation (Johnson 1975; Langness and Frank
.981:50; Pelto and Pelto 1978:74; Riley and Nelson 1974; Spradley
.979:32; Webb et al. 1966; Whyte 1943:29–30; Williams 1967:28).

My recommendation goes beyond this basic principle. I am rather
oroposing a *systematic* integration of a wide range of metacommunica-
ive routines into research methodological guidelines. I would also like
o suggest that the process of selecting these routines and determining
heir role in the research be based on a preceding analysis of the
.ociety's communicative patterns.

One methodological concern that is generally seen as relatively mi-
1or weighs quite heavily in this type of analysis. The abbreviatory
1ature of notes taken during or after interviews or other interactions
nay preserve a good deal of the *referential content* of the utterances,
out the *form* will prove elusive. On the other hand, tape-recording
nterviews and other events is quite important. This enables the re-
.earcher to conduct a detailed study of the form of the discourse in
:hese events. One of the most important issues I have raised is that
'ormal features, from the smallest details to the largest structural units,
ndex the metacommunicative properties of the speech. The sensitive
:esearcher may be able to discern some of the metacommunicative
'eatures; such properties are, however, extremely subtle, and most are
1ot consciously accessible in the course of an event. Tape recordings,
on the other hand, can be reviewed time after time, transcribed
:losely, and can be presented to one's consultants for comment.

Tape recordings are also interpretively open-ended, like any text in
the native language. As the researcher's social–cultural and linguistic
:ompetence grows, new dimensions become apparent. New theoretical
understandings can similarly be applied to the original recordings to
see if they can resolve persistent problems. Notes are frozen at the
level of competence possessed by the researcher at the time of their
writing, and they are much less useful in exploring new theoretical
orientations.

The situation with videotaping is less clear, in my opinion. I have
used it, and quite successfully, I think, during my two most recent field
stays. I formerly based my hypotheses about the nonverbal correlates
of speech events on my memory of the most salient gestures, body
postures, and so on. The videotapes show the nonverbal components
in detail, and this has greatly added to my understanding of the contextualization of the verbal forms. I have also had much better results in

eliciting commentary from participants with video rather than audio
recordings. Consultants greatly enjoy seeing themselves on their own
television sets, and they often become quite voluble. One elder became nearly ecstatic while viewing the tape of the conversation we had
just completed, and commented in detail on the historical and cultural
bases of his statements. After the tape was over, he noted 'This is a
very important day for me, Carlos. I had never even heard the sound
of my own voice before now.'

On the other hand, video equipment is vastly more intrusive than a
small cassette tape recorder with built-in condenser microphone. I find
that the presence of the video camera often gives me, as the researcher, much more control over the interaction. Although awareness
of the recording equipment decreases over time, the participants do
not become oblivious, as witnessed by references to the presence of
the camera. This enhanced self-consciousness can lead to a shaping of
one's behavior in accordance with the image one wishes to project.
Speakers thus focus more on monitoring the referential content of
their words; this frequently inhibits the use of very context-sensitive
forms, such as proverbs.

This process of accommodating interactional patterns to the presence of the camera does not render the data invalid or useless. The
point is not to attempt to eliminate the effects of the researcher's own
presence, a fruitless and theoretically unsound goal. The impact of the
video equipment on the speech event can provide fascinating insights
with regard to which facets of communication lie within the limits of
awareness and the conscious control of natives. Nevertheless, video
taping should be carefully complemented by audiotaping and observation. As is the case with tape-recording, awareness of local communicative norms will help the researcher gauge when it will be appropriate
to record and how taping is likely to affect the interaction.

Phase 3: reflexivity in the interviewing process

Once the interviewing has begun, this sketch of the local communicative economy should inform periodic checks on the effectiveness of
one's interviews. A good means of undertaking such an evaluation is to
analyze a selected interview in detail; a tape-recorded example is a far
more reliable source for this task than a reconstruction. Some revision
of the Jakobson–Hymes model of the communicative event, such as
the one I presented in Figure 2, provides a good starting point for
initiating such evaluations. Each of the components – interviewer, respondent, audience, message form, reference, channel, code, social

oles, interactional goals, social situation, and type of communicative
vent (along with key, genre, and other factors that prove to be impor-
ant to one's own situation) – should be examined in terms of their role
n shaping the meaning of what is said by both parties.

This analysis of the manner in which the researcher's and the consul-
ants' conversational norms are juxtaposed in the interview will in-
rease the former's awareness of the conversational loci of procedural
roblems. It will enable the investigator to discern where she or he has
misconstrued the meaning of the responses, thus heading off possible
errors in the interpretation of the data. Likewise, periodic evaluations
vill enable the researcher to progressively reduce the scope of the
difficulties that procedural problems pose for the success of the re-
earch. This awareness can permit researchers to avoid the faux pas
hat reduce the coherence of the discourse and render their interview-
es less willing and able to respond.

Going over selected interviews with consultants can be quite useful.
Such assistance can be obtained by soliciting aid in transcribing and/or
interpreting the interview. I have learned a great deal by turning on a
ape recorder while I replay a videotape of an interview or other
peech event with the participants. They frequently go into great detail
vith respect to why they made a given statement, why it is true, how
others would disagree, and so on. My experience suggests, however,
hat the interviewees themselves are less likely to point out the ways in
vhich the researcher has violated the norms of the speech situation or
misconstrued the meaning of an utterance than are persons who did
not participate in the initial interview.

Microanalyses of interviews will in turn provide a new source of
comparison with data from other communicative events. Paying atten-
ion to the different ways in which topics are addressed in different
social situations will help round out, so to speak, impressions derived
from a given means of data acquisition. Once again, such comparisons
will enable the researcher to see more clearly where interviews will
produce gaps in the data. Analysis of the interviews and their juxtaposition with metacommunicative material from other events will permit
ongoing revisions in research plans. It may be necessary to explore a
wider range of speech events or to change one's mode of participation
n them in order to obtain information on certain topics. It might, for
example, be wise to ask a native or a co-researcher of the opposite sex
o record a given event if one's presence is precluding certain types of
discussion. I also think it is particularly important to look over as many
of the research results as possible about three months before complet-
ng the study. This will minimize the possibility that major hiatus will
plague the interpretation and write-up of the materials.

Phase 4: analyzing interviews

If I were to try to put my finger on the single most serious shortcoming relating to the use of interviews in the social sciences, it would certainly be the commonsensical, unreflexive manner in which most analyses of interview data are conducted. As Cicourel (1974c:22) has put it, "questions and answers are presumed to possess 'obvious' significance." It is simply assumed that different responses to roughly the same question are comparable. The usual practice thus consists of extracting statements that pertain to a given theme, event, symbol, or what have you from field notes or transcriptions. These responses are then juxtaposed, yielding a composite picture of things that seem to go together in the eyes of the researcher on the basis of referential, decontextualized content.

With respect to anthropological fieldwork, this technique used to serve as a starting point for analysis when ethnographers were urged to file their field notes directly into categories provided by Murdock et al.'s *Outline of Cultural Materials* (1950) or the Royal Anthropological Institute's *Notes and Queries on Anthropology* (1951). Some researchers now index their field notes and/or transcriptions in terms of major dates, events, names, and the like; they then feed this information into a computer. At the push of a button, the machine accomplishes their decontextualization for them automatically.[1]

The development of a more sophisticated approach to the analysis of interview data is imperative. The communicative blunders described in Chapter 3 point to the complexity of the interview process and to the many factors that can give rise to procedural problems. Yet the goal of analysis cannot simply be to control for or eliminate such problems. This approach would preserve the fallacy that underlies the "bias" research on the interview I critiqued in the first chapter. Interviews are cooperative products of interactions between two or more persons who assume different roles and who frequently come from contrasting social, cultural, and/or linguistic backgrounds. A mode of analysis that envisions interview data as, even ideally, a direct outpouring of the interviewees' thoughts or attitudes obscures the nature of the interview as a social interaction and a communicative event. Such a perspective also misses the point that the interview situation itself is a rich source of data if it is viewed as an object of analysis as well as a research tool.

One of the major findings that emerged from an analysis of my own communicative blunders is that *the communicative structure of the en-*

ire interview affects the meaning of each utterance. To cite one instance: My initial interviews with Silvianita and George López were
strained and relatively unproductive, and it was many years before I
was able to appreciate why this had been the case. I had never considered the possibility that the Lópezes might not accept my definition
of our interactions as interviews. The Lópezes viewed these sessions as
pedagogical encounters between two elders and a young person with
little knowledge of the community, *Mexicano* culture, or New Mexican
Spanish. Even after I published a volume on the Lópezes and other
carvers (1980), the couple told their visitors that I had come to learn
how to carve. (They noted that I had indeed become a proficient
carver but then, for some reason, had given up the work.)

My initial questions met with responses that seemed superficial or
irrelevant or with a strident 'Who knows!' Overlooking their perception of our relationship would lead me to believe that they were
fairly ignorant of the history of their family and its carving. What
they were really trying to get across, in fact, was that I had to learn
to respect them as elders as well as to discover which questions were
relevant to them and the basic cultural assumptions that underlie the
answers.

A different sort of example is provided by my misinterpreting statements when I did not take the speaker's interactional goals into account. For instance, my question, 'Were there any *ricos* here in bygone
days?' emerged from my desire to collect data on the history of social
inequality in the community. Mr. Trujillo was willing to help me satisfy
my need for such information. But his answer also addressed his own
desire to induce me to internalize basic *Mexicano* values of religiosity
and corporatism. This anecdote exposes a very general phenomenon.
The unifunctional utterance, one that accomplishes only one communicative function, is rare, at least in conversation. Statements nearly
always relate to two or more features of the communicative situation,
such as distinct interactional goals, at the same time. If one considers
each "answer" only in the context of the preceding question, then a
great deal of meaning will be lost.

What is needed is a means of interpreting interview data that will
assess the manner in which each statement fits into this communicative
web and will thus have the best chance of yielding an adequate interpretation of its meaning. I thus propose a two-step process, one that
begins with the structure of each interview as an interactional whole
and then proceeds to the identification of the metacommunicative properties of the individual utterances.

The structure of the interview

I will draw on the Jakobson–Hymes model of the communicative event (see Figure 2) in framing my remarks on the structure of the interview as a whole. The model simply serves as a heuristic device in assessing the range of elements that *might* be of importance in a given interview. Researchers will certainly have discovered by this point, however, that some of the Jakobson–Hymes components may play a relatively insignificant role in any particular interaction or perhaps in a given speech community as a whole. Similarly, elements that do not figure in the analytic model may prove crucial. Researchers should have developed a good working sense of each major type of speech situation regarding the range of components that should be checked and of the range of communicative functions they can convey.

Perhaps the most basic maxim to be followed is that the interview must be analyzed as a whole before any of its component utterances are interpreted. This process can proceed much more quickly and adequately if the researcher takes relatively detailed notes on each interview. Once the interview is over (and generally after returning to one's residence), the investigator should note important facts that will not appear on the record of the interview itself, be it a tape recording or a video recording or a set of notes. Detailed notes on the setting, participants, time of day, ongoing social or ritual events, and so forth should be complemented by the researcher's perceptions of the interaction. This procedure may be impractical when the project focuses on quantitative analysis of data from a large survey. The inclusion of even minimal contextual information at the end of the schedule would, however, greatly facilitate interpretation of the statistical patterns.

In beginning the analysis, compare such notes with the transcript (if available). What major themes were stressed in each participant's statements? How was each reacting to the interview and to the other participants? As argued in Chapter 3, it is particularly important to look for possible divergences in interactional goals, perceptions of the nature and purpose of the interaction, and the like. If these cues are missed, they are likely to lead the researcher to misconstrue his or her consultants' remarks.

A second step is to map out the linear structure of the interview. Many interviews proceed from informal conversation to introductory statements and/or questions, to broad questions, to more detailed questions, and then return to informal dialogue before the participants shift to other activities or the researcher leaves. Significant interactional units may also be segmented by the arrival or departure of

participants, movements from one topical focus to another, activities
(such as cooking, eating, or working) occurring simultaneously, and
the like. This sketch should indicate major changes in key, tone, or
genre.

The initial stage of the analysis thus consists of identifying the components of the interview and interpreting their communicative functions. It may be useful to plot the most important features on a series
of sheets of paper. A visual representation is helpful in discerning the
outlines of the communicative forest from amid its many trees. However one may approach it, a synthesis of the components and functions
is the next step. As Jakobson (1960), Mukařovský (1977a, 1977b), and
others have argued, the meaning of an utterance or other sign is tied to
the *interaction* of its constituent components and their functions. Even
if a response appears to be oriented toward the referential function –
providing information on the topic specified in the question – its meaning is dependent as well on the coexisting communicative functions.
The interview is a gestalt produced by the interaction of all these parts.
In assessing the role each element plays in this process, consider the
manner in which the functioning of each component is affected by the
roles of the others. For example, code-switching between Spanish and
English is affected by the competence of the participants in each language, the social relationship between them, the topics under discussion, the social situation (e.g., formal vs. informal, ritual vs. everyday), the genre and key of the discourse, and so on.

Interpreting individual utterances

We are now in a position to be able to address the needs of the
researcher who is really not interested in the interview qua speech
event, but in the bearing of a series of responses on the topic at hand.
The proposed mode of analysis provides both a head start and some
insurance for the interpretation of individual statements. Having identified the utterances that address the subject in question, the analyst
can focus on ascertaining how the specific utterances fit into the broad
communicative outlines that have been sketched for the interview as a
whole. As Agar and Hobbs (1982) have shown, the meaning of a
response may emerge from its relation to utterances at any point in the
preceding discourse. A few hours of auditing tapes, reading notes and
transcripts, and thinking about the interview places one in the best
position for discerning the broader significance of the responses. This
greatly decreases the danger of coming up with narrow or erroneous
interpretations.

Metacommunicative features. Two concepts, metacommunication and contextualization, provide excellent keys to the interpretation of individual statements. In studying the metacommunicative properties of utterances, we are examining their capacity for simultaneously commenting on communicative processes (including the interaction itself) and indicating a referent.[2] This task has been stimulated in recent years by the advent of ethnopoetics. Hymes (1981) in particular has shown how a close analysis of the *form* of oral literature provides a sounder basis for interpretation than deductions based on content alone.

This leads me to the proposition that speech, whether contained in interviews, myths, or "natural" conversations, provides an ongoing interpretation of its own significance. This interpretation is conveyed mainly in stylistic terms. Thus, if the analyst pays close attention to how a statement is made, he or she will find clues to the interpretation the speaker wishes to attach, so to speak, to the words. These stylistic cues can be (and usually are) embedded in any part of the message form, including its visual (gesture, gaze, proxemics, etc.), prosodic (intonation, loudness, stress, vowel length, phrasing, pitch, etc.), and verbal dimensions. Lexical selection, pronominalization, verb tense and aspect, the operation of optional syntactic transformations, and the like enable speakers to choose between referentially equivalent forms that will convey entirely different messages about the topic in question.

Both the range of stylistic devices within individual languages and the variation between languages preclude offering any simple formulas for discerning the interpretations embedded in texts. But the researcher will already have two useful tools for interpreting utterances. First, the researcher can draw on her or his analysis of the overall structure of the interview. This should provide a good sense of the range of factors that shape specific statements. Here the exceptions prove the rule: The key to the meaning of individual utterances often lies in their *departure* from the communicative norms of the conversation as a whole. Sudden changes in prosodic features, lexical range, or other stylistic elements frequently point to the presence of a new interpretive frame, such as sarcasm or joking. Likewise, many metacommunicative devices function similarly to the conversational metasigns described in Chapter 3 in that they serve to articulate the relationship between individual utterances and the overall structure of the discourse. Having this broader frame in mind is the best insurance against overlooking the presence of these forms and the ways in which they shape the meaning of responses.

A second tool for discerning the metacommunicative properties of interview responses will already be in the researcher's hands at this point. The findings from Phase 1 of the research will have attuned the investigator to a wide range of metacommunicative forms and functions used in that speech community. The analysis of native metacommunicative routines is particularly useful in this regard. Our ability to interpret the role of metacommunication in interviews is frustrated by the nature of the interview as a communicative event. Interviews are attractive in that they present the possibility of gathering a mass of data on topics selected by the researcher in a short amount of time. Researcher and interviewee implicitly agree to foreground the referential function of language and to suppress most of the stylistic and social constraints that normally impinge on transmission of information on these topics (i.e., as they are conveyed in ritual, production, etc.).

This does not engender a total dearth of metacommunicative elements; it does, however, greatly reduce the degree to which they rise into consciousness, particularly that of the interviewer. When it comes to native metacommunicative routines, however, this bias toward the referential coding and the decontextualization of forms is generally absent. In transferring awareness of the role of metacommunicative elements from the latter realm to the former, we increase our chances of perceiving the role of these processes.

Contextualization. I have argued that discourse contains features that signal (generally implicitly) how messages are to be read. This led me to suggest ways of enhancing our ability to read the interpretation embedded in the text. These procedures are designed to reduce our tendency to propound interpretations that have little basis in the text itself. This does not mean, however, that "reading" texts, be they interviews or anything else, is a mechanical process that draws on the interpreter's consciousness as a mere scanning instrument. The basic task is still the same: trying to figure out what the devil that person was trying to get across. The procedure is similarly analogous – examining the myriad details of what is said and done in order to connect them in such a way that the interpreter feels relatively confident that she or he has made sense of the discourse.

Looking for metacommunicative elements enables the researcher to base his or her interpretation on what the speaker is saying not only about "the world out there" but also about the researcher's own words and the manner in which the utterances as a whole relate to the circumstances of their production. This does not, however, guarantee that the interpreter will have identified all of the metacommunicative features and grasped their communicative functions. Is there no way of rechecking one's perceptions against the text, that is, asking the speakers if we have understood them?

Taken literally, the notion is absurd. The researcher can, of course, go back to the interviewee and ask if the interpretation is correct. This can produce interesting data on native textual analysis or literary criticism, but it hardly solves the problem. Human introspective capacities do not necessarily extend to recalling exactly what one was intending to say at some point in the past. Likewise, most metacommunicative features are not fully conscious, and speakers are unlikely to have perceived them at all (cf. Gumperz 1982:131–2; Silverstein, 1979, 1981a). In any case, taking a tape or transcript back to the interviewee(s) creates *another* speech event, and its contextual elements will shape the consultant's remarks along other lines. What is needed is some means of rechecking one's perceptions against those of the participants at the time.

One can do precisely that, if in a slightly roundabout manner, while analyzing the conversation. Participants are constantly exchanging implicit messages as to how they perceive the speech event and how they want their utterances to be interpreted. They are also continually checking to see if their perceptions are shared by the other participants. This process has been captured by Cook-Gumperz and Gumperz (1976) under the aegis of "contextualization." They argue that communicative contexts are not dictated by the environment but are *created by the participants in the course of the interaction*. Similarly, contexts are not conditions that are fixed at the beginning of an interaction, remaining stable until its termination.

Cook-Gumperz and Gumperz suggest it is accordingly necessary for speakers to provide contextualization cues to signal which features of the social and linguistic setting provide frameworks for interpreting their remarks. Participants monitor each other's words and actions in order to see how their interlocutors perceive the context, and this is particularly useful to researchers in their efforts to assess the validity of their own interpretations.

A variety of types of signals are used by co-conversationalists in ascertaining whether or not their perceptions of the communicative event are shared. Some of these are explicit, such as when we ask, "Are you being sarcastic?" "Is that a joke?" "Do you really mean that?" and the like. Although such queries generally present themselves as responses to the ambiguity of the preceding utterance, this is not always the case. As I noted above, *Mexicano* elders continually interject interrogatives such as ¿*ves*? 'do you see?' ¿*sabes cómo*? 'do you know what I mean?', ¿*no*? 'no?' or 'really?' in the course of pedagogical dialogues to assess the comprehension of their pupils. Conversational uses of proverbs and other genres feature an elicitation of the listener's comprehension of and agreement with the speaker's point as a central component of the performance (Briggs 1985a).

It is, however, far more common to use implicit messages, features that hide, so to speak, behind the referential context of what is said, in contextualizing utterances. Specialists in nonverbal communication have conducted a great deal of research on the way speakers use visual signs in providing interpretive frames for verbal messages (cf. Birdwhistell 1970; Hall 1959, 1966, 1977; Kendon 1972, 1973, 1977, 1978; Kendon, Harris, and Key 1976; Scheflen 1965, 1966). Interlocutors use visual contact to provide a near-constant means of monitoring the contextual cues of their fellow participants. Speakers draw on a wide range of signals, including extending one's hands with cupped, upturned palms, shrugging the shoulders, and lifting the head and/or eyebrows, to elicit indications of comprehension and agreement. They shape their utterances from moment to moment in keeping with both solicited and impromptu responses from their listeners. A look of boredom may prompt a reassessment of the relevance of one's remarks, while a visual sign that the hearer is confused often elicits an elaboration of material that had been presupposed, together with a repetition of the utterance. The value of the visual track as a means of assessing the meaning speakers attach to their words provides a strong incentive for videotaping at least some interviews.

The conversational analysis group has identified a host of devices that enable co-conversationalists to coordinate their turns at talk (cf. Duncan 1973, 1974; Duncan and Niederehe 1974; Jefferson 1972; Sacks 1967; Sacks, Schegloff, and Jefferson 1974). "Huh?", "right?", "yes?", "okay?", "you know?", "see?", and so forth have traditionally been viewed as mere fillers, phatic signals used to keep the channel open until we think of something to say. Research has shown, however, that they provide the person who dominates the floor with a great deal of feedback with respect to the manner in which her or his interpretations of the interaction are shared by the other participants.

This process is requisite to adequate comprehension in dialogue. As Gumperz (1982a, 1982b) and others have shown, interpretive frames are often divergent, leading co-conversationalists to misjudge their interlocutors' intents. Gumperz (1982a) has shown that such miscommunication frequently occurs in interactions between members of different classes and/or ethnic groups within a single society, and interviewers are hardly exempt from this process. Researchers similarly encounter difficulties in communicating with members of another society or a different group within their own society using a pattern of interaction possibly unfamiliar to the latter. Discerning such malcomprehension is important for two reasons. First, it is important that the researcher does not simply preserve the misunderstandings of the interview, both his or her own and those of the interviewees, in the course of the analysis. If the respondent did not understand the question and the analyst does not realize this, the meaning of her or his "answer" will be distorted.

The second reason involves the value of these "errors" as sources of data. As scholars have long noted with respect to metaphor and ambiguity (cf. Fernandez 1972, 1974, 1977; Ricoeur 1977; Sapir and Crocker 1977), disentangling cases in which interpretive frameworks are not fully specified or are shared only in part can provide powerful insights into the nature of social–cultural and communicative norms. Some of the most interesting situations emerge when the participants realize that something has gone awry. This usually invokes procedures for renegotiating a common frame. (See Jefferson [1972] on "side sequences" and Churchill [1978] on mechanisms for repairing procedural problems.)

These moments provide particularly fruitful means of comprehending interpretive frames: Calling the contextualization process into question brings it much closer to the surface of consciousness. Both referential and other communicative functions are brought to bear reflexively on the task of interpretation. Researchers may thus profit from paying close attention to the way their consultants check to see if they share a common interpretation of the meaning of what is being said and how they deal with situations in which this is not the case.[3]

Studying the manner in which participants in interviews monitor each other's interpretive frames still does not guarantee the analyst that his or her account is correct and/or exhaustive. It and the other steps outlined in this chapter do, however, enable researchers to base their interpretations as much as possible on those of the respondents. The technique leads the analyst away from literal, narrowly referential meanings and toward grasping the broader pragmatic significance of what is said. The procedure helps the investigator avoid the errors in interpretation that result from differences in communicative as well as basic social–cultural norms between researcher and consultants. The preceding discussion of malcomprehension points to the way in which greater methodological sophistication can turn interviewing pitfalls into important sources of data. In a word, developing interview techniques that fit the metacommunicative norms of the society in question provides a basis for overcoming a number of the problems that have diminished the depth and the accuracy of social-scientific research.

Presuming that the researcher has now grasped the significance of the interview data, the question then becomes one of the best way to present these findings. Obviously, this process follows from the proclivities and the research interests of the individual. I would like to argue, however, for the importance of describing not only the content of respondent statements but their interpretive framework as well. Since the metacommunicative dimensions inform the investigator's analysis, readers must be provided with at least a sketch of such features if they are to be in a position to judge the interpretation competently.

One way to answer this challenge is to provide substantial excerpts from the transcripts, either in the text or in appendixes. It is important to resist standard editorial policies and the urgings of many manuals[4] that prescribe deletion of both the interviewer's questions and all back channel cues from the transcripts. As the reader will certainly have gathered from the preceding pages, this method does expose the role of the researcher, including his or her ungrammatical sentences, faux pas, and general naiveté. Now that arguments for the obligation of the practitioner to account for her or his own contribution to the data-collection process are becoming more prevalent and more forceful,[5] however, the mask of "scientific objectivity" no longer provides such an effective means of avoiding this kind of exposure.

6. Conclusion: theoretical quagmires and "purely methodological" issues

The preceding pages have hardly eschewed theoretical issues. Thus far, however, theory has been used primarily as a means of highlighting the problems inherent in interview techniques, exploring their theoretical roots, and pointing the way to methodological progress. Such discussion is not, in and of itself, sufficient to show that the adoption of a critical perspective on interviewing is requisite to theoretical advances in the social sciences and linguistics. But the lack of a critical perspective on interview techniques is tied to a number of fundamental theoretical obstacles.

My thesis is that methodological shortcomings have both emerged from and in turn reinforced these theoretical quagmires. The problem is that the goals of social-scientific and linguistic research lie beyond the confines of this highly circumscribed process. The only way to break this pattern is to raise methodological questions from the inferior status they currently enjoy, explore the interpenetrations of theoretical and methodological problems, and revise methodology in the light of theory *and vice versa*.

A number of important theoretical advances have been made in the last two decades. Scholars from diverse disciplinary and theoretical perspectives have moved away from an emphasis on static structures and codes as abstracted from human conduct. Research has focused increasingly on the way codes relate to messages, or structure to action, and the manner in which the system is transformed through use. Social–cultural anthropology, for example, has moved away from viewing culture as monolithic and static toward analyzing the way in which cultural systems are instantiated in individual events by concrete persons (cf. Crick 1976; Geertz 1973). As the authors of a recent assessment of the field put it, symbolic anthropology is based on the assumption that "the constant tension between individual experience and the collective means for expressing and interpreting that experience is the dynamic relationship by which culture comes to be and through which it is constantly changing" (Dougherty and Fernandez 1981:413).

112

Linguistics has taken a similar turn. Saussure (1959) deemed the units of *langue,* the abstract entities in language that hold constant between contexts, the real objects of linguistic inquiry. The role of context in determining the meaning of signs was accordingly relegated to the periphery. The Chomskyian revolution in syntax and ethnoscientific approaches to semantics advanced this concern with ideally context-independent units and their relations in linguistic systems to a new level of abstraction.

Now few practitioners adhere to Saussure's rigid dichotomy between *langue* and *parole,* and even fewer are willing to accept his banishment of the latter from the sphere of serious scholarly study. Many linguists have similarly rejected Chomsky's (1957, 1965) emphasis on "competence" apart from "performance" and his reliance on introspective data. Hymes (1964, 1972, 1974a), Fishman (1964; Fishman, Ferguson, and Das Gupta 1968), Labov (1966, 1972a, 1972b), and others elevated the study of *parole* 'speaking', to the status of a major field of linguistics – sociolinguistics. A concern with close analyses of conversations and various kinds of texts has stimulated the growing areas of conversational and discourse analysis. The application of such techniques to oral literatures has given rise to ethnopoetics (cf. Hymes 1981; Tedlock 1983). Practitioners have become increasingly aware that the meaning of what is said is shaped by accompanying prosodic and nonverbal cues; a priori assumptions regarding the nature of the relationship between communicative modes is giving way to collaborative research between specialists in these different areas.

The most encouraging facet of these developments is their relationship to advances in other disciplines. A number of philosophical movements have contributed insights into questions of meaning and communication. "Speech act" theorists, particularly Austin (1962) and Searle (1969; 1979; 1983), have heightened awareness of the formulaic and performative character of speech. Phenomenological and hermeneutic traditions have the increased sophistication of textual interpretation (Gadamer 1975, 1979; Rabinow and Sullivan 1979; Ricoeur 1979, 1981).

In sociology, the work of Goffman (1959; 1974, 1981) and the ethnomethodologists, particularly Garfinkel (1967, 1972) and Sacks (1967, 1974), has greatly influenced the study of communication and social behavior in general. Cicourel (1964, 1974a, 1982a, 1982b, 1983) has challenged social scientists to pay more attention to the linguistic underpinnings of their research and to make explicit the ethnographic background information that informs their analysis. These approaches echo Schutz's (1962) concern with the phenomenological underpinnings of the reality of everyday life. These writers have stimulated a great deal of research on the nature of the interpretive activities through which social structures are created and understood. This work, along with that of Gouldner (1970) and others, has challenged sociologists to be more explicit about the nature of their own interpretive procedures.

Social scientists and linguists have increasingly looked to literary criticism for insights into the process of textual analysis (see, for example, Bakhtin 1981; Bloom et al. 1979; Culler 1975; Derrida 1976, 1978; Jameson 1971, 1972; Kristeva 1980; Vološinov 1973; Williams 1977). Folkloristic research on genre and performance has expanded the range of speech acts examined by linguists and anthropologists and has pointed to the importance of oral textual traditions (cf. Abrahams 1983; Bauman 1975; Ben-Amos 1976; Glassie 1982; Paredes and Bauman 1971). This convergence is apparent in the growing tendency of practitioners to abandon narrow disciplinary lines in favor of exploring broader approaches to research problems.

Unfortunately, this major theoretical reorientation has not produced a corresponding methodological revolution. Although interviews constitute the central mode of data collection in the social sciences and linguistics, they are probably the least understood. Only occasionally have interviews formed the focus of theoretical analyses or ethnographic descriptions. Scholars have begun to compile descriptions of native metacommunicative routines and to demonstrate their usefulness as sources of sociolinguistic and ethnographic data. Because few practitioners have used research on specific routines in exploring the nature of metacommunicative competence as a whole, this body of research has not generated a rethinking of the way we communicate with our consultants. Cicourel, Dexter, and others have pointed to the problems inherent in received techniques (see Chapter 1). Nevertheless, their calls for research on the communicative nature of interviews and for the incorporation of such findings into research methodology have, by and large, gone unheeded.

Our inability to translate theoretical insights into solid methodological reformulations must be examined. Why does the gap between theory and methodology appear to be so large? Why are we so reluctant even to examine these questions? I suggest that these methodological shortcomings are not arbitrary or inexplicable. I also believe that the apparent hiatus between theoretical and methodological concerns is illusory. It is rather the case that we have banished a number of fundamental preconceptions, like Freudian neuroses, from the realm of conscious theory, only to re-create them on a subconscious methodological level.

In Chapter 1, I related our uncritical acceptance of interview techniques to their ubiquity in social-scientific and linguistic research as well as in the native linguistic communities of scholars. I now want to advance the proposition that the received perspective on interviewing emerges primarily from two basic assumptions. I contend that interview techniques are prima facie expressions of our underlying, generally unstated theories of communication and of reality. If we look just below the surface of interviews, we encounter the same persistent, problematical preconceptions whose existence as conscious theoretical models has come under increasing attack. Discovering this connection is requisite to achieving a better grasp on the nature of the interview and to making theoretical headway.

Referential bias and the problem of awareness

One set of preconceptions emerges from our folk views of language. As Silverstein has argued, scientists and philosophers who study language operate under the influence of their own "linguistic ideologies, . . . sets of beliefs about language articulated by the users as a rationalization or justification of perceived language structure and use" (1979:193). These ideologies draw on the conscious beliefs that native speakers have formulated with respect to the nature of language and language use. One of the most interesting facets of Silverstein's work is his demonstration that the relationship between language structure and native linguistic awareness is both selective and patterned. His thesis is that certain elements will be accessible to native exegesis, whereas others will evade conscious formulation and explication. These are, in his terms, unavoidably referential, surface segmentable, and relatively presupposing (1981a:5–7). These features are, I want to argue, encapsulated in the interview.

Unavoidable referentiality entails, in Jakobson's (1960:353) terms, the predominance of the referential or descriptive function of language. Native speakers will thus see the meaning as resting primarily on the ability of a stretch of speech to designate one or more aspects of their cultural universe and to convey a proposition about such. "Mary is a brave girl" thus delimits a specific human object and suggests that she falls within a recognized cultural category, that of "brave girls." The referential function focuses the attention of speaker and hearer on the referential *object,* not on the speech act itself. On the other hand, the referential content of Chomsky's (1957:15) famous example, "colorless green ideas sleep furiously," is both avoidable and beside the point. Rather, it directs our attention to the ability of grammatical systems to generate utterances that conform to syntactic rules but are devoid of sense. Similarly, as Bloch (1975a) has pointed out, political rhetoric is frequently lacking in new informational content.[1] Nevertheless, such discourse can be extremely effective if this lack of emphasis on content is coupled with a clever use of stylistic features to create the desired effect on the audience. (I owe this point to Ronald Reagan.)

The axis of *surface segmentability* revolves around the way in which forms are analyzed. The meaning of "surface segmentable forms" accrues to units such as affixes, lexemes, and phrases that are susceptible to traditional syntactic and semantic analysis. In other words, speakers will be able to identify specifiable stretches of the words as they are spoken in decoding their meaning. In the above example, "Mary" is decodable as a designation for a specific individual, "is a brave girl" makes a statement about that person. Each component of the predicate phrase is in turn analyzable for its contribution to the meaning of the utterance as a whole. On the opposite end of this continuum we find stylistic features. Intonational changes, for instance, necessarily overlap in production with the referential content of speech. The meaning of the sentence "John is a very brave fellow," uttered with a "sarcastic" tone of voice, would be interpretable by native speakers. They would, however, have more difficulty identifying the elements of the utterance that signaled the fact that its overt meaning was precisely the opposite of what the speaker sought to convey.

A third axis of comparison, *relative presupposition,* entails the manner in which the context enters into the meaning of what is said. The most highly presupposing forms are interpretable only when certain facts concerning the context of utterance are apparent to all participants before the act of speaking. Use of the token "she," for example, presupposes a shared understanding of the fact that a nonpresent female is the subject of discourse. Lacking such knowledge, the hearer will be forced to ask "Who are you talking about?" A sudden shift in the formality index of speech, on the other hand, can change the social context of the conversation itself. When a status superior changes from formal to familiar forms or both interlocutors shift from the standard language to a local dialect, for example, this alters the manner in which the participants interact. Relatively presuppositional forms are thus opposed to their *creative* counterparts. The latter are not present before the time of utterance, are brought into being by the speech act itself, and themselves effect a change in the social situation.

Silverstein's argument is that linguistic forms that are unavoidably referential, surface segmentable, and relatively presupposing are the most readily available to consciousness. Interestingly, these are precisely the areas in which the interview is strongest. Interviews foreground the referential function. Both researcher and respondent implicitly agree to amass as much information about a given topic as possible. We accordingly see the meaning of interview data as emanating from the contribution of the surface forms to this propositional knowledge. Similarly, all statements are ideally decodable vis-à-vis the information shared by all participants in addition to that made available to them in the course of the interview. These canons pertain to interpretation as well as production, because the interview frame alerts the participants that messages will be decoded (and should be decodable) via the contribution of surface segmentable units to propositions under specifiable (presuppositional) conditions.

Interestingly, invocation of the interview frame also selects negatively for metacommunicative events that are less surface segmentable and more creative, and whose meaning hinges less on reference. This description closely fits nearly all of the *Mexicano* metacommunicative routines I presented in Chapter 4. Here stylistic features, such as tonality, pitch register, stress, phrasing, laryngeal constriction, Spanish/English code-switching, and so on, convey crucial information regarding meanings that are not decodable vis-à-vis business-as-usual referentiality. The less segmentable and referential messages provide the juxtaposition of clarity with indirectness that is the sine qua non of more advanced rhetorical strategies. The emphasis on creativity is obvious; speakers use their words to transform the parameters of the interaction itself.

The reluctance of researchers to pay more serious attention to native metacommunicative routines is also linked to standard modes of analyzing data. I argued in Chapter 4 that *Mexicano* metacommunicative routines, such as eliciting repetitions from young children, political rhetoric, and scriptural allusions, present native analyses of basic *Mexicano* cultural premises. These analyses are, however, not immediately apparent in the referential content of the surface forms. Discerning them entails learning how value-laden statements are embedded in formulaic (and in many cases folkloric) expressions. Similarly, the relationship between the referential content of the words and what is really being said is generally indirect. Such forms are also pregnant with indexical features that point to details of the ongoing context. Here we are more aware that limiting one's interpretation to the referential content of the surface forms constitutes taking the joke (or what have you) literally. It is harder to delude ourselves into thinking that the meaning of the interaction is independent of the context in which it was articulated.

But this is precisely what we do with interviews. Researchers ask for conscious models of social–cultural and linguistic events and processes – "Tell me what you . . ." Because we are drawing on knowledge that lies within the limits of native awareness, the data are rich in forms that are unavoidably referential, surface segmentable, and relatively presupposing. The natives presumably also sing, dance, pray, feast, labor, and so forth about these issues. Such events generally convey this information indirectly, embedding it in elaborate metaphors and in the minute details of specific interactions. Interviews, on the other hand, are designed to extract this social–cultural or linguistic information from the contexts in which it is usually conveyed.

As Silverstein (1981a) has argued, submitting such knowledge to introspection leads to the transformation of the signs actually used in such contexts into maximally referential, segmentable, and presupposing expressions. In other words, relying on interviews allows us to accomplish an initial decontextualization of the data even before we begin the analysis. We are, in effect, asking the natives to reduce the information to precisely the type of forms that fit our native-speaker bias for unavoidably referential, surface segmentable, and relatively presupposing forms.

Overreliance on interviews thus frustrates theoretical progress in two ways. First, interviews suppress precisely the types of data needed to elucidate current theoretical concerns. Many researchers have sought, for example, to counter the structuralists' concern with codes as abstracted from use by studying what makes specific messages unique. Interviews reduce the variation between referentially equivalent messages and focus instead on the way messages elucidate the code. Analyses that center on interview data will thus frustrate efforts to appreciate the role of social and linguistic context, variation, performance and performativity, poetic structure, and the like.

Second, scholars from a wide range of disciplines have urged their colleagues to reject timeworn modes of analysis that isolate the referential content of what is said and then extract that content from its social and linguistic context (see, for example, Bauman 1975; Geertz 1972, 1973; Hymes 1974a, 1981; Silverstein 1976). But interviews provide us with forms that are maximally referential, surface segmentable, and presupposing. This leads us to believe that we can analyze responses simply in terms of a referential analysis of surface forms in keeping with explicit presuppositions. In other words, interview data lull us into being content with business-as-usual interpretive techniques.

A major theme of the present work has been that this practice is fraught with danger. Interview data are indeed decontextualized with respect to the social behavior they describe. But interview responses are equally contextualized; their form and content are shaped to fit the exigencies of the interview situation. This reversion to unsophisticated modes of analysis unconsciously undermines our attempts to expand analytic techniques to reflect theoretical advances, just as it jeopardizes the accuracy of our findings.

In short, recent trends in theorizing have made us increasingly skeptical of the bias toward referential, context-independent signs that is part and parcel of our own native theory of communication. The methodological underpinnings of accepted research techniques are, however, still based on these preconceptions. This leads us to place little reliance on speech events that confront us with linguistic forms that challenge the premises of our native theory. Rather, we concentrate on obtaining masses of data that precisely fit our vision of what talk is all about. Analysis then rejects the course charted by our own theoretical understandings in favor of following the dictates of our linguistic ideology. Research thus ultimately serves to reinforce our preconceptions rather than to draw on our consultants' understandings in broadening our horizons and deepening our comprehension.

Reflexivity

A second major obstacle to methodological progress is our implicit ontology, particularly our theory of social reality. Karp and Kendall (1982) have neatly characterized the degree to which our perspective on fieldwork follows "from behaviorist, reductionist, and naturalist premises, namely, that the object of anthropological inquiry is the 'stuff out there' and that that 'stuff' has as two of its primary attributes *stability* and *observability*."[2] In other words, if social facts are, as Durkheim (1938) would have it, like rocks, we need not concern ourselves with the effects of our actions (including the asking of questions) on our consultants' behavior, or with the fact that our perceptions are mediated by our own personal, cultural, and conceptual orientations. This conception neatly excuses the social scientist from the task of examining his or her own role in the process.

Articulating such claims has become highly unfashionable, and many practitioners have admitted the importance of reflexivity, or reflection on one's relation to the research situation (cf. Babcock 1980; Ruby 1980, 1982). Theorists have similarly replaced the objectivity-*versus*-subjectivity question with an awareness of the fact that social scientific investigations entail intersubjectivity, the creation of a psychological link between two or more minds. The role of social–cultural, theoretical, and personal predilections in the perception, interpretation, and translation of data is now well known.

Karp and Kendall's (1982) discussion of anthropological research provides a case in point. They argue that fieldwork does not simply involve learning to think like the natives. It is rather a means of learning to provide a rapprochement between native meanings and the requirements of anthropological discourse. The last two decades have witnessed the emergence of an anthropological genre in which ethnographers detail their actions in and reactions to the field situation (see, for example, Belmonte 1979; Berreman 1962; Crapanzano 1977, 1980; Dwyer 1982; Rabinow 1977, 1982; Ruby 1980, 1982). If discussion of one's relation to the fieldwork process is treated as a task that is independent of interpreting the data, however, the status quo of linguistic and ethnographic reporting will be preserved. The problem of translating awareness of the need for reflexivity into procedures for systematically analyzing the effect of the fieldworker's presence on the data has scarcely been discussed.

Our reliance on interviews and our uncritical approach to them is partly responsible for this lack of progress. When we begin an interview, our questions direct the attention of the participants *away* from the ongoing social situation. We collaborate in using the referential power of speech to transport researcher and interviewee(s) alike to another place and perhaps another time. Ordinarily, the researcher will have played no role in the events or processes under discussion. This facilitates our false consciousness of objectivity – the illusion that the object of scrutiny is "out there" and operates independently of our actions; we accordingly excuse ourselves from the need to consider our relation to it.

Nothing could be farther from the truth. This collectively created portrait of "the real world" is produced to satisfy the goals of an interaction in which we have a leading role. Given the fact that the researcher plays the dominant interactional role in interviews, her or his participation must be assessed in analyzing each datum that emerges from this setting. Decontextualizing what is said by focusing exclusively on the referential content of responses irrevocably separates the act of self-examination from the task of interpreting the meaning of what is said. As was the case with Humpty-Dumpty, no methodological sleight of hand can ever reunite them.

Politics and methodology

What, then, does it mean to rely primarily on interviews in one's research and to analyze the data in the received fashion? I have argued that interviews constitute remarkably clear encapsulations of our theories of communication and of social reality. I have also tried to show that many speech communities possess quite different norms with respect to what constitutes knowledge and how one goes about acquiring it. In the case of anthropological fieldwork, for example, recall that the standard modus operandi is to seek out individuals who are particularly good at answering our questions and to "train the informants to conceptualize cultural data in the frame of reference employed by the anthropologists" (Pelto and Pelto 1978:72). In other words, rather than learn the natives' means of acquiring information, we commonly impose our communicative norms on our consultants. This practice amounts to *communicative hegemony*.

Given the degree to which interview techniques form powerful encapsulations of our folk views of life and language, what we are exporting is not simply an approach to research. The formula is classic: members (primarily) of the middle and upper middle classes of dominant, Western societies enter into other communities. Once there, they impose a priori notions of the most efficient means of accomplishing their goals. The goals themselves are not intrinsically malignant; I firmly believe in the merits of seeking a deeper understanding of ourselves and of human conduct in general. But the ways in which we go about doing it indicate that many of our efforts are fraught with the same contradictions inherent in more exploitative journeys to other lands. This suggests that communicative hegemony is a rather more subtle and persistent form of *scientific colonialism* (cf. Galtung 1967; Hymes 1969b).

This process holds grave consequences for research within our own society as well. Let us take an example that is of both immediate and central concern – research on gender roles and gender-based discrimination.

Carol Gilligan's *In a Different Voice* has received much scholarly and popular attention, and it has greatly stimulated discussion of the ways in which social scientific models contain sexist biases. She specifically argues that "theories formerly considered to be sexually neutral in their scientific objectivity are found instead to reflect a consistent observational and evaluative bias" (1982:6). She suggests that women speak "in a different voice," in other words, that "women perceive and construe social reality differently from men" (1982:171). Men, she argues, tend to view development in terms of separation and achievement, whereas women stress attachment. For women, this places awareness of the "reality of interconnection" with other individuals in interpersonal relationships at the core of perceptions of self and other (1982:172). She also notes that women are more likely to base their decisions on "a contextual judgment, bound to the particulars of time and place" (1982:58–9).

It thus comes as a surprise to learn that the "three studies [which] are referred to throughout this book and reflect the central assumptions of my research . . . all . . . relied on interviews and included the same set of questions" (1982:2). Gilligan's conclusions regarding the importance of context and interpersonal relationships in women's experiences never moved her to question the advisability of using interviews as the sole source of data acquisition in her research. It should be stated in her defense that her choice of open-ended interviews may well have been motivated by the desire to avoid even more highly constrained encounters, such as questionnaires or experimental procedures. If so, however, this concern would seem to have led her to pay careful attention to the role of the interview as a social encounter in shaping the interview texts. Unfortunately, this is not the case. Gilligan analyzed the interview data in a highly decontextualized fashion; the reader does not even learn in a given instance whether the interviewer was female or male.

In the case of the abortion-decision study, for example, the twenty-nine participants ranged in age from fifteen to thirty-three, and they were quite diverse in terms of social class and ethnicity. The women were encouraged to participate in the study by clinic counselors for essentially therapeutic reasons (1982:3). It seems quite likely that some of the women perceived the interviews as therapy, others, as a contribution to research, while others may simply have viewed them as bureaucratic preliminaries to getting an abortion. These differences suggest that the interviews may have constituted vastly different types of communicative encounters in the eyes of the respondents; the role of such factors is, however, not explored (cf. Constantinople 1984:16; Nails 1983).

There is one exception. An eleven-year-old girl and boy named Amy and Jake both comment on a hypothetical situation in which a man must steal to save his wife's life. In a fascinating analysis, Gilligan notes that "the different logic of Amy's response calls attention to the interpretation of the interview itself" (1982:31). The answers initially suggest that the boy is more advanced in terms of moral development. Gilligan notes, however, that "it immediately becomes clear that the interviewer's problem in understanding Amy's response stems from the fact that Amy is answering a different question from the one the interviewer thought had been posed."

Gilligan thus comes face-to-face with the sort of problems inherent in interview techniques. Her argument with respect to the more contextual and interpersonal nature of women's responses should have led her quickly away from placing such heavy reliance on interview data or at least led her to analyze such data contextually. Rather than seize on her insight into Amy's response and radicalize her research methodologically, Gilligan reverts to a decontextualized mode of analysis.

My goal in criticizing Gilligan's methodology is not to undermine the importance of her research. I am certainly in agreement with the con-- clusion: "Among the most pressing items on the agenda for research in adult development is the need to delineate *in women's own terms* the experience of their adult life" (1982:173; emphasis in original). I am, rather, concerned with the way that an uncritical acceptance of the methodological status quo reintroduces the very sorts of ontological and political biases that are being called into question. If her analysis is correct, then one could hardly find a less effective mode of capturing this "voice" than traditional interview-based research. Gilligan's methodology severs the data from a set of contextual factors and an interpersonal relationship that has profoundly affected the respondent's self-expression – the interview situation itself.

Research on gender roles provides a striking example of the methodological conservatism that characterizes social-scientific research. Feminist writers have addressed the crucial task of exposing cases in which research has added "scientific" legitimacy to gender-based discrimination. This has involved a radical critique of taken-for-granted concepts based on sexist assumptions. The same critical spirit has not fostered a comparable examination of the assumptions that underlie our reliance on naive interview techniques.

I have tried to show that interviews provide a particularly effective means of assuring oneself in advance that the discourse inscribed in the course of the research will be filtered and codified in keeping with predominant Western institutions and ideologies. Because interviews constitute powerful encapsulations of the societal status quo, sole reliance on interviews and decontextualized modes of analysis provide faulty means of collecting data that are less colored by "a consistent observational and evaluative bias." An exclusive reliance on interviews and decontextualized modes of analysis places feminist research in the unusual position of drawing female as well as male researchers into a relationship of communicative hegemony vis-à-vis women in order to understand women's experiences. I would accordingly add another item to the agenda for gender-related research – the need to listen to the way that women ordinarily articulate their experiences to other women.

My argument is that the close relationship between methodology and theory is paralleled by an equally intimate connection between methodology and politics. Just as interview techniques contain hidden theoretical and ideological assumptions, they are tied to relationships of power and control. The same patterns of inequality emerge from the relationship between controlling and subordinate groups within societies, between "developed" and "underdeveloped" societies, and between interviewers and interviewees. This leads me to suggest that our reluctance to examine the assumptions that underlie interview techniques and to adopt more socially, culturally, and linguistically sensitive research techniques is rooted, at least in part, in the desire to hold on to a rather comfortable position in a number of unequal relationships.

Most researchers will deny the existence of a political dimension to their methodological choices. Regardless of their possible incompatibility with the metacommunicative norms of the population in question, interviews will still be seen by many as providing the most rational and efficient means of acquiring large bodies of information that bear on the issues of greatest moment to social-scientific inquiry. After all, it will be argued, such research is undertaken in order to address "our" questions, not "theirs." But there is a hidden irony here. Given the state of interviewing practice, we often learn more about our own preconceptions and communicative norms than about the daily-life issues of the group in question. It is the objectivist ideology that underlies interview techniques rather than an empirical assessment of their strengths and weaknesses that leads us to believe we are capturing features of our subjects' behavior and belief.

The prevalent ideology of interviewing precludes us from ever seriously addressing the ecological validity problem raised in Chapter 1. Our methodology thus ultimately seems to hurt "us" more than it hurts "them." The opposite is true, however, in those cases in which the failure of our efforts to impose communicative hegemony, say on inner-city ethnic children, prompts us to label them cognitively, linguistically, and/or socially "deficient." In the case of inner-city ethnic children, this fallacy has often been legitimized by "scientific" research and enshrined in educational policy (cf. Labov 1972a).[3]

That the political dimensions of methodological issues are seldom examined or discussed should come as no surprise. We gather our data in encounters that focus on the topics under discussion rather than on the research encounter itself. We further this process in our analysis of interview data. By failing to consider the effects of the interview situation on responses, we circumvent the vital process of examining our own contribution to the generation of the data. Focusing on what the natives say and do thus keeps us from having to ask tough questions with regard to the effect of our actions on the data, and on the people we are studying.

If communicative hegemony were to be made explicit and propounded as a theoretical position, few scholars would find it acceptable. As an implicit methodological premise, however, it encounters little resistance. Methodology is, after all, "purely methodological," and it is not a valid object of serious study. A historian friend of mine once quipped that theory for historians is like underwear: It's all right to have it, just as long as it doesn't show. This sort of repression seems to be directed at methodology in linguistics and the social sciences. But it prevents us from coming to terms with the fact that the received methodology acts as a hidden filter, blocking our ability to hear what "they" are saying while allowing the comforting sound of our own preconceptions about language and life to be echoed in the data. Our neglect of methodological questions and refusal to examine our role in generating the data preclude any departures from the status quo.

The path from theoretical obstacles to methodological shortcomings thus forms a tight circle. Only by considering methodology in the light of theory and pondering the theoretical baggage hidden on the methodological plane will we finally be able to chart a new course. But where are we to begin? Because we have spent so much time avoiding these questions, the first steps will not come easily. What we need is a specific, concrete focus for our initial efforts. I submit, by way of conclusion, that the most fruitful point of departure is learning how to ask.

Notes

1. Introduction

1 Bauman (1975), Ben-Amos (1976), Hymes (1981), and other practitioners have addressed this problem in stressing the need to identify the signals that frame a given interaction as a performance of a given type. The same type of analysis has not, however, been used in grasping the nature and significance of the interview data that practitioners use in interpreting performances. Similarly, the signals that point to the role the collector plays in the interaction are seldom stressed. This hiatus often thwarts the efforts of some researchers to examine the dialogic character of narrative and other performances and to analyze their role in creating the text. The transcripts presented in such sophisticated works as those by Glassie (1982) and Tedlock (1983) provide no clues as to the verbal and/or nonverbal reactions of the collector.

2 The work of Cicourel (1964, 1974c, 1981, 1983, 1985) is quite pertinent here. I will reserve discussion of his research on the interview, however, to the section that focuses on the use of interviews in sociological research.

Churchill (1978) devotes a short monograph to the examination of procedural problems in question–answer sequences, cases in which the hearer has not heard the question clearly or does not understand what it means. His analysis is quite pertinent because he derives a number of maxims that underlie question–answer sequences among speakers of American English. His data are taken, however, from transcripts of noninterview speech; although he is interested in the application of his results to interviewing, he does not extend his analysis to the interview.

3 Albert (1972:104) similarly argues, "Observation of speech behavior, noting spontaneous statements that are obviously or potentially about speaking, systematic questioning, and confirmatory observation should provide the data required for a comprehensible view of speech behavior."

4 The placement of greater reliance on the analysis of speech collected in "natural" settings – that is, those the least affected by the researcher's presence – now characterizes the work of many sociolinguists. For example, Sherzer (1983:10) frames the contribution of his major study of *Kuna Ways of Speaking* as "the first book-length treatment of the complete range of forms of discourse in a nonliterate society, based entirely on naturally occurring and recorded speech." Although observation is preferable to interviewing in many contexts, it is hardly immune from the need for critical attention. Observation-based techniques also raise problems regarding sampling, selec-

126

tivity, and the effect of the interviewer (and her or his tape recorder) on speech events. Moreover, some exegesis is necessary to enable the outsider to comprehend what is said, and the relationship between observational and exegetic data must be considered.

Some sociolinguists have distanced themselves from practitioners who claim that researchers should rely primarily or exclusively on such data. Hymes (1974b:444) notes, for example, "the failure inherent in a conception of sociolinguistics as a method of obtaining 'real' data"; he accordingly points to the need to obtain data on underlying competence that can be obtained through participants' views of a speech event that has already taken place.

5 Interestingly, an "Outline Guide for the Ethnographic Study of Speech Use" (Sherzer and Darnell 1972) proposes a number of topics for investigation, but it does not even broach the question of the types of methodologies that may be appropriate for addressing them.

6 Labov (1972b:207) notes, for instance, that "the elementary steps of locating and contacting informants, and getting them to talk freely in a recorded interview, are formidable problems for students. It is an error for anyone to pass over these questions, for in the practices and techniques that have been worked out are embodied many important principles of linguistic and social behavior. Close examination of these methodological assumptions and findings will tell us a great deal about the nature of discourse and the functions of language."

7 Some writers do not distinguish the senses of these two sets of terms. "Standardized" is accordingly used synonymously with "scheduled" in reference to interviews that follow a fixed set of questions, whereas "nonstandardized" and "nonscheduled" both refer to interviews that do not draw on a fixed set of questions.

8 Some writers, such as Bailey (1978:93), use the terms "schedule" and "questionnaire" interchangeably, whereas others (e.g., Gorden 1969:62) keep their senses distinct. I will adhere to the latter usage. My focus, however, is on face-to-face interviews. I will refer to questionnaire-based research, like telephone polling, only en passant.

9 Gorden's (1969:59–60) discussion includes a third category, based on the purpose of interviews, in which he includes such forms as the focused interview (Merton, Fiske, and Kendall 1956), the assessment interview (Shoulksmith 1968), the depth interview (Banaka 1971), the problem-solving interview (Beveridge 1968), and the helping interview (Benjamin 1969).

2. The setting: Mexicano society and Córdova, New Mexico

1 The existence of the Pueblo Quemado is first noted in a reissuing of the grant to Santo Domingo de Cundiyó in 1743. The document indicates that Pueblo Quemado constituted the northern border of the Cundiyó Grant (Spanish Archives of New Mexico, 1, no. 211). More extensive material on Córdova's early history is provided by documents dated 1748 and 1749. The first is a petition for permission for the withdrawal of the settlers of three communities, Abiquiu, Ojo Caliente, and Pueblo Quemado, to more secure locations (Spanish Archives, 1, no. 28). The following year, the Pueblo Quemado settlers asked the governor for permission to return to their fields (Spanish Archives, 1, no. 718).

2   In 1935 the number of people finding work outside the state had dropped to fewer than 2,000, and their earnings were estimated at $350,000 (Harper et al., 1943:77). Although earnings rose in the following years (Soil Conservation Service 1937:5), a large gap was left between the income of most villagers and the amount needed for subsistence. This gap was filled by relief dollars from the Works Project Administration, the Soil Conservation Service, the Civilian Conservation Corps, the Farm Security Administration, the Water Facilities Administration, the Rural Rehabilitation Administration, and many other governmental relief projects. Estimated relief income for *Mexicanos* in the Middle Rio Grande Valley in 1936 was $1,143,051 (Soil Conservation Service 1937:5).

3   This information was provided by Charles Hart (1973: personal communication) on the basis of a public voucher for work performed under provisions of the Federal Aid and Federal Highways acts, as amended. The voucher was filed with the New Mexico State Highway Commission in 1955.

4   Phonological features include the loss of intervocalic *-d* at the end of past participles of *-ar* verbs (e.g., *tirao* instead of *tirado*), the aspiration of sibilants and, in some cases, of *f* and *h* (e.g., *ji* for *sí*, *jumo* for *humo*, *jui* for *fui*), diphthongization of stressed words (e.g., *pais* for *país*), and the addition of a paragogic *i* at the end of infinitives and oxytones ending in *l, n, r,* and *s* when in isolation or at the end of a breath group (e.g., *¿quiéni?* for *¿quién?* and *a veri* for *a ver*). Lexically, some forms have been retained from sixteenth- and seventeenth-century Spanish (e.g., *asina* for *así; croque* for *creo que*). English loan words, such as *troca* 'truck', *yonque* 'junk', and *shantear* 'to shack up' are common, although they are used less frequently in Córdova than in urban areas. (See Bowen 1952; Cobos 1983; Espinosa 1911, 1930; Rael 1937.)

5   That language use is closely related to social identity at many levels of social organization is, of course, a widespread phenomenon. See Gumperz (1982a, 1982b) for recent research on this problem.

6   See Bloch (1975b) for analyses of the importance of stylistic features in political discourse in other societies.

3. Interview techniques vis-à-vis native metacommunicative repertoires or on the analysis of communicative blunders

1   It is particularly important to avoid reifying the model, taking it as a blueprint of the interview itself. These components are not simply givens, determined at the outset and remaining constant through the interview. They are, rather, emergent in the course of the interview; the role each plays in determining the meaning of what is said thus changes as the interaction progresses. (Cf. Cicourel 1964, 1974c; Cook-Gumperz and Gumperz 1976; Gumperz 1982a)

2   I am relying primarily on Peirce's (1932:2.230–1) definition of indexicality and on Silverstein's (1976:14–16) characterization of the relationship between referential and indexical functions. It must be stressed that these terms do not refer to one-to-one relationships between linguistic forms and communicative functions. Referentiality and indexicality are types of "semiosis," in Peirce's terms; a single form may accordingly be tied to several semiotic functions, including both referential and indexical modes.

3 See Benveniste (1966). Note that the relationship between personal pronouns and speech event participants is more complex in such cases as pronouns within direct (or quoted) discourse; here the "I" that I may utter may in fact identify the source of the quotation rather than the speaker.
4 This is not to say, however, that Grimshaw or Strauss and Schatzman actually present an in-depth analysis of communicative norms for such speech communities. Although they are to be commended for raising the problem, it should be pointed out that these works are based primarily on the authors' intuitive understanding of these processes rather than on systematic research on the norms that underlie the interview.
5 This problem is hardly peculiar to *Mexicano* society. Ben-Amos (1976) argues that generic definitions are culture-specific components of a given communicative repertoire. Genres from two different societies that can be classified within the same analytic, cross-cultural "type" (e.g., the proverb) may nevertheless be identified in each tradition with quite different performance features. Knowledge of the analytic type is thus unlikely to enable a researcher to identify and interpret examples of a related genre; this ability must be acquired.
6 Hudson (1980:134) has used the term "encyclopedic structure" in dealing with the problem of providing a referential frame for the production and interpretation of utterances.
7 This is only true, however, of questions that do not pertain to the current topic, for example, where the utterance of a question effects a change in topic. Questions that fall within the present frame of reference can be intelligible even if they do not include a triplex sign.

4. The acquisition of metacommunicative competence

1 The following symbols bear these meanings in the transcriptions and in passages from them that appear in the analysis:

/ /	Material enclosed within slashes is in phonemic transcription
[ ]	Material enclosed within brackets has been placed within the text by the author to clarify meaning; in text (2), brackets indicate that the enclosed transcription is phonetic
( )	Indications of nonverbal signals on tape (e.g., laughter, special tone of voice, etc.)
(( ))	Material within double parentheses is unclear on tape; transcription is only approximate
' '	English glosses are placed within single quotation marks
. . .	Ellipsis within a text indicates that the speaker interrupted his or her utterance to begin a new utterance
/	a slash at the end of one utterance and another at the beginning of the next speaker's turn indicates an overlap
ALL CAPS	Text set in small capital letters is uttered with unusual force (quantity)

2 *Chongo* is used for 'braid' in New Mexican Spanish. In its marked sense, it refers to the queue-style hair worn by some Rio Grande Pueblo Indians (Cobos 1983:48), hence the association of *shongos de indio* 'Indian braids'. Recall that /š/ is realized as [č] in the Córdovan dialect.

3 See McDowell (1975, 1979, 1982) for research on the sociolinguistic complexity of Chicano children's folklore in Texas.

4 The discourse transcribed as texts 3 and 4 is formally elaborated. Such features as tone groups, pauses, and stress parallel the semantic and pragmatic content of the words, creating carefully constructed rhetorical structures. In keeping with the ethnopoetic principles elucidated by Hymes (1981), McLendon (1982), and Tedlock (1971, 1972), I have used these formal features in attempting to preserve a sense of the rhetorical structure in the transcriptions and translations.

5 This comment is based on the discussion in Geertz's famous article "Deep Play: Notes on the Balinese Cockfight" (1972). It should be noted, however, that Geertz seems no more concerned with the problems inherent in interviewing than other ethnographers. In his similarly well-known essay "Thick Description: Toward an Interpretive Theory of Culture" (1973:3–30), Geertz examines in detail the "interpretive activity" involved in making sense of an account of a sheep raid that took place in the highlands of central Morocco in 1912. Interestingly, this "interpretive activity" does not include any mention of who presented the account in what manner and in what type of situation and for what reasons.

6 It should be noted that Pelto and Pelto do express some reservations regarding the use of key informants and do allude to the fact that "the interaction between fieldworker and informants is a complex social process" (1978:74). Nevertheless, they simply allude to sources of potential bias rather than urge fieldworkers to be constantly aware of their patterns of interaction with their consultants, especially in comparison with native norms of interaction. (See Karp and Kendall [1982] for a penetrating critique of the book.)

5. Listen before you leap: toward methodological sophistication

1 I do not wish to suggest that the use of computers in social scientific and linguistic research is inherently misguided. My characterization simply applies to the use of computers in providing modern aids to the age-old task of locating statements that bear on the same topic (as judged on the basis of their referential content) and extracting them from their interactional contexts.

2 Insights into the nature of metacommunication can be drawn from the work of the Russian Formalists on the way literature and poetry can 'make strange' (*ostrannanie*) or distort language in order to convey plot and character (cf. Matejka and Pomorska 1978; Erlich 1955). Similarly, the Prague Linguistic Circle, particularly in the work of Mukařovský (1977a, 1977b) and Jakobson (1960), pioneered the study of the manner in which the components of literary and other modes of expression form a semiotic system that superimposes distinct types of communicative functions (also see Garvin 1964; Matejka & Titunik 1976). Silverstein (1976, 1979, 1981a, 1981b) has brought this tradition in line with new advances in linguistics, systematized its theoretical base, and applied it to a broader range of communicative acts. Bateson (1972, 1979; Bateson and Ruesch 1951) brought the term "metacommunication" into general currency and established its status as a major element of communicative processes, verbal and nonverbal.

3 Manuals on interviewing frequently urge researchers to interview only one person at a time. Although I do not find the arguments for this position entirely unconvincing, this practice does seem to reflect an interest in enabling the interviewer to retain as much control over the speech event as possible. A one-on-one situation greatly impoverishes the data on crosschecks of interpretive frames. When I interviewed two or more *Mexicano* elders, for example, they frequently sought their peers' assessments of their own interpretive frames and of my questions and statements in addition to the queries that were directed to me. This provided me with a basis for assessing my own interpretation of the discourse, both at the time of the interview and in the course of the analysis.

4 Allen and Montell (1981) suggest that "Our recommendation is to transcribe tapes verbatim, then edit the transcription to remove false starts, *uhs, ahs,* and stutterings, and 'crutch' words and phrases such as 'well,' and 'you know.' " Hoopes (1979:118) similarly argues that "Some deletions are easy to decide upon. 'Uh' is probably the most commonly spoken monosyllable, often used unconsciously by even the most fluent speakers while mentally reaching for the right word. Except in the rare instances where 'uh' adds something to meaning (perhaps by suggesting nervous hesitation), there is no point in reproducing it in the transcript." Hoopes goes on to include false starts and " catch phrases" (e.g., "you know") in his list of items that should be deleted. As studies of turn-taking in conversation have shown, such cues provide important information on the structure of discourse (cf. Duncan 1972, 1973; Duncan and Niederehe 1974; Jefferson 1972; Sacks 1967; Sacks et al. 1974). Their deletion deprives the reader of important information on how both speaker and hearer(s) are relating to each other and to the meaning they attach to their statements.

5 See, for example, Babcock (1980), Belmont (1979), Berreman (1962), Crapanzano (1977, 1980), Dwyer (1982), Glassie (1982), Hymes (1969b), Karp and Kendall (1982), Rabinow (1977), and Ruby (1980, 1982).

6. Conclusion: theoretical quagmires and "purely methodological" issues

1 I should note that I am only in partial agreement with Bloch's (1975a) theory of redundancy in political rhetoric. Because such discourse is generally formulaic and the referential content offers little new information, Bloch concludes that its communicative content is also nil. As any sensitive observer of Western political rhetoric will tell you, however, stylistic features can convey messages that can shape the course of history. Most announcements of nuclear arms negotiations between the Soviet Union and the United States are specifically intended to limit referential content. Lexical choices, prosodic features, and nonverbal signs create a "tone," however, that tells persons who are skilled in reading such messages if anything significant is being said. Bloch's attempt to interpret the rhetorical dimensions of politics is thus thwarted by the same referential bias that equates the information value of speech with its referential content alone.

2 It should be noted that Karp and Kendall are specifically critiquing the work of Pelto (1970) at this point in the text. Emphasis is in the original.

3 I am indebted on this point to an anonymous reviewer for Cambridge University Press.

References

Ablon, Joan (1977). Field method in working with middle class Americans: new issues of values, personality and reciprocity. *Human Organization* 36(1):69–72.

Abrahams, Roger (1976). *Talking black.* Rowley, Mass.: Newbury House.
  (1983). *The man-of-words in the West Indies: performance and the emergence of Creole culture.* Baltimore: Johns Hopkins University Press.

Agar, Michael H. (1980a). *The professional stranger: an informal introduction to ethnography.* New York: Academic Press.
  (1980b). Stories, background knowledge and themes: problems in the analysis of life history narrative. *American Ethnologist* 17:223–39.

Agar, Michael H., and Hobbs, Jerry R. (1982). Interpreting discourse: coherence and the analysis of ethnographic interviews. *Discourse Processes* 5:1–32.

Akinnaso, F. Niyi, and Seabrook Ajirotut, Cheryl (1982). Performance and ethnic style in job interviews. In John J. Gumperz (ed.), *Language and social identity.* Cambridge University Press, pp. 119–44.

Albert, Ethel M. (1972). Culture patterning of speech behavior in Burundi. In John J. Gumperz and Dell Hymes (eds.), *Directions in sociolinguistics: the ethnography of communication.* New York: Holt, Rinehart & Winston, pp. 72–105.

Allen, Barbara, and Montell, William Lynwood (1981). *From memory to history: using oral sources in local historical research.* Nashville, Tenn.: The American Association for State and Local History.

Austin, J. L. (1962). *How to do things with words.* Cambridge, Mass.: Harvard University Press.

Babbie, Earl B. (1973). *Survey research methods.* Belmont, Calif.: Wadsworth.

Babcock, Barbara (1980). Reflexivity: definitions and discriminations. *Semiotica* 30(1–2):1–14.

Backstrom, Charles H., and Hursh, Gerald D. (1963). *Survey research.* Evanston, Ill.: Northwestern University Press.

Bailey, Kenneth D. (1978). *Methods of social research.* New York: Free Press.

Bakhtin, M. M. (1981). *The dialogic imagination: four essays* (Michael Holoquist, ed.; Caryl Emerson and Michael Holoquist, trans.). Austin: University of Texas Press.

Banaka, William H. (1971). *Training in depth interview.* New York: Harper & Row.

Bates, Elizabeth. (1976). *Language and context: the acquisition of pragmatics.* New York: Academic Press.

132

Bates, Elizabeth, Camaioni, Luigia, and Volterra, Virginia. (1979). The acquisition of performatives prior to speech. In E. Ochs and B. B. Schieffelin (eds.), *Developmental pragmatics*. New York: Academic Press, pp. 111–29.

Bateson, Gregory. (1936). *Naven: a survey of the problems suggested by a composite picture of the culture of a New Guinea tribe drawn from three points of view* (2nd ed., 1958). Stanford, Calif.: Stanford University Press.

(1972). *Steps to an ecology of mind*. New York: Ballantine.

(1979). *Mind and nature: a necessary unity*. New York: Dutton.

Bateson, Gregory, Jackson, Don D., Haley, Jay, and Weakland, John H. (1972 [1956]). Toward a theory of schizophrenia. Reprinted in Gregory Bateson, *Steps to an ecology of mind*. New York: Ballantine, pp. 201–27.

Bateson, Gregory, and Ruesch, Jurgen (1951). *Communication: the social matrix of psychiatry*. New York: Norton.

Baum, Willa K. (1971). *Oral history for the local historical society* (2nd rev. ed., 1974). Nashville, Tenn.: American Association for State and Local History.

Bauman, Richard. (1975). Verbal art as performance. *American Anthropologist* 77(2):290–311.

Beattie, John. (1965). *Understanding an African kingdom: Bunyoro*. Studies in Anthropological Method. New York: Holt, Rinehart & Winston.

Belmonte, Thomas (1979). *The broken fountain*. New York: Columbia University Press.

Ben-Amos, Dan (1976). *Folklore genres*. Austin: University of Texas Press.

Benjamin, Alfred (1969). *The helping interview*. New York: Houghton Mifflin.

Bennett, John W., and Thaiss, Gustav (1970). Survey research in anthropological field work. In Raoul Naroll and Ronald Cohen (eds.), *A handbook of method in cultural anthropology*. New York: Doubleday, pp. 316–37.

Benveniste, Emile (1971). *Problems in general linguistics*. Miami Linguistics Series, no. 8. Coral Gables, Fla.: University of Miami Press.

Bermosk, Loretta L., and Mordan, Mary J. (1964). *Interviewing in nursing*. New York: Macmillan.

Bernard, H. Russell, Killworth, Peter, Kroenfeld, David, and Sailer, Lee (1984). The problem of informant accuracy: the validity of retrospective data. In Bernard J. Siegel, Alan R. Beals, and Stephen A. Tyler (eds.), *Annual review of anthropology*, vol. 13. Palo Alto, Calif.: Annual Reviews, pp. 495–517.

Berreman, Gerald D. (1962). *Behind many masks: ethnography and impression management in a Himalayan village*. Monograph no. 4. Lexington, Ky.: Society for Applied Anthropology.

Beveridge, Wilbert E. (1968). *Problem-solving interviews*. London: Allen & Unwin.

Birdwhistell, Ray L. (1970). *Kinesics and context: essays on body motion communication*. Philadelphia: University of Pennsylvania Press.

Bloch, Maurice. (1975a). Introduction. In Maurice Bloch (ed.), *Political language and oratory in traditional society*. New York: Academic Press, pp. 1–28.

Bloch, Maurice (ed.) (1975b). *Political language and oratory in traditional society*. New York: Academic Press.

Bloom, Harold, de Man, Paul, Derrida, Jacques, Hartman, Geoffrey, and Miller, J. Hillis (1979). *De-construction and criticism*. New York: Continuum.

Boas, Franz (1920). The method of ethnology. *American Anthropologist* 22:311–21.

Bowen, J. Donald (1952). The Spanish of San Antonito, New Mexico. Ph.D. dissertation, University of New Mexico, Albuquerque.

Brenner, Michael (1978). Interviewing: the social phenomenology of a research instrument. In M. Brenner, P. Marsh, and M. Brenner (eds.), *The social contexts of method*. London: Croom Helm.

(1980). Skills in the research interview. In M. Argyle (ed.), *The handbook of social skills*. London: Methuen.

(1981a). Aspects of conversational structure in the research interview. In Paul Werth (ed.), *Conversation and discourse: structure and interpretation*. London: Croom Helm, pp. 19–40.

(1981b). Patterns of social structure in the research interview. In Michael Brenner (ed.), *Social method and social life*. New York: Academic Press, pp. 115–58.

Briggs, Charles L. (1980). *The wood carvers of Córdova, New Mexico: social dimensions of an artistic "revival."* Knoxville: University of Tennessee Press.

(1983). Questions for the ethnographer: a critical examination of the role of the interview in fieldwork. *Semiotica* 46(2–4):233–61.

(1984). Learning how to ask: native metacommunicative competence and the incompetence of fieldworkers. *Language in Society* 13(1):1–28.

(1985a). The pragmatics of proverb performances in New Mexican Spanish. *American Anthropologist* 87(4):793–810.

(1985b). Treasure tales and pedagogical discourse in *Mexicano* New Mexico. *Journal of American Folklore* 98(389):287–314.

(1986). Getting both sides of the story: oral history in land grant research and litigation. In Charles L. Briggs and John R. Van Ness (eds.), *Land and cultural survival: the Spanish and Mexican land grants of New Mexico and Colorado*. Albuquerque: University of New Mexico Press.

Briggs, Charles L., and Van Ness, John R. (eds.) (1986). *Land and cultural survival: the Spanish and Mexican land grants of New Mexico and Colorado*. Albuquerque: University of New Mexico Press.

Brim, John A., and Spain, David H. (1974). *Research design in anthropology: paradigms and pragmatics in the testing of hypotheses*. New York: Holt, Rinehart & Winston.

Brogdan, Robert, and Taylor, Steven J. (1975). *Introduction to qualitative research methods: a phenomenological approach to the social sciences*. New York: Wiley.

Burawoy, M. (1979). *Manufacturing consent*. Chicago: University of Chicago Press.

Burnett, Jacquetta Hill (1976). On the analog between culture acquisition and ethnographic method. In Joan I. Roberts and Sherrie K. Akinsanyal (eds.), *Educational patterns and cultural configurations: the anthropology of education*. New York: McKay, pp. 221–6.

Campa, Arthur L. (1946). *Spanish Folkpoetry in New Mexico*. Albuquerque: University of New Mexico Press.

(1979). *Hispanic Culture in the Southwest*. Norman: University of Oklahoma Press.

Cancian, Frank (1963). Informant error and native prestige ranking in Zinacantan. *American Anthropologist* 65(5):1068–75.

(1965). *Economics and prestige in a Maya community: the religious cargo system in Zinacantan*. Stanford, Calif.: Stanford University Press.

Catron Papers. Special Collections, University of New Mexico, Case no. 212.

Chagnon, Napoleon A. (1974). *Studying the Yɑnomamö*. New York: Holt, Rinehart & Winston.

Chomsky, Noam. (1957). *Syntactic structures*. The Hague: Mouton.

(1965). *Aspects of the theory of syntax*. Cambridge, Mass.: MIT Press.

(1968). *Language and mind* (enlarged ed., 1972). San Diego, Calif.: Harcourt Brace Jovanovich.

Churchill, Lindsey (1978). *Questioning strategies in sociolinguistics*. Rowley, Mass.: Newbury House.

Cicourel, Aaron V. (1964). *Method and measurement in sociology*. New York: Free Press.

(1970). The acquisition of social structure: towards a developmental theory of language and meaning. In J. Douglas (ed.), *Understanding everyday life*. Hawthorne, N.Y.: Aldine.

(1974a). *Cognitive sociology: Language and meaning in social interaction*. New York: Free Press.

(1974b). Some basic theoretical issues in the assessment of the child's performance in testing and classroom settings. In Aaron V. Cicourel et al., *Language use and school performance*. New York: Academic Press.

(1974c). *Theory and method in a study of Argentine fertility*. New York: Wiley Interscience.

(1981). Pragmatic issues in the construction of recent history from interview narratives. In H. Parret, M. Sbisà, and J. Berschueren (eds.), *Possibilities and limitations of pragmatics*. Studies in Language Companion Series, vol. 7. Amsterdam: John Benjamins, pp. 105–21.

(1982a). Interviews, surveys, and the problem of ecological validity. *American Sociologist* 17:11–20.

(1982b). Language and belief in a medical setting. In Heidi Byrnes (ed.), *Contemporary perceptions of language: interdisciplinary dimensions*. Washington, D.C.: Georgetown University Press, pp. 48–78.

(1983). Social measurement as the creation of expert systems. Paper presented at conference on potentialities for knowledge and social science. University of Chicago, September 11–14, 1983.

(1986). Elicitation as a problem of discourse. In *Sociolinguistics: An international handbook of the science of language and society*. Berlin: Walter De Gruyter.

Cobos, Rubén (1983). *A dictionary of New Mexico and southern Colorado Spanish*. Santa Fe: Museum of New Mexico.

Conklin, Harold C. (1968). Ethnography. In David L. Sills (ed.), *International encyclopedia of the social sciences*. New York: Macmillan, vol. 5, pp. 172–78.

Constantinople, Anne (1984). Justice and care: toward an ethics of adulthood. Unpublished manuscript in possession of author.

Cook-Gumperz, Jenny, and Corsaro, William A. (1976). Social-ecological constraints on children's communicative strategies. In J. Cook-Gumperz and J. J. Gumperz, *Papers on language and context*. Working Paper no. 46. Language Behavior Research Laboratory, University of California, Berkeley.

Cook-Gumperz, Jenny, and Gumperz, John J. (1976). *Papers on language and context*. Working Paper no. 46, Language Behavior Research Laboratory, University of California, Berkeley.

Corsaro, William A. (1979). Sociolinguistic patterns in adult-child interaction. In Elinor Ochs and Bambi B. Schieffelin (eds.), *Developmental pragmatics*. New York: Academic Press, pp. 373–89.

Court of Private Land Claims, New Mexico Land Grants Collection of the State Records Center and Archives, Santa Fe, Case no. 212.

Crapanzano, Vincent (1977). On the writing of ethnography. *Dialectical Anthropology* 2(1):69–73.

   (1980). *Tuhami: portrait of a Moroccan*. Chicago: University of Chicago Press.

Crick, Malcolm. (1976). *Explorations in language and meaning: towards a semantic anthropology*. New York: Wiley.

Culler, Jonathan (1975). *Structuralist poetics: structuralism, linguistics, and the study of literature*. Ithaca, N. Y.: Cornell University Press.

Cutler, William, III (1970). Accuracy in oral history interviewing. *Historical Methods Newsletter* 3: 1–7. Reprinted in David K. Dunaway and Willa K. Baum (eds.), *Oral history: an interdisciplinary anthology*. Nashville: American Association for State and Local History, pp. 79–86.

Davis, Cullom, Back, Kathryn, and MacLean, Kay (1977). *Oral history: from tape to type*. Chicago: American Library Association.

Davis, John D. (1971). *The interview as arena*. Stanford, Calif.: Stanford University Press.

Dean, John P., and Whyte, William Foote (1958). How do you know if the informant is telling the truth? *Human Organization* 17(2): 34–8.

Denzin, Norman K. (1970). *The research act: a theoretical introduction to sociological methods*. Hawthorne, N.Y.: Aldine.

Derrida, Jacques (1976). *Of grammatology*. (Gayatri Chakravorty, trans.) Baltimore: Johns Hopkins University Press.

   (1978). *Writing and difference*. (Alan Bass, trans.). Chicago: University of Chicago Press.

Dexter, Lewis Anthony (1970). *Elite and specialized interviewing*. Evanston, Ill.: Northwestern University Press.

Dougherty, Janet W. D., and Fernandez, James W. (1981). Introduction to Symbolism and cognition. Special issue of the *American Ethnologist* 8(3):413–21.

Duncan, Starkey (1972). Some signals and rules for taking speaking turns in conversation. *Journal of Personality and Social Psychology* 23(2):283–92.

   (1973). Towards a grammar for dyadic conversation. *Semiotica* 9(1):29–46.

   (1974). On the structure of speaker–auditor interaction during speaking turns. *Language in Society* 3(2):161–80.

Duncan, Starkey, and Niederehe, G. (1974). On signalling that it's your turn to speak. *Journal of Experimental Social Psychology* 10:234–47.

Durkheim, Emile (1938). *The rules of sociological method,* 8th ed. (Sarah A. Solovay and John H. Mueller, trans.; George E. G. Catlin, ed.). New York: Free Press.

Dwyer, Kevin (1982) *Moroccan dialogues: anthropology in question*. Baltimore: Johns Hopkins University Press.

Edgerton, Robert B., and Langness, L. L. (1974). *Methods and styles in the study of culture*. San Francisco: Chandler & Sharp.

Eisenberg, A. R. (1982). Language acquisition in cultural perspective: talk in three Mexicano homes. Ph.D. dissertation, University of California, Berkeley.

Erickson, Frederick, and Shultz, Jeffrey (1982). *The counselor as gatekeeper: social interaction in interviews.* New York: Academic Press.

Erlich, Victor (1955). *Russian Formalism: history–doctrine* (4th ed., 1980). The Hague: Mouton.

Ervin-Tripp, Susan (1972). On sociolinguistic rules: alternation and co-occurrence. In John J. Gumperz and Dell Hymes (eds.), *Directions in sociolinguistics: the ethnography of communication.* New York: Holt, Rinehart & Winston, pp. 213–50.

(1979). Children's verbal turn-taking. In Eleanor Ochs and Bambi B. Schieffelin (eds.), *Developmental pragmatics.* New York: Academic Press, pp. 391–414.

Espinosa, Aurelio M., Sr. (1910–16). New Mexican Spanish folklore. *Journal of American Folklore* 23:395–418 (1910); 23:397–444 (1911); 26:97–122 (1913); 27:105–47 (1914); 28:205–6, 319–52 (1915); 29:505–35 (1916).

(1911). *The Spanish language in New Mexico and southern Colorado.* Santa Fe: Historical Society of New Mexico, Publication no. 16.

(1930). *Estudios sobre el español de Nuevo Mejico,* 2 vols. (A. Alonso and Angel Rosenblat, trans. and eds.). Buenos Aires: Imprenta de la Universidad.

(1953). *Romancero de Nuevo Méjico.* Madrid: C. Bermejo.

Fenlason, Anne, Beals, G., and Abrahamson, A. (1962). *Essentials of interviewing.* New York: Harper & Row.

Fernandez, James W. (1972). Persuasions and performance: of the beast in every body . . . and the metaphors of Everyman. *Daedalus* 101(1):39–60.

(1974). The mission of metaphor in expressive culture. *Current Anthropology* 15(2):119–45.

(1977). The performance of ritual metaphors. In J. David Sapir and J. Christopher Crocker (eds.), *The social use of metaphor: essays on the anthropology of rhetoric.* Philadelphia: University of Pennsylvania Press.

Firth, Raymond (ed.) (1957). *Man and culture: an evaluation of the work of Bronislaw Malinowski.* London: Routledge & Kegan Paul.

Fishman, Joshua. (1964). Language maintenance and language shift as fields of inquiry. *Language* 9:32–70.

(1966). *Language loyalty in the United States.* The Hague: Mouton.

Fishman, Joshua, Ferguson, Charles A., and Das Gupta, Jyotirindra (1968). *Language problems of developing nations.* New York: Wiley.

Frake, Charles O. (1972). How to ask for a drink in Subanum. In John J. Gumperz and Dell Hymes (eds.), *Directions in sociolinguistics: the ethnography of communication.* New York: Holt, Rinehart & Winston, pp. 127–32.

Franklin, Billy J., and Osborne, Harold W. (eds.) (1971). *Research methods: issues and insights.* Belmont, Calif.: Wadsworth.

Freilich, Morris (ed.) (1970). *Marginal natives at work: anthropologists in the field* (2nd ed.). Cambridge, Mass.: Schenkman.

Friedlander, Peter (1970). *The emergence of a UAW local, 1936–1939: a study in class and culture.* Pittsburgh: University of Pittsburgh Press.

Froelich, Robert, and Bishop, F. M. (1969). *Medical interviewing.* St. Louis, Mo.: Mosby.

Gadamer, Hans-Georg (1975). *Truth and method.* New York: Crossroad.

(1979). The problem of historical consciousness. In Paul Rabinow and William M. Sullivan (eds.), *Interpretive social science: a reader.* Berkeley: University of California Press, pp. 103–60.

Galtung, Johann (1967). After Camelot. In Irving L. Horowitz (ed.), *The rise and fall of Project Camelot: studies in the relationship between social science and practical politics.* Cambridge, Mass.: MIT Press, pp. 281–312.

Garfinkel, Harold (1967). *Studies in ethnomethodology.* Englewood Cliffs, N. J.: Prentice-Hall.

(1972). Remarks on ethnomethodology. In John J. Gumperz and Dell Hymes (eds.), *Directions in sociolinguistics: the ethnography of communication.* New York: Holt, Rinehart & Winston, pp. 301–24.

(1974). 'Good' organizational reasons for 'bad' clinical records. In Roy Turner (ed.), *Ethnomethodology.* New York: Penguin.

Garner, Van H. (1975). *Oral history: a new experience in learning.* Dayton, Ohio: Pflaum/Standard.

Garrett, Annette (1942). *Interviewing: its principles and methods.* New York: Family Service Association of America.

Garvin, Paul L. (ed.) (1964). *A Prague School reader on esthetics, literary structure, and style.* Washington, D.C.: Georgetown University Press.

Geertz, Clifford (1972). Deep play: Notes on the Balinese cockfight. *Daedalus* 101:1–37.

(1973). *The interpretation of cultures.* New York: Basic.

(1974). "From the native's point of view": On the nature of anthropological understanding. *Bulletin of the American Academy of Arts and Sciences* 28(1). Reprinted in Keith H. Basso and Henry T. Selby (eds.), *Meaning in anthropology.* Albuquerque: University of New Mexico Press, pp. 221–37.

Georges, Robert A., and Jones, Michael O. (1980). *People studying people: the human element in fieldwork.* Berkeley: University of California Press.

Gilligan, Carol (1982). *In a different voice: psychological theory and women's development.* Cambridge, Mass.: Harvard University Press.

Glassie, Henry (1982). *Passing the time in Ballymenone: culture and history of an Ulster community.* Philadelphia: University of Pennsylvania Press.

Goffman, Erving (1959). *The presentation of self in everyday life.* New York: Doubleday.

(1974). *Frame analysis.* New York: Harper & Row.

(1981). *Forms of talk.* Philadelphia: University of Pennsylvania Press.

Golde, Peggy (1970). *Women in the field: anthropological experiences.* Hawthorne, N.Y.: Aldine.

Goldstein, Kenneth S. (1964). *A guide for field workers in folklore.* Hatboro, Penn.: Folklore Associates, Inc.

Goody, Esther N. (ed.) (1978). *Questions and politeness: strategies in social interaction.* Cambridge University Press.

Gorden, Raymond L. (1969). *Interviewing: Strategy, technique, and tactics* (rev. ed., 1975). Homewood, Ill.: Dorsey.

Gossen, Gary H. (1974). *Chamulas in the world of the sun: time and space in a Maya oral tradition.* Cambridge, Mass.: Harvard University Press.

Gouldner, Alvin W. (1970). *The coming crisis of Western sociology.* New York: Basic.

Grice, H. P. (1975). Logic and conversation. In P. Cole and J. L. Morgan (eds.), *Syntax and semantics 3: speech acts.* New York: Academic Press, pp. 41–58.

Grimshaw, Allen D. (1969). Language as data and as obstacle in sociological research. *Items* 23:17–21.

(1969–70). Some problematic aspects of communication in cross-racial research in the United States. *Sociological Focus* 3(2):67–85.

(1974). Data and data use in an analysis of communicative events. In Richard Bauman and Joel Sherzer (eds.), *Explorations in the ethnography of speaking.* Cambridge University Press, pp. 419–24.

Gumperz, John J. (1972). Introduction. In John J. Gumperz and Dell Hymes (eds.), *Directions in sociolinguistics: the ethnography of communication.* New York: Holt, Rinehart & Winston, pp. 1–25.

(1982a). *Discourse strategies.* Cambridge University Press.

Gumperz, John J. (ed.) (1982b). *Language and social identity.* Cambridge University Press.

Halberstam, Sandra (1978). Interviewing in sociology: a brief review. In Lindsey Churchill, *Questioning strategies in sociolinguistics.* Rowley, Mass.: Newbury House, pp. 5–18.

Hall, Edward T. (1959). *The silent language.* New York: Doubleday.

(1966). *The hidden dimension.* New York: Doubleday.

(1977). *Beyond culture.* New York: Doubleday.

Harper, Allan G., Córdova, Andrew R., and Oberg, Kalvero (1943). *Man and resources in the Middle Rio Grande Valley.* Albuquerque: University of New Mexico Press.

Henry, Frances, and Saberwal, Satish (eds.) (1969). *Stress and response in fieldwork.* New York: Holt, Rinehart & Winston.

Herskovits, Melville J. (1954). Some problems in method in ethnography. In Robert J. Spencer (ed.), *Method and perspective in anthropology: papers in honor of Wilson D. Wallis.* Minneapolis: University of Minnesota Press, pp. 3–24.

Herzfeld, Michael (1980). The dowry in Greece: terminological usage and historical reconstruction. *Ethnohistory* 27(3):225–41.

Herzog, George. (1945). Drum-signaling in a West African tribe. *Word* 1:217–38.

Hobbs, Jerry R., and Robinson, Jane. J. (1979). Why ask? *Discourse Processes* 2:311–18.

Hoffman, Alice (1974). Reliability and validity in oral history. Reprinted in David K. Dunaway and Willa K. Baum (eds.), *Oral history: an interdisciplinary anthology.* Nashville, Tenn.: American Association for State and Local History (1984), pp. 67–73.

Hoinville, Gerald, Jowell, Roger, et al. (1978). *Survey research practice.* London: Heinemann Educational Books.

Hollander, A. N. J. den (1967). Social description: the problem of reliability and validity. In D. G. Jongmans, and P. C. W. Gutkind (eds.), *Anthropologists in the field.* Assen, Netherlands: Van Gorcum, pp. 75–88.

Hoopes, James (1979). *Oral history: an introduction for students.* Chapel Hill: University of North Carolina Press.

Hotchkiss, J. C. (1967). Children and conduct in a Ladino community of Chiapas, Mexico. *American Anthropologist* 69(4):711–18.

Hudson, R. A. (1980). *Sociolinguistics.* Cambridge University Press.

Hyman, Herbert H., with Cobb, William J., Feldman, Jacob J., Hart, Clyde W., and Stember, Charles Herbert (1954). *Interviewing in social research* (2nd ed., 1975). Chicago: University of Chicago Press.

Hymes, Dell H. (1964). Introduction: toward ethnographies of communication. In John J. Gumperz and Dell Hymes (eds.), The ethnography of communication. *American Anthropologist* 66(6) pt. 2:1–34.

(1969a). Linguistic aspects of comparative political research. In Robert T. Holt and John Turner (eds.), *Methodology of comparative research*. New York: Free Press.

(1969b). *Reinventing anthropology*. New York: Pantheon.

(1969c). The use of anthropology: critical, political, personal. In Dell Hymes (ed.), *Reinventing anthropology*. New York: Pantheon, pp. 3–79.

(1971a). Competence and performance in linguistic theory. In R. Huxley and E. Ingram (eds.), *Language acquisition: models and methods*. New York: Academic Press, pp. 3–28.

(1971b). Sociolinguistics and the ethnography of speaking. In Edwin Ardener (ed.), *Social anthropology and linguistics*. London: Tavistock, pp. 47–93.

(1972). Models of the interaction of language and social life. In John J. Gumperz and Dell H. Hymes (eds.), *Directions in sociolinguistics: the ethnography of communication*. New York: Holt, Rinehart & Winston, pp. 35–71.

(1974a). *Foundations in sociolinguistics: an ethnographic approach*. Philadelphia: University of Pennsylvania Press.

(1974b). Ways of speaking. In Richard Bauman and Joel Sherzer (eds.), *Explorations in the ethnography of speaking*. Cambridge University Press, pp. 433–51.

(1981). *'In vain I tried to tell you': essays in Native American ethnopoetics*. Philadelphia: University of Pennsylvania Press.

Irvine, Judith T. (1978). Wolof "magical thinking": culture and conservation revisited. *Journal of Cross-Cultural Psychology* 9(3):300–310.

(1979). Formality and informality in communicative events. *American Anthropologist* 81:773–90.

Ives, Edward D. (1974). *The tape-recorded interview: a manual for field workers in folklore and oral history*. Knoxville: University of Tennessee Press.

Jakobson, Roman (1957). *Shifters, verbal categories, and the Russian verb*. Cambridge, Mass.: Harvard University Russian Language Project.

(1960). Closing statement: linguistics and poetics. In Thomas A. Sebeok (ed.), *Style in language*. Cambridge: MIT Press, pp. 350–77.

Jameson, Frederic (1971). *Marxism and form*. Princeton, N.J.: Princeton University Press.

(1972). *The prison house of language: a critical account of structuralism and Russian Formalism*. Princeton, N.J.: Princeton University Press.

Jefferson, Gail (1972). Side sequences. In David Sudnow (ed.), *Studies in social interaction*. New York: Free Press, pp. 294–338.

Johnson, John M. (1975). *Doing field research*. New York: Free Press.

Jongmans, D. G. and Gutkind, P. C. W. (eds.) (1967). *Anthropologists in the field*. Assen, Netherlands: Van Gorcum.

Joyner, Charles W. (1975). A model for the analysis of folklore performance in historical context. *Journal of American Folklore* 88(349):254–65.

(1979). Oral history as communicative event: a folkloristic perspective. *Oral History Review* 7:47–52.

Kahn, Robert L., and Cannell, Charles F. (1957). *The dynamics of interviewing*. New York: Wiley.

Karp, Ivan, and Kendall, Martha B. (1982). Reflexivity in field work. In P. F. Secord (ed.), *Explaining social behavior: consciousness, human action, and social structure*. Beverly Hills, Calif.: Sage, pp. 249–73.

Kastenbaum, R., and Sherwood, S. (1967). *VIRO: A new scale for assessing the interview behavior of elderly people.* Proceedings of the 20th Annual Meeting of the Gerontological Society.

Keenan, Elinor Ochs (1973). A sliding sense of obligatoriness: The polystructure of Malagasy oratory. *Language in Society* 2:225–43.

Kendall, Martha B. (1981). Toward a semantic approach to terms of address: a critique of deterministic models in sociolinguistics. *Language and Communication* 1(2/3):237–54.

Kendon, Adam (1972). Some relationships between body motion and speech: an analysis of an example. In A. Seigman and B. Pope (eds.), *Studies in dyadic interaction: a research conference.* Elmsford, N.Y.: Pergamon Press, pp. 177–210.

(1973). The role of visible behavior in the organization of social interaction. In Mario von Cranach and Ian Vine (eds.), *Social communication and movement: studies of interaction and expression in man and chimpanzee.* New York: Academic Press, pp. 29–74.

(1977). *Studies in the behavior of social interaction.* Atlantic City, N.J.: Humanities Press.

(1978). Differential perception and attentional frame in face-to-face interaction: two problems for investigation. *Semiotica* 24(3/4):305–15.

Kendon, Adam, Harris, Richard M., and Key, Mary Ritchie (eds.) (1976). *Organization of behavior in face-to-face interaction.* The Hague: Mouton.

Kerlinger, Fred N. (1964). *Foundations of behavioral research.* (2nd ed., 1973). New York: Holt, Rinehart & Winston.

Kluckhohn, Clyde, and Leighton, Dorothea (1946). *The Navaho.* (rev. ed., 1962). New York: Doubleday.

Kluckhohn, Florence R. (1940). The participant-observation technique in small communities. *American Journal of Sociology* 46:331–43.

Kobben, A. J. F. (1967). Participation and quantification: Field work among the Djuka (Bush Negroes of Surinam). In D. G. Jongmans and P. C. W. Gutkind (eds.), *Anthropologists in the field.* Assen, Netherlands: Van Gorcum, pp. 35–55.

Kristeva, Julia (1980). *Desire in language.* New York: Oxford University Press.

Labov, William (1966). *The social stratification of English in New York City.* Washington D.C.: Center for Applied Linguistics.

(1972a). *Language in the inner city: studies in the Black English vernacular.* Philadelphia: University of Pennsylvania Press.

(1972b). *Sociolinguistic patterns.* Philadelphia: University of Pennsylvania Press.

(1972c). Some principles of linguistic methodology. *Language in Society* 1(1):97–120.

Labov, William, and Fanshel, David (1977). *Therapeutic discourse: psychotherapy as conversation.* New York: Academic Press.

Labov, William, and Waletzky, Joshua. (1967). Narrative analysis. In June Helm (ed.), *Essays on the verbal and visual arts: proceedings of the 1966 annual spring meeting of the American Ethnological Society.* Seattle: American Ethnological Society, pp. 12–44.

Langdon, Grace (1954). *Teacher–parent interviews.* Englewood Cliffs, N.J.: Prentice-Hall.

Langness, L. L. (1965). *The life history in anthropological science.* New York: Holt, Rinehart & Winston.

Langness, L. L., and Frank, Gelya (1981). *Lives: an anthropological approach to biography.* Novato, Calif.: Chandler & Sharp.

Lawless, Robert., Sutlive, Vinson H., Jr., and Zamora, Mario D. (1983). *Fieldwork: The human experience.* New York: Gordon & Breach.

Leach, Edmund R. (1967). An anthropologist's reflections on a social survey. In D. G. Jongmans and P. C. W. Gutkind (eds.), *Anthropologists in the field.* Assen, Netherlands: Van Gorcum, pp. 75–88.

Levinson, Stephen C. (1983). *Pragmatics.* Cambridge University Press.

Lynd, Robert S., and Lynd, Helen Merrell (1929). *Middletown: a study in contemporary American culture.* New York: Harcourt Brace.

MacDonald, Donald A. (1972). Fieldwork: Collecting oral literature. In Richard M. Dorson (ed.), *Folklore and folklife: an introduction.* Chicago: University of Chicago Press, pp. 305–40.

McDowell, John H. (1975). The speech play and verbal art of Chicano children: an ethnographic and sociolinguistic study. Ph.D. dissertation, University of Texas, Austin.

   (1979). *Children's riddling.* Bloomington: Indiana University Press.

   (1982). Sociolinguistic contours in the verbal art of Chicano children. In Jon Armastae and Lucma Elmas-Olivares (eds.), *Spanish in the United States: sociolinguistic aspects.* Cambridge University Press, pp. 333–53.

McLendon, Sally (1982). Meaning, rhetorical structure, and discourse organization in myth. In Deborah Tannen (ed.), *Analyzing discourse: text and talk.* Georgetown University Round Table on Languages and Linguistics, 1981. Washington: Georgetown University Press, pp. 284–305.

Maker, H. J., Folks, J. J., Anderson, J. U., and Link, V. G. (1973). *Soil associations and land classification for irrigation, Rio Arriba County.* Agricultural Experiment Station, Research Report 254. Las Cruces: New Mexico State University.

Matejka, Ladislav, and Pomorska, Krystyna (eds.) (1978). *Readings in Russian poetics: Formalist and structuralist views.* Michigan Slavic Contributions 8. Ann Arbor: Michigan Slavic Publications.

Matejka, Ladislav, and Titunik, Irwin R. (eds) (1976). *Semiotics of art: Prague School contributions.* Cambridge, Mass.: MIT Press.

Mehan, Hugh (1979). *Learning lessons: social organization in the classroom.* Cambridge University Press.

Mehan, Hugh, and Wood, Houston (1975). *The reality of ethnomethodology.* New York: Wiley.

Menyuk, Paula (1977). *Language and maturation.* Cambridge, Mass.: MIT Press.

Merritt, Marilyn. (1976). On questions following questions in service encounters. *Language in Society* 5:315–57.

Merton, Robert K., Fiske, M. O., and Kendall, Patricia L. (1956). *The focused interview.* New York: Free Press.

Middletown, John (1970). *The study of the Lugbora.* New York: Holt, Rinehart & Winston.

Mintz, Sidney (1979). The anthropological interview and the life history. *Oral History Review* 7:18–26.

Mitchell, R. E. (1965). Survey materials collected in the developing countries: Sampling, measurement, and interviewing obstacles to intra- and international comparisons. *International Social Science Journal* 17(4):666–85.

Moss, William W. (1974). *Oral history program manual.* New York: Praeger.

Mukařovský, Jan (1977a). *The word and verbal art: selected essays by Jan Mukařovský* (John Burbank and Peter Steiner, trans. & eds.). New Haven, Conn.: Yale University Press.

(1977b). *Structure, sign, and function: selected essays by Jan Mukařovský* (John Burbank and Peter Steiner, trans. & eds.). New Haven, Conn.: Yale University Press.

Murdock, George P., et al. (1950). *Outline of cultural materials.* Behavior Science Outlines, vol. 1. New Haven, Conn.: Human Relations Area Files.

Myers, Vincent (1977). Toward a synthesis of ethnographic and survey methods. *Human Organization* 36(3):244–51.

Nails, Kebra (1983). Social-scientific sexism: Gilligan's mismeasure of man. *Social Research* 50(3):643–64.

Naroll, Raoul (1962). *Data quality control – a new research technique: prolegomenon to a cross-cultural study of culture stress.* New York: Free Press.

Naroll, Raoul, and Cohen, Ronald (eds.) (1970). *A handbook of method in cultural anthropology.* New York: Doubleday.

Neisser, Ulric (1976). *Cognition and reality: principles and implications of cognitive psychology.* New York: Freeman.

Neuenschwander, John A. (1976). *Oral history as a teaching approach.* Washington: National Educational Association.

O'Barr, William M., Spain, David H., and Tessler, Mark A. (eds.) (1973). *Survey research in Africa: its applications and limits.* Evanston, Ill.: Northwestern University Press.

Ochs, Elinor (1979). Introduction: what child language can contribute to pragmatics. In Elinor Ochs and Bambi B. Schieffelin (eds.), *Developmental pragmatics.* New York: Academic Press, pp. 1–17.

(1982). Talking to children in Western Samoa. *Language in Society* 11(1):77–104.

Owusu, Maxwell (1978). Ethnography of Africa: the usefulness of the useless. *American Anthropologist* 80(2):310–34.

Paredes, Americo, and Bauman, Richard (eds.). (1971). Toward new perspectives in folklore. *Journal of American Folklore* 84.

Paul, Benjamin D. (1953). Interview techniques and field relationships. In A. L. Kroeber (ed.), *Anthropology today: an encyclopedic inventory.* Chicago: University of Chicago Press, pp. 430–51.

Payne, S. L. (1951). *The art of asking questions.* Princeton, N.J.: Princeton University Press.

Peirce, Charles Sanders (1932). *Collected papers of Charles Sanders Peirce.* Vol. 2: *Elements of logic,* C. Hartshorne and P. Weiss (eds.). Cambridge, Mass.: Harvard University Press.

Pelto, Pertti J. (1970). *Anthropological research: the structure of inquiry.* New York: Harper & Row.

Pelto, Pertti J., and Pelto, G. H. (1973). Ethnography: the fieldwork enterprise. In John J. Honigman (ed.), *The handbook of social and cultural anthropology.* Chicago: Rand McNally, pp. 241–88.

(1978). *Anthropological research: The structure of inquiry* (Rev. ed. of Pelto 1970). Cambridge University Press.

Philips, Susan U. (1974). Warm Springs 'Indian time': How the regulation of participation affects the progression of events. In Richard Bauman and Joel Sherzer (eds.), *Explorations in the ethnography of speaking.* Cambridge University Press, pp. 92–109.

Powdermaker, Hortense (1966). *Stranger and friend: the way of an anthropologist.* New York: Norton.

Rabinow, Paul (1977). *Reflections on fieldwork in Morocco.* Berkeley: University of California Press.

(1982). Masked I go forward: reflections on the modern subject. In Jay Ruby (ed.), *A crack in the mirror: reflective perspectives in anthropology.* Philadelphia: University of Pennsylvania Press, pp. 173–85.

Rabinow, Paul, and Sullivan, William M. (eds.) (1979). *Interpretive social science: a reader.* Berkeley: University of California Press.

Rael, Juan B. (1937). A study of the phonology and morphology of New Mexican Spanish, based on a collection of 410 folktales. Ph.D. dissertation, Stanford University.

(1951). *The New Mexican alabado.* Stanford University Publications, University Series, Language and Literature, vol. 9, no. 3. Stanford, Calif.: Stanford University Press.

[1957]. *Cuentos españoles de Colorado y de Nuevo Méjico* (2 vols.). Stanford, Calif.: Stanford University Press.

Rich, J. (1968). *Interviewing children and adolescents.* New York: Macmillan.

Richardson, Stephen A., Dohrenwend, B., and Klein, D. (1965). *Interviewing: its forms and functions.* New York: Basic.

Ricoeur, Paul (1977). *The rule of metaphor: multidisciplinary studies on the creation of meaning in language* (Robert Czerny, trans.). Toronto: University of Toronto Press.

(1979). A model of the text: meaningful action considered as a text. In Paul Rabinow and William M. Sullivan (eds.), *Interpretive social science: a reader.* Berkeley: University of California Press, pp. 73–101.

(1981). *Hermeneutics and the human sciences.* (John B. Thompson, ed. and trans.). Cambridge University Press.

Riesman, David (1958). Introduction to D. Lerner, *The passing of traditional society: modernizing the Middle East.* New York: Free Press.

(1959). Some observations on interviewing in a state mental hospital. *Bulletin of the Menninger Clinic* 23:7–19.

(1964). *Abundance for what? and other essays.* Garden City, N.Y.: Doubleday.

Riesman, David, and Benney, Mark (1956). Asking and answering. *Journal of Business* 29:225–36.

Riley, Matilda White (ed.) (1963). *Sociological research: a case approach.* New York: Harcourt Brace & World.

Riley, Matilda White, and Nelson, Edward E. (1974). *Sociological observation: a strategy for new social knowledge.* New York: Basic.

Robb, John Donald (1980). *Hispanic folkmusic of New Mexico and the Southwest: a self-portrait of the people.* Norman: University of Oklahoma Press.

Royal Anthropological Institute (1951). *Notes and queries on anthropology* (6th ed.). London: Routledge.

Ruby, Jay (1980). Exposing yourself: reflexivity, film, and anthropology. *Semiotica* 30(1–2):153–79.

(ed.) (1982). *A crack in the mirror: reflective perspectives in anthropology.* Philadelphia: University of Pennsylvania Press.

Sacks, Harvey (1967). Unpublished lecture notes. University of California, Irvine.

    (1974). An analysis of the course of a joke's telling in conversation. In Richard Bauman and Joel Sherzer (eds.), *Explorations in the ethnography of speaking*. Cambridge University Press, pp. 337–53.

Sacks, Harvey, Schegloff, Emanuel A., and Jefferson, Gail (1974). A simplest systematics for the organization of turn-taking for conversation. *Language* 50:696–735.

Sapir, J. David, & Crocker, J. Christopher (1977). *The social use of metaphor: essays on the anthropology of rhetoric*. Philadelphia: University of Pennsylvania Press.

Saussure, Ferdinand (1959). *Course in general linguistics* (Charles Bally and Albert Sechehaye, eds.; Wade Baskin, trans.). New York: McGraw-Hill.

Schatzman, Leonard, and Strauss, Anselm L. (1973). *Field research: strategies for a natural sociology*. Englewood Cliffs, N.J.: Prentice-Hall.

Scheflen, Albert E. (1964). Communication and regulation in psychotherapy. *Psychiatry* 27:126–36.

    (1965). *Stream and structure of communicational behavior: context analysis of a psychotherapy session*. Behavioral Studies Monograph 1. Philadelphia: Eastern Pennsylvania Psychiatric Institute.

    (1966). Natural history method in psychotherapy: communications research. In Louis A. Gottschalk and A. H. Auerbach (eds.), *Methods of research in psychotherapy*. East Norwalk, Conn.: Appleton-Century-Crofts.

Schieffelin, Bambi B. (1979). Getting it together: an ethnographic approach to the study of the development of communicative competence. In Elinor Ochs and Bambi B. Schieffelin (eds.), *Developmental pragmatics*. New York: Academic Press, pp. 73–108.

Schuman, Howard, and Presser, Stanley (1981). *Questions and answers in attitude surveys: experiments on the effects of question form, wording and context*. New York: Academic Press.

Schutz, Alfred (1962). *Collected papers I: the problem of social reality*. The Hague: Martinus Nijhoff.

Searle, John R. (1969). *Speech acts: an essay in the philosophy of language*. Cambridge University Press.

    (1979). *Expression and meaning: studies in the theory of speech acts*. Cambridge University Press.

    (1983). *Intentionality*. Cambridge University Press.

Sherwood, Hugh C. (1969). *The journalistic interview*. New York: Harper & Row.

Sherzer, Joel (1973). Nonverbal and verbal deixis: the pointed lip gesture among the San Blas Cuna. *Language in Society* 2:117–31.

    (1983). *Kuna ways of speaking: an ethnographic perspective*. Austin: University of Texas Press.

Sherzer, Joel, and Darnell, Regna (1972). Outline guide for the ethnographic study of speech use. In John J. Gumperz and Dell Hymes (eds.), *Directions in sociolinguistics: the ethnography of communication*. New York: Holt, Rinehart & Winston, pp. 548–54.

Shotter, H. (1979). The cultural context of communication studies: theoretical and methodological issues. In A. Lock (ed.), *Action, gesture and symbol: the emergence of language*. New York: Academic Press, pp. 43–79.

Shoulksmith, G. (1968). *Assessment through interviewing.* Elmsford, N.Y.: Pergamon.

Shumway, Gary L., and Hartley, William G. (1973). *Oral history primer.* Fullerton: California State University at Fullerton.

Siegel, Bernard J. (1959). Some structure implications for change in Pueblo and Spanish New Mexico. In Verne F. Ray (ed.), *Intermediate societies, social mobility, and communication.* Proceedings of the 1959 annual spring meeting of the American Ethnological Society. Seattle: American Ethnological Society, pp. 37–44.

Silverstein, Michael (1976). Shifters, linguistic categories, and cultural description. In Keith Basso and Henry A. Selby (eds.), *Meaning in anthropology.* Albuquerque: University of New Mexico Press, pp. 11–55.

    (1979). Language structure and linguistic ideology. In Paul R. Clyne, William Hanks, and Carol L. Hofbauer (eds.), *The elements: a parasession on linguistic units and levels.* Chicago: Chicago Linguistic Society, pp. 193–247.

    (1981a). *The limits of awareness.* Sociolinguistic Working Paper 84. Austin, Texas: Southwest Educational Development Laboratory.

    (1981b). Metaforces of power in traditional oratory. Unpublished manuscript.

    (1985). The culture of language in Chinookan narrative texts; or, on saying that . . . in Chinook. In Johanna Nichols and Anthony Woodbury (eds.), *Grammar inside and outside the clause.* Cambridge University Press.

Simon, Julian L. (1969). *Basic research methods in the social sciences: the art of empirical investigation.* (2nd ed., 1978). New York: Random House.

Simmons, Marc (1969) Settlement patterns and village plans in colonial New Mexico. *Journal of the West* 8:7–21.

Sitton, Thad, Mehaffy, George L., and Davis, O. L., Jr. (1983). *Oral history: a guide for teachers (and others).* Austin: University of Texas Press.

Smith, Sherolyn K., and Briggs, Charles L. (1972). *A report of attitudes and needs for new city programs in Gallup, New Mexico.* Boulder, Colo.: Western Interstate Commission for Higher Education.

Snow, Catherine (1977). Mother's speech research: An overview. In Catherine Snow and Charles Ferguson (eds.), *Talking to children: language input and acquisition.* Cambridge University Press, pp. 31–49.

Soil Conservation Service, U.S. Department of Agriculture (1937). *Village livelihood in the Upper Rio Grande area and a note on the level of village livelihood in the Upper Rio Grande area.* Regional Bulletin no. 44, Conservation Economics Series no. 17. Albuquerque, N.M.: Soil Conservation Service.

Spanish Archives of New Mexico. Vol. 1: Wills and Land Transfers, nos. 28, 211, 718. Santa Fe: State Records Center and Archives.

Speckman, J. D. (1967). Social surveys in non-Western areas. In D. G. Jongmans and P. C. W. Gutkind (eds.), *Anthropologists in the field.* Assen, Netherlands: Van Gorcum, pp. 56–74.

Spencer, Robert F. (ed.) (1954). *Method and perspective in anthropology: papers in honor of Wilson D. Wallis.* Minneapolis: University of Minnesota Press.

Spindler, George (ed.) (1970). *Being an anthropologist.* New York: Holt, Rinehart & Winston.

Spradley, James P. (1979). *The ethnographic interview.* New York: Holt, Rinehart & Winston.

Stanislawski, Dan (1947). Early Spanish town planning in the New World. *Geographical Review* 37(1):94–105.

Stano, Michael E., and Reinsch, N. L., Jr. (1982). *Communication in interviews.* Englewood Cliffs, N.J.: Prentice-Hall.

Stocking, George W. (1968). *Race, culture, and evolution: essays in the history of anthropology.* New York: Free Press.

(1983). *Observers observed: essays on ethnographic fieldwork.* History of Anthropology, vol. 1. Madison: University of Wisconsin Press.

Stocking, George W. (ed.) (1974). *The shaping of American anthropology, 1883–1911: a Franz Boas reader.* New York: Basic.

Strauss, Anselm, and Schatzman, Leonard (1955). Cross-class interviewing: an analysis of interaction and communicative styles. *Human Organization* 14(2):28–31.

Sullivan, Harry Stack (1954). *The psychiatric interview.* New York: Norton.

Tedlock, Dennis (1971). On the translation of style in oral narrative. In Americo Paredes and Richard Bauman (eds.), Toward new perspectives in folklore. *Journal of American Folklore* 84:114–33.

(1972). *Finding the center: narrative poetry of the Zuni Indians.* Lincoln: University of Nebraska Press.

(1975). Learning to listen: oral history as poetry. In Ronald J. Grele (ed.), *Envelopes of sound: six practitioners discuss the method, theory, and practice of oral history and oral testimony.* Chicago: Precedent, pp. 106–25.

(1983). *The spoken word and the work of interpretation.* Philadelphia: University of Pennsylvania Press.

Thompson, Paul (1978). *The voice of the past: oral history.* New York: Oxford University Press.

Trevarthen, Colwyn (1979). Communication and cooperation in early infancy: a description of primary intersubjectivity. In Margaret Bullowa (ed.), *Before speech.* Cambridge University Press.

Trotter, Robert T., II, and Chavira, Juan Antonio (1981). *Curanderismo: Mexican American folk healing.* Athens: University of Georgia Press.

Turner, David (1968). *Employment interviewer.* New York: Arco.

Van Ness, John R. (1979). Hispanos in northern New Mexico: the development of corporate community and multicommunity. Ph.D. dissertation, University of Pennsylvania, Philadelphia.

Vansina, Jan (1965). *Oral tradition: a study in historical methodology* (H. M. Wright, trans.). Chicago: Aldine.

Vološinov, V. N. (1973). *Marxism and the philosophy of language* (Ladislav Matejka and I. R. Titunik, trans.). New York: Seminar Press.

Warner, W. Lloyd and Lunt, Paul (1941). *The social life of a modern community.* Yankee City Series 1. New Haven, Conn.: Yale University Press.

Wax, Rosalie H. (1971). *Doing fieldwork: warnings and advice.* Chicago: University of Chicago Press.

Webb, Eugene J., et al. (1966). *Unobtrusive measures: nonreactive research in the social sciences.* Chicago: Rand McNally.

Westphall, Victor (1983). *Mercedes reales: Hispanic land grants of the Upper Rio Grande region.* Albuquerque: University of New Mexico Press.

Whorf, Benjamin Lee (1956). *Language, thought, and reality: selected writings of Benjamin Lee Whorf* (John B. Carroll, ed.). Cambridge, Mass.: MIT Press.

148 *Bibliography*

Whyte, William Foote (1943). *Street corner society: the social structure of an Italian slum.* Chicago: University of Chicago Press.

Whyte, William Foote (with the collaboration of Kathleen King Whyte) (1984). *Learning from the field: A guide from experience.* Beverly Hills, Calif.: Sage.

Williams, Raymond (1977). *Marxism and literature.* New York: Oxford University Press.

Williams, Thomas Rhys (1967). *Field methods in the study of culture.* New York: Holt, Rinehart & Winston.

Wolfson, Nessa (1976). Speech events and natural speech: some implications for sociolinguistic methodology. *Language in Society* 5:189–209.

(1979). The conversational historical present alternation. *Language* 55(1):168–82.

Young, Frank W., and Young, Ruth C. (1961). Key informant reliability in rural Mexican villages. *Human Organization* 20(3):141–8.

INDEX

Abrahams, Roger D., 94, 114
acquisition of metacommunicative competence, *see* metacommunicative competence, acquisition of
active phase, of research, 97
adjacency pairs, 73
adolescence, and language acquisition, 75–6
Agar, Michael, 9, 10, 105
age, 21, 56, 57; as factor in communication, 63, 64, 69, 82, 83, 84, 86, 88, 103; as source of "bias" in interviewing, 21
Albert, Ethel M., 16, 94, 126n
ambiguity, 81, 108, 110
American English, 56, 91–2
anthropology, use of interviewing in, 7–10, 120–1
applied research, 96–7
aspect, verbal, 86
Austin, J. L., 15, 45–6, 113
awareness, of linguistic structure and language use, 98, 100, 107, 108, 110, 115–19

Babcock, Barbara, 119
back channel cues, 14, 84, 108, 109, 110, 131n
background knowledge, 42, 52, 113
Bailey, Kenneth D., 24
Bakhtin, M. M., 113
Bates, Elizabeth, 66
Bateson, Gregory, 28, 130n
Bauman, Richard, 11, 114, 118, 126n
Beattie, John, 9
Belmonte, Thomas, 9, 131n
Ben-Amos, Dan, 114, 126n, 129n
Benveniste, Emile, 129n
Berreman, Gerald D., 9, 120, 131n
"bias," 2, 13, 21, 24, 36, 91–2, 102, 123
Birdwhistell, Ray C., 109
Bloch, Maurice, 116, 131n
Brenner, Michael, 25, 26

Campa, Arthur L., 37
Cancian, Frank, 45
canons, of interpretation, 47, 48, 49, 57
caregivers, and language acquisition, 66, 67, 69–74
Chagnon, Napoleon A., 8, 9
channel, as component of communicative event, 40, 44, 100
Chavira, Juan Antonio, 69
Chicago school, of sociology, 19
Chomsky, Noam, 15, 17, 43, 113, 115
Churchill, Lindsey, 43, 90, 110, 126n
Cicourel, Aaron, 15, 22, 24–5, 26, 49, 50, 75, 102, 113, 114
class, social, *see* social class
closed-ended scheduled interviews, 20
closings, in conversation, 53
code, as component of communicative event, 40, 41, 44, 100, 105, 118
code-switching, 71, 86, 105, 117
Cohen, Ronald, 9
coherence, in discourse, 101, 104, 105
cohesion, in discourse, 88, 89, 90
collection, folkloristic, 11
common sense, and interpretive processes, 18, 21, 25, 26, 49, 83; *see also* background knowledge
communicative blunders, 39, 43, 44–5, 50, 58, 59, 64, 89–90, 101, 102, 110; *see also* procedural problems
communicative competence, 2, 15, 75, 76; acquisition of, 39, 43, 50, 60; defined, 43; evaluation of, 37–8, 55, 62, 77; *see also* metacommunicative competence
communicative event, 26, 41, 57; components of, relationship between, 40, 41, 42, 103, 105; Jakobson/Hymes model of, 40–2, 100, 104
communicative functions, 46, 74, 104, 105; *see also* multifunctionality, in discourse
communicative hegemony, 4, 58, 90, 91–2, 121, 123, 124

149

150   *Index*

competence, communicative, *see* communicative competence
competence, syntactic, 43, 113
concentración 'concentration', 63, 66, 88
conflict, in discourse, 78
consciousness, 98, 108; *see also* awareness, of linguistic structure and language use
Constantinople, Anne, 122
context: concept of, 12–13, 25, 71–2, 108; and indexical function, 42
context-independence, 113, 119
context-sensitivity, 50, 65, 77, 100, 117, 121
contextualization, 37, 71–3, 86, 88, 89, 99, 106, 107–10, 113, 116, 117–18, 121, 122–3; defined, 12, 108; in performances, 37, 87
contradictions, methodological, 19, 27
control, in interview situation, 27–8, 56, 89, 123
conversational analysis, 93, 113
conversational historical present tense, 23
conversational implicature, 49, 83
conversational inference, 49
conversational maxims, 49, 57, 83, 97
conversational structure, 51–4, 89; *see also* discourse structure; global structure, of discourse
Cook-Gumperz, Jenny, 12, 14, 70, 71–2, 75, 108
Córdova, Federico, 91–2
Córdova, Lina Ortiz de, 92
Córdova, N. M., 31–6, 48, 57, 78–83, 127n; climate, 31; dialectal characteristics, 37, 129n; history, 32–3, 34–6, 52–3, 54; location, 31, 32; political economy, 33–6; wood carving in, 33, 91
Córdova, Pedro, 52–3
corporatism, 36, 46, 48, 56, 80–1, 103
Corsaro, William A., 75
counseling, use of interviewing in, 21
Crapanzano, Vincent, 120
creativity: pragmatic, 116; syntactic, 43; in verbal art, 76
Crick, Malcolm, 112
Crocker, J. Christopher, 110
crutch words, 14, 131n
cryptotypes, 54
cultural premises, *see* cultural values
cultural stereotypes, 86, 87
cultural values, 37, 47, 48, 55–6, 57, 58, 63, 69, 76, 80–1, 82, 83, 84, 87, 88, 89, 117
Cundiyó, N.M., 34
Cutler, William, III, 13

Darnell, Regna, 94, 127n
Dean, John P., 22
decontextualization, 42–3, 44, 87, 98, 102, 107, 118, 120, 122
deixis, 44
Derrida, Jacques, 114
Dexter, Lewis Anthony, 24, 25, 27, 114
dialect, 36–7
dialogism, 13, 14, 108
dignidad de la persona 'personal dignity', 70, 80
discourse analysis, 18, 107, 113
discourse structure, 53–4, 91–2, 102; *see also* conversational structure; global structure, of discourse
dominance, in relationship between components of communicative event, 41, 56
Dougherty, Janet W. D., 112
Duncan, Starkey, 109, 131n
Durkheim, Emile, 22, 119
Dwyer, Kevin, 9, 120, 131n

ecological validity, 24, 28, 124; *see also* validity
Edgerton, Robert, 8
education, 15, 96; as factor in discourse, 91–2; use of interviewing in, 124
effectiveness, of discourse, 79, 89; *see also* metacommunicative competence, evaluation of
egalitarian values, 80–1
Eisenberg, A. R., 74
elicitation techniques, 16
employer interviews, 20
encyclopedic structure, 53, 129n
epistemology, of fieldwork, 91
errors, as source of data, 110; *see also* communicative blunders
Ervin-Tripp, Susan, 73
Espinosa, Aurelio M., 36, 37, 128n
ethnicity, 26, 39, 43, 61, 96, 122
ethnocentrism, 16
ethnography, of communication, 15, 93; *see also* sociolinguistics
ethnography, use of interviewing in, *see* anthropology, use of interviewing in
ethnomethodology, 18, 113
ethnopoetics, 106, 113
ethnoscience, 113
exegesis, 44, 52, 101, 108, 115

face, in interaction, 75–6
feast days, 36
Fernandez, James W., 110–2
field notes, 102, 104
field research, in sociology, 9, 19

fieldwork: in anthropology, 8, 9–10, 54, 62; defined, 7; in folklore, 62
fillers, in discourse, 14, 131n
Fishman, Joshua, 15, 96, 113
fixed-alternative scheduled interviews, 20
folklore, 11–13, 15, 64, 82, 88, 117; *see also* performance
folkloristics, 114, 126n; use of interviewing in, 11–13
folktales, 37
form, in discourse, 13, 75, 79, 80, 99, 106, 129n; *see also* message form; stylistic features
Frake, Charles O., 45
frames, in discourse, 12, 24, 49–50, 51–4, 56, 57, 64, 72, 73, 79–80, 82, 86, 95, 104, 106, 108
Freilich, Morris, 9, 97–8
funding, for research, 96

Gadamer, Hans-Georg, 113
Gallup, N.M., 96–7
Galtung, Johann, 121
Garfinkel, Harold, 49, 51, 113
gaze, 106, 109; *see also* nonverbal communication
Geertz, Clifford, 90, 112, 118, 130n
gender: as factor in comunication, 56, 69, 89, 95, 101, 122; as source of "bias" in interviewing, 21
gender-based discrimination, 121–3
genre, 12, 37, 83, 88, 89, 108, 114, 129n; as component of communicative event 46–7, 101, 105
Georges, Robert A., 9
gesture, 42, 44, 88, 99, 106, 109; *see also* nonverbal communication
Gilligan, Carol, 121–3
Glassie, Henry, 114, 126n
global structure, of discourse, 52–4, 104, 106; *see also* conversational structure; discourse structure
Goffman, Erving, 46, 47, 76, 113
Golde, Peggy, 9
Goldstein, Kenneth S., 11–13
Goody, Esther N., 45
Gorden, Raymond L., 20, 24
Gossen, Gary H., 94
Gouldner, Alvin W., 114
Grice, H. P., 49, 83
Grimshaw, Allen D., 15, 16, 26, 45, 46, 129n
Gumperz, John J., 12, 14, 15, 16, 70, 71–2, 107, 108, 109
Gutkind, P. C. W., 9

Hall, Edward, T., 109
Henry, Frances, 9

hermeneutics, 113
Herzfeld, Michael, 47
Herzog, George, 44
Hobbs, Jerry R., 56, 105
Hoffman, Alice, 13
Hotchkiss, J. C., 76
Human Organization, 9
Hyman, Herbert H., 19, 23–4, 26
Hymes, Dell H., 11, 15, 16, 40, 46, 94, 100, 104, 106, 113, 118, 121, 126n, 127n, 130n

iconic sign mode, 87, 88
idealization, 98
ideology, linguistic, 115–19; *see also* native models, of language acquisition; awareness, of linguistic structure and language use
imitation, 63, 64, 65, 67–77, 87, 89; *see also* repetition, and language acquisition; repetition elicitation routines
indexical sign mode, 42, 43, 44, 45, 83, 116, 117, 118; defined, 22
indirection, 38, 42, 46, 80–3, 109, 117
individualism, 22, 33, 35, 37, 48
individual true value (ITV), 21, 102; *see also* validity; ecological validity
induced natural context method, 11
informants, 90–2
inobtrusive measures, 20
interactional goals, as component of communicative events, 41, 47–8, 101, 103, 104
interactional style, 21
interés 'interest', 63, 66, 88
interpretive framework, 12, 25, 72, 73, 76, 80, 82, 99, 101, 105, 106, 107, 108, 109–10, 117, 118, 121, 131n; *see also* frames, in discourse
interruptions, 80
intersubjectivity, 119
interview: *see* anthropology, use of interviewing in; folkloristics, use of interviewing in; oral history, use of interviewing in; sociolinguistics, use of interviewing in; sociology, use of interviewing in
intonation, *see* prosody
introspection, 108
Irvine, Judith T., 16, 18
Ives, Edward D., 14

Jakobson/Hymes model of the speech event, 40–2, 100, 104
Jakobson, Roman, 40, 41, 45, 53, 100, 104, 105, 115, 130n
Jameson, Frederic, 114

Jefferson, Gail, 51, 109, 110, 131n
jokes, 47, 88, 106, 108
Jongmans, D. G., 9
Joyner, Charles W., 14

Karp, Ivan, 9–10, 22, 119–20, 131n
Kendall, Martha B., 9–10, 22, 46, 119–
    20, 131n
Kendon, Adam, 109
key, as component of communicative
    event, 46–7, 101, 105
key informant interviewing, 8, 90–1, 120–
    1, 130n
Kluckhohn, Florence, 7, 97
Kobben, A. J. F., 8
Kristeva, Julia, 114
Kuna of Panamá, 44

Labov, William, 15, 16, 17–19, 96, 113,
    124, 127n
land grants, 34
Langness, L. L., 8
language acquisition, *see* metacommunica-
    tive competence, acquisition of
langue 'language system', 113
la plática de los viejitos de antes 'the talk
    of the elders of bygone days', 37, 82,
    83–7, 88
Lawless, Robert, 9
legitimation, in discourse, 82, 86–7
Leighton, Dorothea, 97
lexical range, 45
lexical selection, 106
limits of awareness, *see* awareness, limits
    of
linear structure, of interview, 104
linguistic variation, 15, 17, 43, 94, 96;
    quantitative study of, 17–19
literacy, 91–2
literary criticism, 5, 114
locatives, 53
López, George, 44, 55, 57, 58, 61, 64–5,
    91–2, 103
López, Silvianita Trujillo de, 44, 55, 57,
    58, 61, 64–5, 91–2, 103
Los Alamos National Laboratory, 33, 36
Lunt, Paul, 19
Lynd, Helen Merrel, 19
Lynd, Robert S., 19

MacDonald, Donald A., 13
McDowell, John H., 130n
McLendon, Sally, 130n
manuals, 27, 130n; for anthropological
    fieldwork, 9, 90; for sociological re-
    search, 19; for oral historical interview-
    ing, 13, 14, 131n

markedness, 53
materialism, 35, 37, 86
medicine, use of interviewing in, 21, 49
Mehan, Hugh, 25, 26
memory, 14
message form, as component of commu-
    nicative event, 40, 41, 100; *see also*
    form, in discourse
metacommunication, 10, 44, 47, 61, 82,
    99, 130n; as basic property of inter-
    views, 91, 106–7
metacommunicative competence, 28, 82;
    acquisition of, 61–87, 93, 95, 117, 120–
    1; evaluation of, 28, 61, 62–3, 64, 71,
    80, 82, 87–90; *see also* communicative
    competence; native metacommunicative
    routines
metaphor, 110, 117, 118
metasigns, conversational, 53, 54, 106
Mexicano: folklore, 37, 47, 82, 83–7; land
    expropriation, 34–6; migration, 34, 35–
    6; oral history, 47; political economy,
    33–6, 38, 128n; political rhetoric, 47,
    77–83; term defined, 31
Middletown, 19
Middletown, John, 9
miscommunication, 109–10
misinterpretation, 3, 27
moral values, 28, 55; *see also* cultural
    values
motherese, 66, 72
Mukařovský, Jan, 105, 130n
multifunctionality, in discourse, 103, 110
Murdock, George Peter, 102
myth, 106

Nails, Kebra, 122
Naroll, Raoul, 9
native metacommunicative repertoires,
    39–40, 46, 48, 56, 57–8, 61–2, 94–5,
    98, 101
native metacommunicative routines, 2, 3–
    4, 59–60, 65–88, 92, 96, 107, 114, 117–
    18
native models: of language acquisition,
    62–5, 76; of language structure and
    use, 3, 16, 39, 115–19; of reality, 22,
    115, 119–20
Navajos, 96–7
negotiation, 25, 102, 108, 109
Neisser, Ulric, 24
Nelson, Edward E., 19
New Mexican Spanish, 55, 92, 103, 128n
    129n
New York City, 17, 96
Niederehe, G., 109
nonscheduled interviews, 20, 127n

nonstandardized interviews, 20, 127n
nonverbal communication, 40, 44, 46, 58,
    64–5, 72, 75, 88, 94, 99, 106
norms, communicative, 2, 3, 15, 26, 89,
    90
norms, of interaction, 28, 48, 56, 57, 97
Notes and Queries on Anthropology, 102
note taking, 99
nursing, use of interviewing in, 21

objectivity, 22, 87, 119–20, 124
observability, 119
observation, 7, 11, 17, 19–20, 54, 65, 66,
    67, 76, 89, 94, 99, 100, 126n; and ac-
    quisition of metacommunicative compe-
    tence, 57, 63–4, 87–8
occupation, 56
Ochs, Elinor, 62, 66, 70, 74, 75
ontology, 119–20
open-ended scheduled interviews, 20
openings, in conversation, 53
oral historical vignettes, 82
oral history, 54–5, 58, 83–7; use of inter-
    viewing in, 13–15
oral tradition, 64, 88
Outline of Cultural Materials, 102
Owusu, Maxwell, 10

paciencia 'patience', 88
Paredes, Américo, 114
parents, interviewing of, 20
parole 'speaking', 113
participant observation technique, 19
participants in interview, relationship be-
    tween, 41, 46, 56–9, 87, 103, 105; *see
    also* social roles
passive phase, of research, 97
pauses, in speech, *see* prosody
pedagogical discourse, 57, 84, 89, 92, 108
pedagogy, 49, 61
Peirce, Charles Sanders, 22, 40, 87, 128n
Pelto, G. H., 8, 90, 121, 130n
Pelto, Pertti J., 8, 90, 121, 130n
performance, 11–13, 37, 47, 58, 82, 83,
    88, 114, 118, 126n; *see also* folklore
performance features, 37–8
performativity, 45–6, 86, 113, 117, 118
personality of interviewer, as source of
    "bias," 21
personal narratives 17–18, 23, 58
persuasiveness, of discourse, 77, 88; *see
    also* metacommunicative competence,
    evaluation of
phatic function, 109
phenomenology, 25, 113
Phillips, Susan U., 46

philosophy of language, 45–6, 49, 83, 113
phonological variables, 18
pitch, *see* prosody
poetic structure, of discourse, 80, 118;
    see also ethnopoetics; form, in
    discourse
political dimensions of discourse, 36–8,
    45, 64
political oratory and rhetoric, 38, 63, 77–
    83, 116, 117
political science, use of interviewing in,
    16, 17
political underpinnings of methodology,
    120–5
positivism, 22, 119–20, 124
Powdermaker, Hortense, 7, 9
power relations, in interviewing, 56, 86,
    121
pragmatics, 2, 45, 73, 88, 110, 112, 118
Prague Linguistic Circle, 130n
presupposition, 50, 54, 56, 83, 103, 109,
    116, 117, 118
pretesting, of survey instruments, 96
procedural problems, 39, 44, 89–90, 93,
    94, 98, 102, 110, 126n; defined, 43; *see
    also* communicative blunders
pronominalization, 86, 106
prosody, 24, 42, 66, 72, 73, 78, 79, 80,
    88, 106, 113, 116, 117, 130n
proverbs, 37, 47, 82, 83, 100, 108–9
proxemics, 106
psychiatry, use of interviewing in, 21

quantitative analysis, of interview data,
    17–19, 20, 24, 104; *see also* linguistic
    variation
quantity (loudness) of speech, *see* pro-
    sody
question–answer sequences, 25, 42, 47–8,
    88–90
questionnaires, 20, 127n
questions, "loaded," 13
question wording, 24
quotation-framing devices, 73, 95; *see
    also* repetition elicitation routines

Rabinow, Paul, 113, 120
race, as source of "bias" in interviewing,
    21
Rael, Juan B., 36, 37
rapport, 13, 28, 50, 98
rate of speech, *see* prosody
reductionism, 119–20
referential frames, 46, 64, 89, 90, 91
referential function, 13, 18–19, 40, 43,
    44, 45, 50–6, 76, 80, 95, 98, 99, 102,
    105, 106, 107, 109, 110, 115–17, 118,

referential function (*cont.*)
124, 128n; and ambiguity, 51; and canons of interpretation, 47; as component of communicative event, 40, 41; defined, 42; and definition of the interview, 48–49; and linguistic ideology, 115–19; scope of, 54; specificity of, 55
reflexivity, 102, 110, 119–20, 124; and research design, 100–1
reliability, 13, 21, 23–5, 28; defined, 23
religiosity, 48, 56, 103
religious values, 80–1, 84–6
repair procedures, in conversation, 90, 110
repetition, and language acquisition process, 57, 63, 65, 87–8, 89, 109; *see also* imitation
repetition elicitation routines, 66–76, 117; and interview techniques, 76–7
reported speech, 73, 95; see also *la plática de los viejitos de antes;* repetition elicitation routines
reruns, 52, 54, 56
respeto 'respect', 63, 76, 83
rhetoric, *see* political oratory and rhetoric
Ricoeur, Paul, 110, 113
Riley, Matilda White, 19
Robb, John Donald, 37
Robinson, Jane J., 56
roles, *see* social roles
Royal Anthropological Institute, 102
Ruby, Jay, 119, 120
Russian Formalism, 130n

Saberwal, Satish, 9
Sacks, Harvey, 47, 109, 113
sampling, 90, 98
Sankoff, Gillian, 15
Sapir, J. David, 110
sarcasm, 106, 108, 116
Saussure, Ferdinand de, 40, 113
Schatzman, Leonard, 19, 45, 46, 129n
scheduled interviews, 20, 127n
schedules, 20, 127n
Scheflen, Albert E., 109
Schegloff, Emmanuel A., 109
Schieffelin, Bambi B., 74
Schutz, Alfred, 113
scientific colonialism, 121; *see also* communicative hegemony
scriptural allusions, 37, 47, 82, 83–7, 117
Searle, John, 113
second pair parts, 47; *see also* adjacency pairs
semantics, 113, 116
Sherzer, Joel, 44, 94, 126n, 127n
Shotter, H., 66

side sequences, 51, 110
Silverstein, Michael, 42, 65, 86, 95, 98, 108, 115–19, 128n, 130n
Smith, Sherolyn, 96
Snow, Catherine, 66
social class, 24, 26, 37, 39, 43, 56–7, 61, 95, 96, 109, 122
social inequality, 48, 55
social roles, as component of communicative event, 2, 7, 24, 41, 56–9, 89, 70–1, 76, 101, 102; *see also* participants in interview, relationship between
social situation, as component of communicative event, 41, 43, 45–6, 72, 94, 101, 105
social work, use of interviewing in, 21
sociolinguistic competence, *see* communicative competence
sociolinguistics, 94, 96, 113; use of interviewing in, 15–19; *see also* ethnography of communication
sociology, 15, 113–14; use of interviewing in, 19–23
Spanish, New Mexican, *see* New Mexican Spanish
speech acts, 16, 45, 58, 73, 74, 75, 87–8, 89, 113, 114, 115, 116
Spindler, George, 9
stability, as property of social reality, 22, 119
standardization, of research methodology, 24, 28
standardized interviews, 20, 127n
statistical analysis, 17–19, 20, 24, 104
Strauss, Anselm L., 19, 45, 56, 129n
Street Corner Society, 19
stress, in discourse, *see* prosody
structure, of interviews, 51–4, 104; *see also* conversational structure; discourse structure; global structure, of discourse
stylistic features, 106, 107; *see also* form, in discourse
subjectivity, 119
Sullivan, Harry Stack, 21
Sullivan, William M., 113
surface segmentability, 116, 117, 118
survey research, 17–19, 50, 93, 94, 95–7, 104
Sutlive, Vinson H., Jr., 9
syntax, 106, 113, 115, 116

talento 'talent', 63, 77
tape recording, 17, 65, 67, 95, 99–100, 101, 104
tautology, methodological, 26, 65
Tedlock, Dennis, 113, 126n, 130n
tense, verbal, 106

tension, in interviews, 27–8
terms of address, 86
theory, in relation to methodology, 2, 3,
    112–25
Thompson, Paul, 13, 14
tone, *see* prosody
topic, 53; topical restrictions, 45; topical
    selection, 56, 58, 89, 92, 101; topical
    shifts, 52, 105
transcription, 4, 13, 95, 99, 102, 104, 110,
    129n
translation, 95
transmission, cultural, 37, 83, 84
Trevarthen, Colwyn, 66
triplex signs, 53, 106
Trotter, Robert T., III, 69
Trujillo, Aurelio, 48, 84–7, 103
Trujillo, Costancia, 48, 85
truth values, 22
turn-taking, 76, 80, 83, 84, 89, 109, 131n
type of communicative event, 41, 48–50,
    58, 101, 103, 122

validity, 13, 21, 22, 23–5, 28; defined, 23;
    see also ecological validity

values, cultural, *see* cultural values
Vansina, Jan, 14
variation, linguistic, *see* linguistic variation
verbal art, 11–13, 106, 114, 117; *see also*
    folklore; performance
videotaping, 17, 99, 100, 101, 104, 109
visual signs, 44–5; *see also* nonverbal
    communication
Vološinov, V. N., 114

Warner, W. Lloyd, 19
Wax, Rosalie H., 9
Webb, Eugene J., 20
Whorf, Benjamin Lee, 54
Whyte, William Foote, 22
Williams, Raymond, 114
Wolfson, Nessa, 18, 23, 26, 57
wood carving, 44, 58, 64–5, 103

Yankee City, 19
Young, Frank W., 8
Young, Ruth C., 8

Zamora, Mario D., 9

interview
   question and answer
   inquiry   reply
   dialectic; maieutic